America's Youth in the 1990s

Robert Bezilla, Editor

The George H. Gallup International Institute ❧ Princeton, NJ

First printing

ISBN 0-924455-06-3 (Hard cover)
ISBN 0-924455-05-5   (Soft cover)

Table of Contents

Detailed Tables

Foreword

This book is based on research by The Gallup Youth Survey, which since March 1977, has been devoted to the study of American teen-agers. The information it contains was gathered in ongoing surveys of persons 13 to 17 years old with regard to all manner of things affecting their lives. In addition to exploring specific attitudes at a given time, the surveys delineate trends in teen thinking on more than 200 issues of continuing importance.

The Gallup Youth Survey was established by Dr. George H. Gallup, a founding pioneer of public opinion studies in America. Dr. Gallup believed that those who would serve the people should first hear the voice of the people, a principle he applied to America's youth no less than to its elders.

AMERICA'S YOUTH IN THE 1990s is an updated companion to an earlier volume, *AMERICA'S YOUTH 1977–1988*, which covered the first 10 years of the program. Together, they provide an unparalleled body of knowledge on habits, hopes, fears and dreams of American youth.

The Gallup Youth Survey was established by Dr. Gallup in 1977, seven years before his death, and now operates through the international institute founded in his memory. We are proud to dedicate this book to the man without whose vision there would have been neither book nor Institute.

George H. Gallup, Jr.

George H. Gallup, Jr., Chairman
The George H. Gallup International Institute
Princeton, N.J.

INTRODUCTION

Overview

America's teen-agers today are very different in many ways from those the Gallup Youth Survey interviewed when it got its start in 1977. At that time teens still were concerned about the aftermath of the Vietnam war, worried about "the bomb," and distrusted the Soviet Union.

Except perhaps on geography quizzes, today's teens need no longer fear the conglomeration of nations that made up the former Soviet Union, are witnessing wholesale weapons disarmament, and view Vietnam as the subject of "Rambo" films and what must seem to them arcane debates about President Bill Clinton's former draft status.

Unlike the Vietnam era, teens and their elders showed no disagreement over America's aims in the Persian Gulf. Most young people were proud of their country and its armed forces during Operation Desert Storm, and most indicated they would serve their nation if asked to do so under similar circumstances.

This spirit of voluntarism extends beyond the military, with many teens indicating they would be willing to serve their nation both at home and abroad in more peaceful pursuits. Already, teens have become a potent force donating many hours in community service. Even more would serve if given the opportunity to do so.

While teens in the 1970s seemed mired in an emergent drug culture, since that time they have increasingly opposed legalization and decriminalization of marijuana and other illicit substances, and in recent years have identified drugs as the most important problem facing both the nation and their generation. When it comes to drugs, there probably is more of a problem among people their parents' age than among teens, themselves.

Unfortunately, alcohol has now become the drug of choice for many teens, who usually find little difficulty in obtaining it even though they are under age. Health officials also express continuing concern about the number of teens who experiment with tobacco with the all too frequent tragic consequence of becoming addicted to the substance at an early age.

The sexual revolution of the 1970s has given way to somber discussions by teens and their parents and teachers about AIDS and other sexually transmitted diseases. Those few teens who were not already aware of the dangers, received sobering instruction through the dramatic announcement by Magic Johnson that he has the AIDS virus. Teens now often endorse the idea of chastity before marriage to ward off AIDS and other diseases, but even more often approve of free distribution of condoms in the schools in case temptation and adolescent hormones overcome prudence.

The great majority of teens aspire to form traditional families through marriage and children, and to work to make their marriages last.

The "generation gap" of a decade ago has all but disappeared: Few teens now name it as a problem and many report at least fairly harmonious relationships with their parents and an appreciation of the pressures they face.

The civil rights and women's rights movements of the 1970s era have been joined by new causes in the 1990s. Teens feel great strides have been made by blacks and by women in securing greater rights, but many feel more improvement is needed. Teens also now are more sensitive to the rights and needs of Hispanics and Asians in their midst. Increasingly, we are becoming a nation of diverse color, and in many school districts, members of minority groups now outnumber white students. To deal with the changes, teens usually express interest in receiving more education that is centered on the heritage and culture of minority groups and that places less emphasis on the literature of "dead white males." Teens, however, still debate the merits of the gay rights movement.

Most teen-agers are very concerned about the environment, both throughout the world and in their own country and community. They do not feel enough progress is being made to protect and restore the environment, and the great majority would willingly enlist in the cause to reverse the trends.

Teens today appear to have more confidence in their country and in themselves. Most appear to set lofty goals for themselves and more and more expect to enter college and obtain employment in a white-collar, technical, or professional field. Young women increasingly are moving beyond sexual stereotypes to seek entry into fields previously considered available or suitable only for men.

Teen-agers generally have a favorable impression of their own school and teachers. Many may rate themselves highly for their academic accomplishments, but they are also aware that perhaps homework, grading, and graduation requirements could be somewhat stricter. Unfortunately, violence in the schools persists in some areas to detract from teen scholastic ambitions.

Teens usually "want it all." For young women, this means not only marriage and children, but also sustaining a career through the family formation years.

America has always been a religious nation, and based upon the survey findings for the current young generation, appears likely to continue on that path. Teens in large numbers still believe in God, pray, read Scripture, and attend worship services.

Even through the materialistic culture of the 1980s decade—the so-called "Age of Greed"— teens appeared to place greater importance on values related to character, integrity, service, and knowledge. While also aspiring to various material goals, they generally try to place these in proper perspective.

Teens Still Know How To Have Fun

The teen-ager is an American invention, alternately envied and feared throughout the world. Whether the rest of the world likes it or not, sooner or later the music they hear will be influenced by American teen musical tastes, and so will the movies and the television fare they see.

Increasingly the diet of the world features "junk food" originally designed to appeal to American teen tastes, while teens throughout the world covet American jeans and black leather jackets that ultimately become incorporated into the designs of the fashion houses of Paris, Milan, and Tokyo.

The Gallup Youth Survey has continuously chronicled changes in American teen fads, tastes, and interests. The heavy and acid rock music that dominated the teen scene in 1977 when the Youth Survey was founded, has given way to the mellower sounds of radio's top-40 format which in turn is yielding to the syncopated beat of rap music.

In the teen music world of today most teens probably could not find the AM radio dial on their boom boxes, preferring the superior sound of FM radio. Similarly, compact discs have driven out LP and 45-rpm records, and cassettes and walkman recorders have replaced reel-to-reel and 8-track tapes.

Ask teens to name their favorite movie stars and many are likely to name a rock video or TV series performer who seldom if ever has been in motion pictures. In today's teen world, movies are not just found in theaters, but are regular fare on broadcast and cable television, or are available on pay-TV, on laser discs, and as rentals from the local video store. Add them all together and the effect is that the typical teens is likely to see over one hundred films a year. By their own admission teens feel they probably should be spending more time reading and doing home work, and less before the video screen.

Home computers have not entered the majority of teen households yet, and a career in computers has lost some of its glamour, but most teens have studied computers at school and know how to use them. For teens, word processors have replaced typewriters, and hand-held calculators have supplanted rote memorization of the multiplication tables. Most importantly, the majority of parents and grandparents in America seemingly would be unable to use their videocassette recorders without the programming expertise of a resident teen-ager. Not surprisingly, the typical teen home is wired wall to wall for sight, sound, and computing. Teens by their own admission say they probably spend too much time with the electronic fare and not enough reading or studying.

The economics of recession and the lure of the electronic media have hurt magazine sales among teens, but many still have access to daily newspapers. In addition to their required texts from school, many teens are likely to read mystery, suspense, action and adventure tales. While young men may dream of distant galaxies of the future when reading science fiction, young women are far more likely to read about the past in a gothic romance novel.

Comics are still read by some younger teens, but the Sunday color strips in the local newspaper attract a far larger audience, as teens catch up on the latest doings of "Garfield," "Peanuts" and "The Far Side."

Physical fitness has become a popular teen goal in recent years, and young women are just as likely as young men now to exercise and participate in sports. Individual sports are enjoying new popularity, and one of the most dramatic developments in the fitness movement has been the great increase in team sports participation by young women. Past stereotypes are falling rapidly as young women in increasing numbers take up such pursuits as weight training and football. The Gallup Youth Survey has had to keep pace with new teen equipment and activities such as cross-training, jazzercize, roller blades, and the latest skate boards.

Basketball is the team sport played most often by teens, and football is their favorite spectator sport. Individual stars such as Michael Jordan and Magic Johnson regularly find their way on to the lists of men in the world teens admire the most.

The American teen's love affair with the automobile has not abated, and it is still considered important to have a car of one's own at school or to cruise around downtown on Saturday night. The recession, however, has led many teens to lower their sights and seek a more economical model than those coveted by the yuppies and preppies of the 1980s.

All in all, nearly all teens probably would disagree strongly with Mark Twain's assessment that youth is wasted on the young.

History

The Gallup Youth Survey was founded in 1977 by the late Dr. George H.Gallup. The youth culture and frequent protests of the 1960s and 1970s era had made it clear to him that systematic, objective information about the values, opinions, attitudes and behavior of young people should be collected through surveys to provide information to parents, citizens, policy makers and social scientists concerning the nation's and the world's youth. Most importantly, Dr. Gallup also wanted to provide information to the young people of the nation about themselves so that they could have a true and proper understanding of the views and behavior of their fellow citizens.

Gallup and others had conducted *ad hoc* surveys among young people in the past, but the lack of a sustained effort severely compromised any attempts to provide comparative analyses with previous generations of teen-agers. Some continuing surveys did exist, but invariably they were either confined to narrow segments of young people such as graduating high school seniors or entering college freshmen, or were focused upon marketing research topics that shed little light upon social, health, moral, religious or political concerns. A continuing effort to sample a wide spectrum of teen-agers on salient topics was needed.

There also was an important need for objective interpretation of the survey data: All too often surveys in the period were seriously flawed by questioning and sampling techniques that would yield results that would fulfill theories popular at the time either by presenting the nation's youth as revolutionaries or by indulging in "teen bashing" depictions of a generation of narcissistic, drug-crazed, sexually promiscuous delinquents. The first Gallup Youth Surveys, through proper sampling and questioning methodology, served to correct the record by showing that the preponderance of teens in the 1970s were already concerned about the impact of drugs upon their generation, often embraced traditional values, and sought to serve their nation, world and humanity.

To provide wide dissemination of the information about youth, the Gallup Youth Survey since its inception has been syndicated nationally as a weekly newspaper column by Associated Press Newsfeatures, first under the by-line of George Gallup, and now under the names of his sons, Alec M. Gallup and George H. Gallup, Jr. James Shriver, III served as the first editor of the Gallup Youth Survey until 1983. Since that time Robert Bezilla has served as editor and director. A compendium of the first decade of research by the Gallup Youth Survey was published in 1988 as *America's Youth 1977–1988*.

Initially, the Gallup Youth Survey was conducted as part of the Gallup Organization's American Institute of Public Opinion, which also conducted the Gallup Poll. In 1988, The George H. Gallup International Institute was founded to carry on the mission of Dr. Gallup, and the Gallup Youth Survey became an integral unit of the new Institute.

The Gallup Youth Survey fits well with the Institute's four primary mission areas of concern: education, health, the environment, and religion and values. While greatest emphasis is being placed upon these areas of concern by the Gallup Youth Survey, it continues to study the full spectrum of the young person's world so that the total context of the youth experience can be better understood. In this way, such forces as popular culture, the media, political events, and economic affairs can be assessed according to their impact upon the education, health, environment and values of youth.

The Institute also provides important and comprehensive direction to the activities of the Gallup Youth Survey through the counsel of its staff and Board of Trustees.

Reading the Tables

These are some of the patterns which have impressed us over the years, and the reader may wish to keep them in mind while reading the statistical tables of the findings.

Gender — This is becoming less and less of a factor. Early analyses of the Gallup Youth Survey frequently called attention to differences. More recently, no significant differences between the sexes in many aspects of their attitudes and behavior can be found.

Age — There often is a difference between older and younger teens. Children usually enter their teen years with optimism, trust, and hope for the future. Their faith and morals often seem stronger than our own. It is not unusual, however, to find they enter a period of rebellion in the early teen years. As teens grow older, rebelliousness often subsides as they gain maturity and become more accustomed to their growing bodies and emotions. By age 16, many appear to have a clearer vision of their future. For some it is exciting and challenging. For others, tragically, there almost seems to be a realization of future failure, with a turning towards self-destructive behavior.

Race — The non-white segment of young people is growing faster than the white segment, because of immigration and higher birth rates. Non-white teens often lack the advantages possessed by whites, and probably bear the burdens of prejudice and bias. Despite this, their interest in seeking peace, harmony, and achieving the betterment of the world's people usually is markedly above-average.

Academic performance — This is a self-reported classification. The majority of teens seem to view themselves as, to use Garrison Keiller's phrase, "slightly above average." Accordingly, the classifications, in addition to giving some measurement of academic achievement, may be useful indicators of self-confidence.

Region — We are becoming an increasingly homogeneous nation, but some regional differences persist. Teens in the East and West usually have more liberal attitudes and are quicker to adapt to new trends and fads than are those in the Midwest and South. Those in the heartland of the country more often show a deeper religious faith and higher ideals.

City size — The majority of young people of the inner city too often are blamed for the miscreant behavior of a few. Living in large cities does not make young people any less optimistic, virtuous, or fun loving. Suburbanites often enjoy the greatest material advantages and frequently have the added benefit of well-educated parents. Teens living in rural areas often have the fewest material and cultural advantages, but often appear to compensate by drawing upon greater inner strength. Teens from small towns sometimes seem to be the most malcontent, perhaps because they suffer from many of the inconveniences of urban life while not enjoying the cosmopolitan offerings of larger cities.

Religious preference — The designation *Protestant* embraces a wide range of beliefs and social contexts, including evangelical Blacks from both the South and northern cities, born-again teens from the "Bible Belt," and mainline Protestant denomination members. Catholics may be somewhat more homogeneous, but past stereotypes of immigrant blue-collar families no longer hold true — Catholics as a group now are more upscale than Protestants.

Interviewing Teen-agers

Initially, the Gallup Youth Survey sampled young people between the ages of 13 and 18. The only rationale perhaps in choosing that particular age span was that these probably are the years most people think of as being the "teen" years. The age could be, and has on occasion, been lowered to 12 or younger. After 1982, the sample dropped 18-year-olds because of an awkward overlap among those who are age 18 between the Gallup Youth Survey and the adult samples such as the Gallup Poll.

The Gallup Youth Survey sample is derived from the Gallup Organization's national adult sample, and is nationally projectible. Initially, sample sizes were about 1,000 to 1,200 interviews each, and surveys were conducted once or twice a year. After 1982, they have been conducted more frequently, but usually with a sample of 500 to 600 interviews.

The interviews are conducted by telephone. In the early days of the Gallup Youth Survey, calls were made by resident interviewers; more recently they have been conducted from Gallup's various central telephone interviewing facilities. The interviews average from 20 to 45 minutes in length. Occasionally, we are asked if it is difficult to keep teens on the telephone for that length of time. In response we can simply say that the question has never been raised by anyone who has ever had a teen-ager in the house.

There was a great deal of experimentation in questioning during the first few surveys. An initial assumption held by some was that, at least among younger teens, the questioning had to be "light;" that is, should not include the weightier topics usually addressed in the Gallup Poll. As a consequence, there were many questions on the order of:

"Do you consider yourself good-looking or attractive, or not?"
"Have you ever been in love?"
"Did you kiss on your first date, or not?"

And, in that early period, quizzes that showed how ignorant teens were about geography, politics, and cultural affairs were very popular. Questions and quizzes of this nature may have been "interesting," but there seldom seemed to be much that one could do with them, particularly in terms of measuring trends. Fortunately, there also were some questions on more essential matters such as Presidential approval, the most important problem facing the generation, and substance abuse. Today, the early findings on these matters are invaluable components of a growing data bank of teen measurements. We only wish that we had comparable measurements going back to even earlier decades.

To provide that kind of continuity we have identified a series of questions we believe should be repeated at systematical periodical intervals. Presidential approval and most-important-problem-facing-the-nation questions are asked on almost every survey to uncover new trends in opinions. Matters such as basic questions on substance abuse, media habits, and most admired men and women usually are asked annually. Slower-changing topics such as values and religion are researched biennially.

We have discovered so far there is no practical limit to the topics that can be asked of younger teens. That is to say, they are generally willing to offer opinions on just about any topic. There are some considerations, however, that should be borne in mind when questioning teens, especially those who are younger.

1. The vocabulary of teens may be more limited than that of adults. In asking adults about education, for example, the wording used is "Students often are given grades A, B, C, D and Fail to *denote* the quality of their work. Suppose the schools in your community. . . ?" For teens, we simply ask "Students often are given grades A, B, C, D and Fail on the quality of . . ." (One might question the use of 'denote' even for an adult general survey. Phrasing questions for teens can be a helpful exercise in developing wordings that usually will be understood by most members of the general populace.)

2. Occasionally, special qualifications should be added to questions for teens. When asking about most admired men and women, the questions are rephrased as "What one man that you have heard or read, alive today in any part of the world, do you admire the most— *not including any of your relatives or personal friends?*"

3. When asking about candidate and political party preferences it is necessary to add qualifiers such as . . . *when you are old enough to vote.*

There may be few restrictions upon what may be asked of younger teens, but there are some definite limitations to the way in which they respond.

The range of response that can be expected from young teens *a priori* should be expected to be more limited than that of older teens or adults for the simple reason that younger teens have not lived as long, and therefore have not been able to accumulate comparable quantities of experience and information.

When we ask younger teens to report on their behavior, we anticipate they will have fewer experiences to report. Care must be exercised in interpreting their limited reports. If, for example, younger teens less often report substance abuse and experimentation, it does not always necessarily follow that they are more virtuous; it may simply be a matter of not having access or the opportunity to use the substances. Indeed, when younger teens report levels of substance abuse or maintain attitudes about the substances that are comparable to those of older teens or adults, this can be a cause for alarm.

The attitudes and opinions of teens can also be limited by their store of knowledge and experience. When people wonder why young people and teens seem to have admired contemporary presidents so much, it must be remembered that for the youngest teens they were the only presidents they have ever known. In the case of a survey taken in 1988 for the youngest teens, Ronald Reagan was the incumbent president since the first moment they became aware there was such a thing as a president. Even for older teens, Jimmy Carter as president would have been only a vague memory at best.

While contemporary presidents benefit from this limitation of knowledge, they also have suffered from it when the tables are turned and teens are asked to give their opinions about "worst presidents."

Greatest U.S. Presidents (First Three Mentions)

Teens	1985		
	Teens 13–15	Adults 16–17	18 & older
Ronald Reagan	28%	23%	21%
Jimmy Carter	10	13	9
Gerald Ford	6	7	*
Richard Nixon	4	9	11
Lyndon Johnson	1	1	5
John Kennedy	38	44	56
Dwight Eisenhower	1	4	16
Harry Truman	3	5	26
Franklin Roosevelt	14	27	41
Herbert Hoover	1	*	1
Abraham Lincoln	54	52	48
Thomas Jefferson	9	6	7
George Washington	52	40	25

* Less than one-half of I percent.

AIPO 837, Q. 116

Note that in 1985 Ronald Reagan drew most mention from young teens, while older teens were most likely to cite Jimmy Carter, Gerald Ford, or Richard Nixon as great presidents. Adults were far more likely to name John Kennedy, Dwight Eisenhower, Harry Truman, Franklin Roosevelt. Eisenhower and Truman are barely mentioned by teens of any age.

Not surprisingly, younger teens make do with the knowledge and experience they have. To give an example: when asked to name whom they admire the most, younger teens are somewhat more likely than those who are older to include entertainers and sports stars on their lists.

Another consequence of their lack of experience is that younger teens often are less likely than their elders to know their limitations and to give optimistic predictions about their futures, e.g., envision themselves as future rock stars, professional athletes, and as achieving success early in life.

Finally, when one looks at the bottom of the table at the "don't know," "no opinion" and other non-response categories that might indicate an inability to respond to standard survey questioning, the proportion of non-responders among younger teens is not much greater than that found among older teens, or, for that matter, among adults. The following table is derived from a sample 144 questions taken from Gallup Youth Survey questionnaires in the period of 1988–1989. Overall, average non-response among younger teens (3.8%) is only one point higher than reported by older teens (2.8%)

Non-Response to Gallup Youth Survey Questions
(Mean non-response for each category of questions)

	Teens 13–15	Teens 16–17
Personal questions	.7%	.1%
Substance abuse	1.3	.7
Entertainment and media	1.5	1.3
Education	1.9	1.8
Economics	2.4	1.0
Political issues	6.0	4.2
Social issues	6.3	4.2
OVERALL	3.8	2.8

Don't Call Them "Kids"

Throughout this report you will probably note that we almost never use the terms "kids" or "boys and girls" when describing the opinions of young people. We have asked those who respond to our surveys about the terms they find acceptable. Accordingly, we follow their wishes and refer to people who are 13 to 17 years of age as "teens," "teen-agers," "young adults," and "young men and women." When writing about those in school we use the term "students" rather than "high schoolers."

About two young people in three (64 percent) say "young adults" is a very acceptable term in describing them, and an additional 30 percent find this somewhat acceptable. The variation of "young men and women" is very acceptable to 59 percent of young people.

The term "youth" finds far less endorsement, with only three young people in 10 (29 percent) saying it is very acceptable. It is rated somewhat acceptable by 55 percent, but 16 percent say it is not acceptable.

The full term "teen-agers " is acceptable to six young people in 10 (60 percent) and an additional 35 percent say it is somewhat acceptable. Fewer young people, however, find "teens" to be very acceptable (53 percent). "Teens" is most acceptable to young men (58 percent) and to those who are ages 13 to 15 (56 percent). Fewer young women (49 percent) or older teenagers (50 percent) say the abbreviated form is very acceptable.

Nearly half of the teens (46 percent) say it is very acceptable to call them "students," and 49 percent find the term somewhat acceptable. The more specific term of "high schooler" finds less favor and is very acceptable to only 37 percent of the young people.

Only one person in five (19 percent) in the "adolescent" years finds it very acceptable to be addressed by that term. Sixty percent acknowledge the term is somewhat acceptable.

"Boys and girls" is found to be very acceptable to just 18 percent of the young people, somewhat acceptable to 49 percent, but rated unacceptable by 32 percent. Even fewer teenagers like to be called "kids," with only 10 percent saying the term is very acceptable, 40 percent somewhat acceptable, and half (49 percent) rating it unacceptable.

Seven teenagers in 10 (71 percent) reject the idea of being called children.

We also avoid using terms such as kids or boys or girls when questioning young people for the Gallup Youth Survey because from teenagers' perspective, kids, children, boys and girls are people younger than themselves. It is better to use a phrase such as "people your own age."

Preferred Descriptions

November 1989

	Very acceptable	Somewhat acceptable	Not acceptable
Young adults	64%	30%	6%
Teen-agers	60	35	4
Young men and women	59	34	7
Teens	53	40	6
Students	46	49	5
High schoolers	37	50	12
Youth	29	55	16
Adolescents	19	60	19
Boys and girls	18	49	32
Kids	10	40	49
Children	7	21	71

Satisfaction with own life

Influences

Greatest problems

Parental relationships

Parental strictness

Stress

Family discussions

SELF, PARENTS, FAMILY, PEERS

Satisfaction with Own Life

Teen-agers' optimism about themselves generally is at a constant high level, but also can be subject to upward and downward swings that often mirror their confidence in the nation (see page 111). Self-confidence among teens was at its lowest point in 1980 when 82 percent said they were satisfied with the way things were going in their personal lives. By 1986, nine teens in 10 said things were going well for them. In 1992, however, the satisfaction level was 86 percent.

1.1 Trend in Satisfaction with Personal Life

In general, are you satisfied or dissatisfied with the way things are going in your own personal life?

1992	86%
1988	85
1987	87
1986	90
1985	88
1983	82
1980	82
1979	87

1.2 Satisfaction with Own Life

	September – October 1992	
	Satisfied	Dissatisfied
National	**86%**	**12%**
Male	88	11
Female	85	12
Ages 13 – 15	88	8
Ages 16 – 17	83	16
White	86	12
Non-white	86	11
White-collar background	89	10
Blue-collar background	85	10
Above-average students	88	10
Average and below	84	13
East	84	14
Midwest	84	13
South	84	13
West	87	10
Large city	92	7
Suburb	91	9
Small town	83	15
Rural	84	12
Republican	89	10
Democrat	85	12
Independent	85	14
Protestant	84	14
Catholic	88	10
Church attender	88	10
Non-attender	84	14

Note: 2 percent of teens held no opinion.

GO 12869; Q. 13

Influences

Friends, families, and schools are named by America's teens as the people and institutions that are having the most influence upon their generation. While the ideas learned from religious leaders and great books may have had considerable impact upon past generations of teens, a high proportion of young people today report that music and television are exerting great influence upon them. Even Hollywood apparently is encountering difficulty in capturing teen imaginations, as few young people now believe the movies are having much impact upon them.

Nearly nine teens in 10 say friends have a great deal of influence on them.

The home environment has great influence upon young people in the opinion of half of the teens. Next in importance are the nation's schools, with 45 percent of the teens rating them as having a great deal of influence.

Social critics and educators have long worried about the disproportionate impact modern music and television are having upon America's youth, and the survey results suggest they may have good reason to be concerned. Three teens in four, for example, say music is having a great deal or some influence upon young people. Similar proportions of teens attach a great deal or some importance to the impact television is believed to have upon their generation.

Movies have long counted upon teens as an important source of their audience and revenues, but now only one young person in five feels the silver screen, be it at the theater or on a television set, has great impact on the contemporary teen scene.

The role of the print media in molding young minds and tastes currently has been seriously diminished in the opinions of young people. Magazine publishers probably will be discomforted to learn that only 9 percent of the nation's teens view their publications as having a great deal of influence upon their generation.

The outlook for the future of book publishing will be even bleaker if current teen attitudes are carried over into their adult lives. Just 3 percent of the teens now feel books are having a great deal of influence upon their contemporaries.

Religion now is believed by only one teen in eight to have a great deal of influence upon America's youth.

1.3 Influences on Teens

Do you feel today's teen-agers are influenced a great deal, some, a little, or very little by ...?

	April 1990			
	Great deal	**Some**	**Little**	**Very little**
Friends	87%	11%	1%	1%
Home	51	31	14	4
School	45	36	14	5
Music	41	35	17	7
Television	32	43	18	7
Movies	19	48	22	11
Religion	13	30	28	28
Magazines	9	41	32	17
Books	3	23	41	32

Note: 1 percent of the teens did not make a choice.

Personal Problems

Ask teen-agers about the greatest personal problems they face, and they most probably will talk about the pressures they are under to get good grades at school or their concerns about college and future careers. Evidence from the Gallup Youth Survey suggests, however, that teens are less willing to recognize or perhaps to admit the friction that so often occurs between parents and teen-agers. Teens are about twice as likely to say their best friend has problems in getting along with parents than to say they, themselves, have similar conflicts. This finding suggests teens may be better in identifying other's family conflicts than in either recognizing or admitting their own domestic tensions.

Teens usually feel they and their friends are about the same in suffering from the growing pains of adolescence Teens, however, may be far more adept in recognizing the various kinds of fears they have themselves than in seeing the fears entertained by their best friend.

1.4 Greatest Problems Facing Teens
(Three greatest problems named by teens)

Which of the following is the single greatest problem you face today? In addition to the above, what are the two next most important problems you face? What are the three biggest problems your best friend faces?

	April 1991	
	Teen's own top-three problems	Best friend's top-three problems
School grades	33%	27%
Career uncertainties	25	11
Growing pains	18	14
Fears	18	7
Getting along with parents	16	31
Being liked	15	15
Financing college	15	9
School problems	14	20
Drug abuse	12	10
Fear of war	12	5
Peer pressures	11	11
Weight problems	11	8
Concern about AIDS	10	5
Economic problems	10	8
Alcohol abuse	9	15
Depression	8	8
Teen pregnancy	7	8
Other	7	7
No response	2	7

Most Important Problems Facing Teens

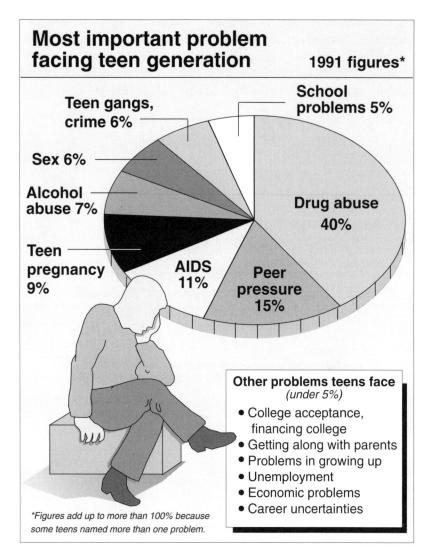

Most important problem facing teen generation

1991 figures*

Teen gangs, crime 6%

Sex 6%

Alcohol abuse 7%

Teen pregnancy 9%

AIDS 11%

Peer pressure 15%

Drug abuse 40%

School problems 5%

Other problems teens face
(under 5%)
- College acceptance, financing college
- Getting along with parents
- Problems in growing up
- Unemployment
- Economic problems
- Career uncertainties

Figures add up to more than 100% because some teens named more than one problem.

Teen-agers for the first time in recent history have the freedom of spending less time worrying about international tensions, the economy, and even the war on drugs, and are able to turn their focus on a variety of problems confronting the nation and their generation.

Drug and alcohol abuse still rank first as the problem of greatest concern to teens, but their importance is diminished as they are joined by other emerging social concerns.

Fifteen years ago, one teen in five was concerned about the "generation gap," and reported that getting along with their parents was the greatest problems faced by young people. Today, only 2 percent still cite this as the most important problem facing their generation.

Grim, new problems, however, now confront the teen generation: One teen in nine cites AIDS as a most important problem. Concern about teen-age pregnancy first appeared on the lists of problems five years ago and is still increasing. In urban areas teen gangs threaten the current generation.

Teen suicide, although statistically not a matter of great concern in national terms, can have devastating impact upon local communities of teens when it occurs.

"Peer pressures" cover a lot of problems and their importance has steadily increased in recent years.

In fact, the problems are so many that only about one teen in 20 appears to be a blissful state of non-awareness of the problems confronting his generation.

1.5 Greatest Problem Facing Teen Generation

What do you feel is the biggest problem facing people your age?

	1992	1991	1987	1985	1983	1977
Drug abuse	40%	49%	54%	40%	35%	27%
Alcohol abuse	7	11	12	14	10	7
Peer pressures	15	13	10	8	8	5
AIDS	11	6	5	–	–	–
Teen-age pregnancy	9	10	11	3	–	–
Sex	6	4	*	*	*	*
Crime, teen gangs	6	9	*	*	*	*
School problems	5	3	1	4	5	3
Getting along with parents	2	2	2	2	5	20
Problems in growing up	2	1	2	5	1	6
Financing college	2	3	1	3	1	–
Unemployment	1	2	2	8	16	6
Fear of war	–	*	1	2	4	–
Economic problems	1	2	1	3	2	3
Career uncertainties	1	1	–	–	3	3
Teen-age suicide	*	1	2	3	–	–
Miscellaneous	4	8	5	7	5	12
Don't know	6	12	8	13	18	14

*Less than one-half of 1 percent

Note: Columns add to more than 100% because some teens named more than one problem.

Parental Relationships

Most teens get on well with their parents, but are twice as likely to get along better with their mothers than with their fathers.

A majority of teens (52 percent) in 1992 said they got on very well with their parents. An additional 44 percent believed they got on fairly well. Only 4 percent of the teens reported their relations with their parents were so strained that they believed they did not get on well with them at all.

Teens were twice as likely to say that they get on better with their mothers (52 percent) than to believe that relationships with their fathers were smoother (26 percent). One teen in five (21 percent) was fortunate enough to report that he got on equally well with both his father and mother.

Opinions by teens that their parents are too strict with them have been increasing slowly but surely over the past several years. In 1985, 29 percent said their parents were too strict. By 1987, the proportion of teens complaining about overly-strict parents rose to 34 percent, and by 1992, to 38 percent. Parents are about right in their amount of strictness according to 37 percent of teens, while 24 percent say they may be too lenient.

1.6 Parental Strictness Trend

Do you think your parents are too strict with you, or not strict enough?

	Too strict	Not Strict enough	About right
1992	38%	24%	37%
1987	34	22	42
1985	29	28	41

How well would say you get along with your parents — very well, fairly well, or not at all well?

	September – October 1992		
	Very well	Fairly well	Not at all well
National	**52%**	**44%**	**4%**
Male	53	43	4
Female	52	44	4
Ages 13 – 15	54	44	2
Ages 16 – 17	50	43	7
White	51	45	4
Non-white	57	40	3
White-collar background	52	44	4
Blue-collar background	49	46	5
Above-average students	59	39	2
Average and below	43	50	7
East	53	40	7
Midwest	55	41	4
South	47	50	3
West	57	39	3
Large city	56	40	4
Suburb	50	49	1
Small town	45	50	5
Rural	63	33	4
Republican	57	40	3
Democrat	51	44	5
Independent	48	46	6
Protestant	56	40	4
Catholic	51	46	3
Church attender	57	40	3
Non-attender	48	48	4

GO 12869. 15

1.8 Get Along Better with Mother or Father?

Would you say you get along better with your mother or your father?

	September – October 1992			
	Mother	**Father**	**Both**	**Neither**
National	**52%**	**24%**	**21%**	**2%**
Male	46	27	25	2
Female	60	21	16	2
Ages 13 – 15	57	22	20	1
Ages 16 – 17	47	28	21	3
White	50	26	21	2
Non-white	61	18	19	2
White-collar background	51	25	21	2
Blue-collar background	55	25	19	1
Above-average students	51	27	21	1
Average and below	55	20	20	2
East	49	17	32	–
Midwest	59	21	16	3
South	51	27	18	2
West	50	29	20	–
Large city	62	21	15	2
Suburb	50	33	15	1
Small town	52	21	24	1
Rural	50	27	20	3
Republican	50	25	22	2
Democrat	57	29	11	3
Independent				
Protestant	52	22	22	3
Catholic	53	30	17	–
Church attender	53	24	21	1
Non-attender	53	25	20	2

Note: 1 percent of the teens did not make a choice.

GO 12869; Q. 16

1.9 How Strict Are Parents?

Do you think your parents are too strict with you, or not strict enough?

| | September – October 1992 | | |
	Too strict	Too lax	About right
National	**38%**	**24%**	**37%**
Male	34	25	39
Female	42	24	34
Ages 13 – 15	37	27	35
Ages 16 – 17	39	21	40
White	35	25	39
Non-white	47	22	30
White-collar background	35	21	43
Blue-collar background	38	32	29
Above-average students	36	22	41
Average and below	39	28	31
East	45	24	31
Midwest	32	29	38
South	42	19	38
West	32	28	39
Large city	49	16	35
Suburb	41	20	39
Small town	35	28	36
Rural	34	25	39
Republican	34	27	39
Democrat	43	22	34
Independent	35	30	34
Protestant	39	24	37
Catholic	34	31	34
Church attender	40	23	36
Non-attender	35	26	38

Note: 1 percent of the teens had no opinion.

GO 12869; Q. 17

Family Stresses

Only one teenager in four (25 percent) thinks he has more problems and pressures than his parents. Two in three teens (65 percent) view their parents as having more stressful lives, and 9 percent feel they are about equal.

A majority of the teens (54 percent) believe their mothers and fathers are coping very well, and an additional 40 percent say they are doing at least fairly well. Just 4 percent of teens feel their parents are not handling pressures too well.

Age makes a difference in how teens view stress in their families. Teens who are 16 and older are slightly more likely than those who are 13 to 15 to believe they have greater problems and pressures than their parents, by a margin of 29 percent to 23 percent. Older teens (58 percent) are also more inclined than those who are younger (51 percent) to think their parents are doing very well in coping with problems.

Teen-agers cite money (38 percent) as the problem their parents are most concerned about. Teens from blue-collar families (43 percent) are more likely than those from white-collar households (37 percent) to say that their parents most often worry about money. Raising children (24 percent) is rated second as the leading problem that parents face. One teen in 10 views work-related pressures as the major problem confronting parents. Another 5 percent report that their parents seem most preoccupied with bettering their lives. Divorced or separated parents are named by only 3 percent of the teens as the leading domestic problem. Only 1 percent of the teenagers interviewed report that health concerns are of paramount importance, and fewer than 1 percent say that drug or alcohol-related pressures are of utmost importance in their parents' lives.

1.10 Parental Stress

| | March – April 1990 | | | | |
	National	Male	Female	Ages 13–15	Ages 16–17
Compared to teens do parents have more or fewer problems and pressures?					
More	65%	66%	65%	69%	61%
About the same	9	9	7	7	9
Fewer	25	24	27	23	29
Not sure	1	1	1	1	1
How well are parents handling problems and pressures?					
Very well	54	53	55	51	58
Fairly well	40	43	38	42	37
Not too well	4	3	6	5	4
Not sure	2	1	1	2	1

Family Dinner Discussions

School-related situations are the most frequent topic of conversation during the dinner hour in teen households. Developments during school hours are discussed during the evening meal by 73 percent of the teens. Young women (77 percent) are more likely than young men (70 percent) to favor school activities as topics for conversations with other family members. About nine teens in 10 (88 percent) reported some form of discussion took place during dinner the day before they were interviewed. Very close to half of the teenagers (49 percent) said they talked about family problems and interests, and 42 percent reported they engaged in conversation centering on the day's news developments.

Young women are more likely than young men to talk about family interests and problems (54 percent to 43 percent). Students with above-average grades discuss current events at the dinner table more often than academic under-achievers (50 percent to 32 percent).

Teenagers report they eat dinner with other family members on an average of five times a week. One teen in three (35 percent) has all dinners at home. Eight percent say they eat dinner alone every night of the week. As teens get older they tend to eat fewer evening meals with others in the household. Those aged 13 to 15 say they have dinner at home with family on an average of more than six times a week. However, by age 16 the average drops to slightly less than four times a week.

In about half of households in which teenagers live (51 percent) grace is said before dinner. Protestant family members pray more often than Catholics (60 percent to 48 percent). Those who are 13 to 15 years of age say grace more often than the 16 and 17 year olds (57 percent to 44 percent).

In almost one half of the households (48 percent) either a television set, or a radio is turned on, or someone is reading a newspaper, magazine or book during dinner. Thirty nine percent said that a TV was on close by while dinner was being consumed. Another 12 percent said radio music programs were heard at dinner time and 13 percent say they read while eating.

1.11 Teen Happenings During Dinner

| | March – April 1990 | | |
	National	Male	Female
Talked about . . .			
School	73%	70%	77%
Family problems and interests	49	43	54
News and current events	42	42	42
Said Grace before the meal	51	52	51
Watched TV	39	38	40
Listened to the radio	12	11	14
Read a book, magazine or newspaper	13	12	14

Marriage intentions

Family planning

Attitudes towards divorce

Abortion

Sex education

AIDS

MARRIAGE, DIVORCE, CHILDREN, SEX

Marriage and Children

In 1992, teens who thought they would marry some day outnumbered those who expected to remain single, by a margin of 88 percent to 9 percent. An additional 3 percent have yet to make up their minds on the subject.

Most teens (84 percent) also said they would like to have children some day. Only 4 percent expected to be married but not have children. The remaining teens either did not plan to marry or had not made any decisions concerning children.

Nearly half of the teens (45 percent) said they would like to have two children. A single child was wanted by 8 percent of the teens, but three was the number named by 21 percent. Four or more children were desired by 9 percent of the teens.

Young men (86 percent) and young women (88 percent) were about equal in expressing beliefs that they would be married some day. Young women however, were slightly more likely than young men to say they would like to have children, by a margin of 88 percent to 81 percent.

2.1 Marriage and Children Trend

	Like to marry	Want to have children
1992	88%	84%
1988	86	76
1987	85	80
1986	88	83
1984	88	83
1983	82	79
1977	84	79

2.2 Marriage Intentions

Do you think you will get married some day, or do you think you will remain single?

| | September – October 1992 | | |
	Get married	Stay single	Not sure
National	**88%**	**9%**	**3%**
Male	86	11	3
Female	88	8	4
Ages 13 – 15	88	8	4
Ages 16 – 17	88	10	2
White	89	8	3
Non-white	85	11	4
White-collar background	94	4	2
Blue-collar background	83	13	4
Above-average students	92	6	2
Average and below	83	12	5
East	85	6	9
Midwest	87	12	1
South	90	8	2
West	89	8	3
Large city	82	16	2
Suburb	94	5	1
Small town	89	8	3
Rural	90	6	4
Republican	92	6	2
Democrat	89	9	2
Independent	88	10	2
Protestant	90	7	3
Catholic	88	10	2
Church attender	89	8	3
Non-attender	88	9	3

GO 12869; Q. 18

2.3 Child Planning

When you do get married, would you like to have children, or not? [Question was asked of only those who said they planned to marry some day.]

	September – October 1992	
	Yes, want to have children	Average number wanted
National	**84%**	**2.3**
Male	81	2.1
Female	88	2.4
Ages 13 – 15	85	2.2
Ages 16 – 17	83	2.4
White	85	2.2
Non-white	84	2.4
White-collar background	88	2.3
Blue-collar background	82	2.2
Above-average students	89	2.3
Average and below	78	2.2
East	84	2.2
Midwest	83	2.4
South	84	2.1
West	86	2.3
Large city	80	2.6
Suburb	90	2.3
Small town	82	2.2
Rural	89	2.3
Republican	86	2.4
Democrat	85	2.3
Independent	83	2.2
Protestant	84	2.3
Catholic	87	2.4
Church attender	86	2.3
Non-attender	83	2.4

GO 12869; Q. 19–20

Important note: These findings are based on all teens, not just those planning to be married.

Attitudes Towards Divorce

Many teens in 1992 believed the divorce laws in the nation are too lax, with 76 percent saying that divorces are too easy to get, compared to only 16 percent who felt they are too difficult to obtain. The laws are about right according to 2 percent of the teens, and another 6 percent had no opinion on the matter.

Seven teens in 10 (71 percent) believed that most people who have been divorced probably have not tried hard enough to save their marriages. Disagreeing were 23 percent of the teens, and 6 percent held no opinion.

Teens who are 16 or older and nearing the age when they may be giving serious consideration to marriage, take the strongest stand against divorce. Older teens (80 percent) are more likely than those who are 13 to 15 years old (73 percent) to believe the divorce laws are too lax. The older teens, by a margin of 80 percent to 65 percent, are also more likely to say that most divorced couples probably did not try hard enough to save their marriages.

2.4 Opinion of Divorce Trends

	Believe divorce laws are too lax	Believe divorced couples try hard to save marriages
1992	76%	23%
1988	72	30
1987	73	25
1986	79	25
1984	75	22
1983	66	23
1981	73	24
1977	55	29

2.5 Ease of Getting a Divorce

Generally speaking, do you think it is too easy, or not easy enough for people in this country to get divorced?

	September – October 1992		
	Too easy	Not easy enough	About right
National	**76%**	**16%**	**2%**
Male	75	18	1
Female	77	15	4
Ages 13 – 15	73	19	3
Ages 16 – 17	80	12	2
White	78	15	2
Non-white	69	22	2
White-collar background	80	12	3
Blue-collar background	75	19	1
Above-average students	82	11	2
Average and below	68	23	3
East	67	22	3
Midwest	81	12	–
South	77	17	3
West	77	16	3
Large city	83	12	2
Suburb	82	12	2
Small town	73	19	3
Rural	77	17	1
Republican	83	11	3
Democrat	80	13	1
Independent	77	18	2
Protestant	79	13	3
Catholic	74	19	1
Church attender	82	13	2
Non-attender	70	20	3

Note: 6 percent of the teens had no opinion.

GO 12869: Q. 21

46

2.6 Opinion of Those Who Got Divorces

Generally speaking, do you think that most people who get divorced have tried hard enough to save their marriages, or not?

	September – October 1992	
	Tried hard	**Did not try**
National	**23%**	**71%**
Male	20	73
Female	26	69
Ages 13 – 15	29	65
Ages 16 – 17	14	80
White	20	74
Non-white	34	62
White-collar background	22	74
Blue-collar background	20	72
Above-average students	21	72
Average and below	25	70
East	25	68
Midwest	22	70
South	21	74
West	25	71
Large city	28	68
Suburb	19	78
Small town	24	70
Rural	18	73
Republican	18	78
Democrat	26	69
Independent	24	73
Protestant	20	75
Catholic	25	69
Church attender	23	73
Non-attender	23	70

Note: 6 percent of the teens had no opinion.

GO 12869; Q. 22

Abortion

The acrimonious and emotional debates on abortion which have so sharply divided our society are not likely to go away in the coming decade. If anything, America's teens appear to be even more closely divided than their parents and elders on the issue. Teens by nearly equal numbers support or oppose the extreme positions of either outlawing all abortions or allowing women to have abortions for any reason they choose.

2.7 Opinion of Abortion

Please tell me how much you support or oppose each of these issues and causes—support very much, support somewhat, oppose somewhat, or oppose very much. Outlawing all abortions for any reason. Allowing a woman to have an abortion for any reason she chooses.

	June – July 1991	
	Allow abortions for any reason	**Outlaw all abortions**
National	**47%**	**44%**
Male	50	45
Female	43	43
Ages 13 – 15	47	48
Ages 16 – 17	46	40
White	45	44
Non-white	53	45
Above-average students	43	46
Average and below	51	42
East	47	43
Midwest	48	49
South	40	47
West	52	34
Protestant	46	44
Catholic	48	45
Church attender	37	51
Non-attender	56	38

GO 224007; Q. 11

Roe v. Wade

A majority of America's teenagers in a 1990 Gallup Youth Survey opposed repealing the U.S. Supreme Court's 1973 Roe v. Wade decision. The judges ruled at that time that states in this country cannot place restrictions on a woman's right to abortion during the first three months of her pregnancy.

In favor of repealing the Court's verdict are 41 percent of the teens, while 54 percent oppose changing it. Support of the law is greater among teens aged 16 or 17 (58 percent) than among those in the 13-to-15 age group (50 percent).

Slightly more than half (52 percent) of the teen-age women interviewed support the pro-choice position, while 43 percent are against it. Male teenagers are even more inclined to back the Supreme Court's regulation (55 percent) than to oppose it (39 percent).

The teens' greatest opposition to abortion comes from the South where pro-lifers edge pro-choice advocates, 48 to 47 percent.

Among those who attended religious services in the seven-day period preceding the interview, 49 percent would like to see the Supreme Court reverse itself, while only 33 percent support its position. Among teenagers who did not attend church recently, those in favor of the law outnumber reformers by a margin of 63 percent to 33 percent.

2.8 Opinion of Roe v. Wade

In 1973 the Supreme Court ruled that states cannot place restrictions on a woman's right to abortion during the first three months of pregnancy. Would you like to see this ruling overturned, or not?

	March – April 1990	
	Favor repeal	**Oppose repeal**
National	**41%**	**54%**
Male	39	55
Female	43	52
Ages 13 – 15	44	50
Ages 16 – 17	36	58
White	41	53
Non-white	39	57
Above-average students	40	54
Average and below	41	54
East	35	58
Midwest	43	52
South	48	47
West	33	62
Republican	44	52
Democrat	38	56
Protestant	45	51
Catholic	42	57

Parental Notification Laws

Most teenagers in 1990 said they would approve state laws requiring a woman under age 18 to obtain consent from at least one parent before having an abortion. Those favoring a parental consent law outnumber opponents by a two-to-one margin, 64 percent to 32 percent.

Similar results were obtained in a Gallup poll of adults in July 1989, showing 67 percent support of requirements for parental notification.

The need for more discussions on the subject between parent and child is emphasized by The Alan Guttmacher Institute's estimate that more than 180,000 abortions are performed on women under age 18 annually, accounting for about one in eleven of the total abortions in the United States.

Younger teens, ages 13 to 15, are more likely than those 16 and older, to support a parental consent law for women under 18 years of age, by a margin of 68 percent to 58 percent.

Strongest support requiring parental consent comes from seven in 10 students (70 percent) who say they are doing above average work in school.

The proposition receives majority approval from teenagers in all areas of the United States.

2.9 Opinion of Parental Approval Laws

Would you favor or oppose a restriction in your state that would require women under 18 years of age to get parental consent before they are allowed to have an abortion?

	March – April 1990	
	Favor	**Oppose**
National	**64%**	**32%**
Male	64	32
Female	64	32
Ages 13 – 15	68	27
Ages 16 – 17	58	38
White	65	32
Non-white	61	33
Above-average students	70	27
Average and below	57	39
East	63	30
Midwest	71	27
South	63	33
West	58	39
Republican	66	31
Democrat	60	37
Protestant	68	30
Democrat	60	37

AIDS

"Say it ain't so, Magic" seemed to be the reaction of many teen-agers when Earvin "Magic" Johnson first announced he was ending his basketball career because he had the AIDS virus. Johnson's revelation unleashed a torrent of commentary and debate in the nation's newspapers that has not gone unnoticed by teen-agers. Should teens practice abstinence or "safe sex?" Was Johnson a hero or a villain? Were President Bush and the Congress doing enough to fight AIDS? Should teens be given sex education or free condoms? The answers teens themselves give to these questions was the subject of a special Gallup Youth Survey taken both before and after the Johnson announcement.

It is only natural that teens would be drawn to the Magic Johnson story. Over half of the nation's teens play basketball themselves, making it the leading participatory sport among America's young people (see page 227). Almost one teen in four names basketball as his favorite spectator sport (see page 229). With this background, the Johnson revelation caught teen attention for AIDS as a leading problem facing both the nation and their generation. Johnson, himself, quickly became an important role model for many teens.

Many teens (77 percent) had already studied AIDS and ways of preventing it at school. More, however, have been alerted to the dangers of alcohol (85 percent) or drug abuse (83 percent). Among those who have held discussions about AIDS at school, most first started talking in class about it in the seventh grade. Now, a majority of teens say discussions about AIDS should be initiated by the sixth grade or even earlier.

Before the Johnson announcement teens had already shown high awareness of the ways people can get AIDS, but the publicity surrounding Magic Johnson may finally have gotten the word through to the few teens who were hazy about the facts of AIDS transmission. As it stands now, over nine teens in 10 know AIDS is caught by drug addicts who share needles, that you can get it through intimate sexual contact with persons of the opposite sex, or through homosexual contact, or by receiving blood transmissions.

2.10 How AIDS Is Caught

Please tell me if the following is or is not a way for people to catch AIDS from someone who has it.

	November 1991	July 1991
By sharing needles	99%	99%
Intimate heterosexual contact	97	94
Intimate homosexual contact	93	89
Receiving blood transfusions	91	95

Fear of Getting AIDS

The fear of getting AIDS has grown from 59 percent of teens in 1987 to 63 percent in late 1991.

2.11 Fear of Getting AIDS

How concerned are you that you, yourself, will get AIDS?

	1991	1987
Very concerned	34%	28%
Somewhat concerned	29	31
Not very concerned	24	22
Not at all concerned	13	19

GO 2150220; Q. 17

Non-white teens (85 percent) show a far greater concern than whites (57 percent) about getting the AIDS virus, themselves.

One teen in three says that because of AIDS he either has changed his behavior (23 percent) or is considering changing it (11 percent). Non-white teens (57 percent) are twice as likely as whites (27 percent) to be in this category. Young men and women are about the same in reporting that they have changed their behavior, but the young men are twice as likely to be considering making changes in their behavior now because of the threat of AIDS, by a margin of 15 percent to 7 percent.

2.12 Behavior Changes Because of AIDS

As I read off four statements, please tell me which one of the statements best applies to you.

	December 1991			
	Have changed	Considered changing	Have not changed	No need to change
National	23%	11%	11%	55%
Male	22	15	14	49
Female	24	7	7	62
White	19	9	13	59
Non-white	37	18	5	40

GO 2150220; Q. 18

Responsibility

Teens believe that many people who have gotten AIDS, including "Magic" Johnson, must bear a large part of the responsibility themselves for their plight. That lesson has not gone unheeded, as many teens now endorse use of condoms, abstinence, and "safe sex" as strategies to help stem the spread of the AIDS epidemic.

The great majority of teens say people such as drug addicts who share needles, those who have had many sex partners of the opposite sex, and gays, must bear at least some of the responsibility for having gotten AIDS. They include Magic Johnson in this category, with many holding the opinion that he, himself, has a great deal of the responsibility for getting AIDS.

2.13 Responsibility for Getting AIDS

Here are some people who have gotten AIDS. For each, please tell me how much you think they, themselves, are responsible for having gotten it — a great deal, some, very little, or not at all.

	December 1991				
	Great deal	Some	Very little	Not at all	Not sure
Needle sharers	92%	3%	2%	3%	*%
Those with many hetero-sexual partners	77	15	3	5	*
Gays	64	25	4	4	3
Magic Johnson	45	33	11	8	3
Hemophiliacs	16	18	17	35	14
Blood transfusion recipients	8	8	22	61	1

*Less than one-half of 1 percent.

GO 2150220; Q. 20

In the aftermath of the Johnson announcement, there have been criticisms by some that his emphasis upon safe sex could be taken as a signal to young people that it is all right to engage in premarital sex. Similar arguments have been made against the highly controversial proposals and programs to distribute free condoms at the nation's schools. Instead, the critics have said that sexual abstinence until after marriage is the most certain way to halt the spread of AIDS among young people. Teen approval of proposals for sexual counseling centers where sexual abstinence could be urged rose from 65 percent before the Johnson announcement to 77 percent afterwards.

At the same time, however, their endorsement of free condom distribution rose even further from 82 percent to 85 percent. Teens would appear to be saying that while they are favorably disposed towards the idea of abstinence, the availability of condoms would be a good idea just in case it does not work.

When specifically asked whether they believe the abstinence or safe sex approach should be emphasized in public education efforts, teens choose safe sex by a margin of two to one. The safe sex approach is chosen over abstinence by teens from all walks in life, and from all regions of the country.

2.14 Safe Sex or Abstinence?

Do you think public education efforts to reduce the spread of AIDS among young persons should focus more on encouraging them to practice safe sex, or more on encouraging them to abstain from sex?

| | December 1991 | |
	Safe Sex	Abstinence
National	**64%**	**31%**
Male	67	29
Female	61	33
Ages 13 to 15	63	32
Ages 16 to 17	65	29
White	64	31
Non-white	66	31
Above-average students	62	34
Average or below	67	28
East	59	35
Midwest	64	29
South	66	29
West	65	30
Protestant	62	31
Catholic	61	35

GO 2150220; Q. 16

The universal distribution of condoms to students has been opposed by some who feel this would send a message to teens that government and schools endorse teen-age premarital sexual activity. Some also have opposed the idea on religious grounds because the use of condoms runs counter to their faith's teachings concerning contraception. Those favoring distribution contend they are being realistic in recognizing that some students will have premarital sex no matter what they are taught, and by giving them condoms serious consequences can be avoided at least in some cases.

Opponents of condom distribution frequently say they support instead the establishment of centers where teens would be counseled and urged to practice sexual abstinence until after marriage. Critics have derisively dubbed these as "chastity centers," and contend that teens would only laugh at the establishments. This might not be the case, however, because a majority of teens give at least preliminary approval to the idea.

2.15 Teen Support for Anti-AIDS Proposals

(Percent of teens who very much or somewhat favor each proposal)

Please tell me how much you support or oppose each of these issues and causes—support very much, support somewhat, oppose somewhat, or oppose very much. How about providing free condoms to students to help prevent the spread of AIDS? Providing counseling centers where students can be taught not to have sexual relations until after they are married?

	June – July 1991	
	Provide free condoms to students	**Provide counseling centers**
National	**82%**	**65%**
Male	81	64
Female	84	65
Ages 13 – 15	83	67
Ages 16 – 17	82	61
White	81	67
Non-white	85	56
Above-average students	83	69
Average and below	80	60
East	85	62
Midwest	89	64
South	83	67
West	69	65
Protestant	84	67
Catholic	86	61

GO 2240097: Q. 11

Teens clearly admire Magic Johnson's candor in talking about AIDS and his pledge to devote his life now to fighting it. They rate his efforts higher than those of the president, the U.S. Surgeon General, their own school and local community efforts, and professional sports teams and leagues.

2.16 Who Is Helping To Fight AIDS?

For each of the following, please tell me if you think the person or group has been doing an excellent, good, fair, or poor job in helping to fight AIDS.

| | December 1991 | | | |
	Excellent	Good	Fair	Poor
Magic Johnson	46%	31%	12%	9%
U.S. Surgeon General	20	45	23	8
Your school	20	37	28	14
Your local church, synagogue, or place of worship	18	30	25	17
Professional sports teams and leagues	14	34	34	16
George Bush	9	33	37	18
Your local community	8	32	32	27
U.S. Congress	5	29	40	21

*Less than one-half of 1 percent.

Note: "No opinion" (1 to 4 percent) is not shown.

GO 2150220; Q. 19

SECONDARY SCHOOL EDUCATION

High school ratings

Teacher ratings

Curriculum revisions

Gender differences

Homework

School discipline

Cheating

School violence and disturbances

Extracurricular activities

Self-grading

Ratings of Schools

Educators and politicians on the local and national levels constantly debate the quality of public education, but students themselves continue to hand out top grades to their local high schools, with 70 percent now giving a grade of A or B. Even in large cities, where public education often is most deficient, 78 percent of students in 1992 gave their schools top grades

3.1 High School Rating Trend

	Grade				
	A	**B**	**C**	**D**	**FAIL**
1992	20%	50%	21%	5%	4%
1991	15	49	26	6	4
1989	14	47	30	6	9
1988	16	47	25	7	4
1987	16	48	27	5	3
1986	22	47	*21*	6	4
1985	19	52	22	4	3
1983	19	53	23	3	2
1982	18	49	23	6	4
1981	17	48	23	7	4
1979	9	39	36	10	5
1978	22	45	24	5	3

3.2 Rating of High Schools

Students often are given grades "A" "B," "C," "D," and "Fail" on the quality of their work. Suppose your own school was graded this way, what grade would you give your own school?

| | September – October 1992 | | | | |
	A	B	C	D	FAIL
National	**20%**	**50%**	**21%**	**5%**	**4%**
Male	17	49	22	5	5
Female	22	51	21	4	2
Ages 13 – 15	21	54	16	5	4
Ages 16 – 17	18	43	28	5	4
White	20	50	20	5	4
Non-white	17	51	25	3	3
White-collar background	19	52	22	5	2
Blue-collar background	19	46	22	4	8
Above-average students	25	52	16	5	2
Average and below	12	46	28	5	6
East	21	50	19	3	5
Midwest	15	47	29	6	1
South	22	50	18	4	5
West	20	51	20	6	2
Large city	25	53	14	3	4
Suburb	21	48	22	6	2
Small town	17	47	26	5	4
Rural	18	55	17	5	4
Republican	18	52	24	4	1
Democrat	20	49	20	5	6
Independent	18	48	23	7	3
Protestant	15	58	19	3	4
Catholic	21	45	23	6	4
Church attender	22	50	21	3	4
Non-attender	17	50	22	7	3

GO 12869; Q. 23

Ratings of Teachers

Three teen-agers in four in 1992 said the overall quality of the teaching in their high schools deserves either an A or a B. Disagreeing were 15 percent of the teens who felt the teaching is just average and merits only a C, but few students thought their teachers should get either a D (6 percent) or failing grade (3 percent) for their efforts.

Teens who themselves are doing well in school usually return the compliment. Among those who said their own grades are above average, 85 percent rated the overall quality of the teaching as superior. Academic under-achievers were less inclined to pass out top grades, with only 65 percent giving above-average marks to their teachers. They were not likely, however, to grade their teachers as failing but to say instead that they were just average and merited a C for their efforts.

3.3 Teacher Grading Trends

	A	B	C	D	FAIL
1992	32%	44%	15%	5%	2%
1989	26	45	23	4	1
1988	24	44	22	6	3
1987	22	48	21	6	2
1986	28	46	21	4	1
1985	25	47	21	5	2
1983	23	52	18	5	1
1982	25	40	27	6	2
1981	24	44	21	7	3
1979	26	42	22	6	3

3.4 Rating of Teachers

What grade would you give the overall quality of the teaching in your school?

	March – April 1990				
	A	**B**	**C**	**D**	**Fail**
National	**32%**	**44%**	**15%**	**5%**	**3%**
Male	30	45	14	6	3
Female	33	44	16	4	2
Ages 13 – 15	37	45	11	3	3
Ages 16 – 17	24	43	22	9	2
White	32	43	16	6	2
Non-white	30	49	12	4	3
White-collar background	33	44	14	6	2
Blue-collar background	28	44	20	3	4
Above-average students	40	45	11	2	1
Average and below	21	44	22	10	4
East	32	43	18	3	2
Midwest	32	42	15	7	3
South	34	41	15	6	3
West	27	53	14	4	1
Large city	39	41	9	4	5
Suburb	30	42	20	7	1
Small town	27	46	19	5	3
Rural	37	43	14	4	2
Republican	32	42	17	7	1
Democrat	31	41	19	3	6
Independent	29	49	12	8	2
Protestant	34	41	16	5	3
Catholic	30	44	18	6	2
Church attender	34	41	15	6	3
Non-attender	29	48	16	4	2

GO 12869; Q. 24

Teacher Fairness

The great majority of teen-agers believe that all or many of their teachers treat them fairly. Especially encouraging is the finding that non-white teens usually feel they are receiving fair treatment at school. Although 61 percent of young blacks feel that members of their race do not receive enough respect in this country, nine in 10 say this prejudice does not extend to their teachers.

Although educational reformers often feel that teachers show a bias in favor of male students, the teens, themselves, on the surface show little difference according to sex in their perceptions of how fairly they are being treated. Only a statistically non-significant one-percentage point difference exists between the number of young men and young women who say they are being treated fairly by all or many of their teachers.

Interestingly, students who are doing just average or below-average work in school are only slightly more likely than above-average students to report they are being treated unfairly by many or all of their teachers.

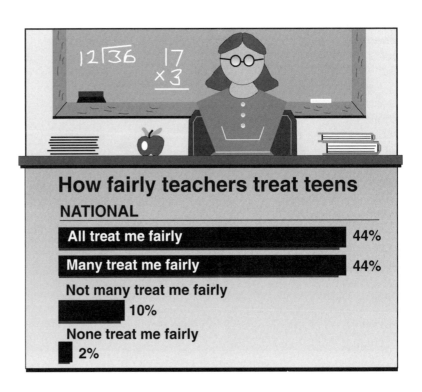

How fairly teachers treat teens

NATIONAL

All treat me fairly	44%
Many treat me fairly	44%
Not many treat me fairly	10%
None treat me fairly	2%

3.5 Teacher Fairness

How would you describe how fairly your teachers treat you — all my teachers treat me fairly, many of my teachers treat me fairly, not many of my teachers treat me fairly, none of my teachers treat me fairly?

	December 1991			
	All fairly	Many fairly	Not many fairly	None fairly
National	**43%**	**44%**	**10%**	**2%**
Male	42	45	8	4
Female	43	43	13	1
Ages 13 – 15	42	45	9	4
Ages 16 – 17	43	44	12	–
White	40	47	10	3
Non-white	55	33	11	2
White-collar background	40	47	10	3
Blue-collar background	41	46	11	1
Above-average students	44	44	9	3
Average and below	40	45	13	2
East	48	41	5	6
Midwest	43	45	9	4
South	36	54	9	1
West	50	36	14	–
Protestant	48	40	11	1
Catholic	32	53	12	2
Church attender	44	43	12	2
Non-attender	41	46	9	3

Note: 1 percent of the teens did not respond to the question.

GO 21504500; Q. 30

Curriculum Revisions

When it comes to what teens want to study at school, "dead white males" are "out," while members of minority groups — male or female — are "in," according to teens.

Many educational reformers, both inside and outside the school systems in this country, have argued in recent years that history, literature, and geography courses in the nation's schools have been placing too much emphasis on white males at the expense of presenting the heritage and ideas of women and peoples of other races and ethnic backgrounds.

Counter-critics have derided these reform suggestions as "political correctness" or "p.c." for short, and feel that the "core curriculum" of the writings and thoughts of white males does not represent political or social manipulation but is instead necessary for a proper understanding of the best in modern thought. The majority of students, themselves, say that coverage of white males is adequate or may be even over-emphasized, and that more attention should be paid to minority groups.

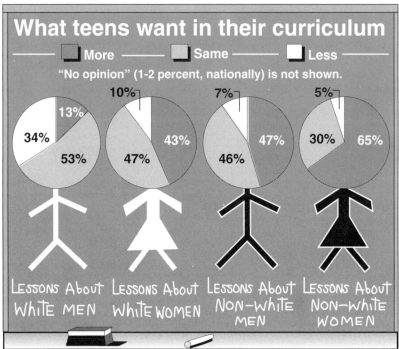

What teens want in their curriculum

More ——— Same ——— Less

"No opinion" (1-2 percent, nationally) is not shown.

Lessons About White Men	Lessons About White Women	Lessons About Non-white Men	Lessons About Non-white Women
13% / 34% / 53%	10% / 43% / 47%	7% / 47% / 46%	5% / 30% / 65%

"In"
- Muslims and their literature (73 percent)
- The history, culture and literature of Africans before they came to this country (66 percent)
- Writings of non-white women (65 percent)
- Curriculum materials on Asian-Americans (61 percent)
- Curriculum materials on Hispanic-Americans (59 percent)

"So – So"
- History and literature of native Americans (49 percent)
- Lives and literature of black Americans of the 20th century (47 percent)
  Literature and deeds of non-white males (47 percent)
- Thoughts and accomplishments of white women (43 percent)

"Out"
- History and literature of white males

3.6 Needed Curriculum Reform

Please tell me whether you think your teachers and textbooks present too much, too little, or the right amount of information about the history of these people and stories and books they have written.

	December 1991		
	Too little information	**About right amount**	**Too much information**
Muslims	73%	21%	4%
Africans before they came to this country	66	28	5
Blacks who were slaves in this country	35	53	12
Blacks in 20th Century America	47	43	10
Asian-Americans	61	32	6
Hispanic-Americans	59	34	6
Native Americans such as Indians	42	48	10
Non-white women	65	30	5
White women	43	47	10
Non-white men	47	45	8
White men	13	53	34

Note: "No opinion" (1% – 2%) is not shown.

GO 21504500; Q. 26

Gender Differences in Academic Performance

For most subjects about half the teens interviewed in a 1991 Gallup Youth Survey felt boys and girls are about the same when their academic abilities are compared. Others, however, still often feel there are many differences between the sexes when their abilities are compared. These perceptions of gender differences tend to increase as teens grow older. There is, however, seldom any agreement about the differences, often with result that there is a fairly even division of opinion on whether boys or girls do better in a particular subject.

The U.S. scientific community has expended considerable effort in recent years in improving opportunities for women in science, but boys still more often are thought to do better in science courses. Overall, sexual parity has been achieved in mathematics, with an even division of opinion between those who think boys or girls do better in math. But one puzzle the mathematics community has not been able to solve is why girls seem to lose interest in math as they grow older. What has often been observed in the classroom is that girls are equal to boys in math in the early grades but as upperclassmen in high school and in college, quickly seem to lose interest in the subject.

There is a clear consensus of opinion that girls do better than boys in English and in writing. Unlike other subjects, only 28 percent of teens feel the sexes are about the same in studying English. Girls, far more often than boys, are viewed as being better at learning foreign languages.

There is a fairly even division of opinion concerning social studies and history, and in art.

One teen in three feels that girls do better than boys in musical studies and talent. (35 percent). Only about one-third as many teens (11 percent) believe boys make better musicians. The sexes are viewed on a par in musical abilities by half of the teens (54 percent).

3.7 Opinion of Differences

	Boys better	Girls better	About the same
Social studies and history	23%	21%	56%
Music	11	35	54
Science	34	14	52
Math	25	24	51
Foreign languages	7	44	49
Art	26	26	48
English and writing	4	68	28

3.8 Gender Differences

Here are some school subjects and activities. Do you think girls do better, boys do better, or are girls and boys about the same?

	November 1991	
	Male	**Female**
Music		
Boys better	12%	9%
Girls better	31	38
About the same	57	53
Social studies and history		
Boys better	27	19
Girls better	19	23
About the same	54	58
Art		
Boys better	24	28
Girls better	25	26
About the same	50	45
Science		
Boys better	40	29
Girls better	13	15
About the same	47	56
Math		
Boys better	31	18
Girls better	25	23
About the same	44	59
Foreign languages		
Boys better	10	5
Girls better	46	42
About the same	43	53
English and writing		
Boys better	6	2
Girls better	68	68
About the same	26	30

GO 21504500; Q. 29

Homework and School Discipline

A majority of teens (56 percent) spent an hour or more doing homework the previous day in a 1992 survey. Those coming from families where parents had attended college more often reported spending this amount of time than those from homes whether neither parent had collegiate experience (64 percent to 47 percent).

Only one teen in eight (12 percent) volunteers that the present homework load is about right. The majority feel instead that they should receive a little less (52 percent) or a lot less homework (10 percent). One teen in four, however, would like to receive more homework, with 4 percent calling for a lot more, and 22 percent for a little more. This represents a sharp drop from 1984, when 40 percent of teens were calling for more homework, and just 49 percent complained they were getting too much.

Most likely to call for the challenge of more homework are non-white students (35 percent) and teens living in large cities (34 percent).

3.9 Homework Trend

	1992	1984
Homework wanted . . .		
Much more	4%	5%
Little more	22	35
About right	12	11
Little less	52	40
Much less	10	9

Most students in 1992 rated discipline at their school as very strict (32 percent) or as somewhat strict (52 percent). Just 11 percent say it is not very strict, and 5 percent that it is not strict at all. By comparison in 1984, just two students in three felt their schools administered strict discipline.

3.10 School Strictness Trend

	1992	1984
Very strict	32%	20%
Somewhat strict	52	44
Not very strict	11	25
Not at all strict	5	7

3.11 Homework

Do you feel that you should have much more homework, a little more homework, a little less homework, or much less homework? ["About right" is a volunteered response.]

	September – October 1992				
	Much more	Little more	About right	Little less	Much less
National	4%	22%	12%	52%	10%
Male	6	23	14	44	13
Female	2	20	9	60	8
Ages 13 – 15	2	25	13	48	12
Ages 16 – 17	6	17	11	58	8
White	4	19	13	52	11
Non-white	5	30	5	52	8
White-collar background	2	21	13	60	5
Blue-collar background	5	23	12	42	18
Above-average students	2	25	12	56	5
Average and below	6	18	12	48	17
East	8	16	15	51	10
Midwest	4	24	9	53	11
South	3	20	8	59	10
West	4	25	18	41	11
Large city	4	30	12	48	6
Suburb	2	23	17	55	3
Small town	3	20	9	50	17
Rural	6	16	12	62	5
Republican	1	22	12	55	10
Democrat	4	22	9	53	13
Independent	7	22	12	52	7
Protestant	3	22	12	54	10
Catholic	2	25	14	48	11
Church attender	5	20	12	51	11
Non-attender	2	23	12	53	9

GO12869; Q.26

3.12 Time Spent Doing Homework

About how much time, if any, did you spend yesterday at each of these activities — doing homework?

	September – October 1992			
	None	**Less than 1 hour**	**1 – 2 hours**	**3 or more hours**
National	**21%**	**22%**	**42%**	**14%**
Male	23	24	41	11
Female	19	20	44	15
Ages 13 – 15	21	22	44	20
Ages 16 – 17	21	21	40	17
White	22	22	42	13
Non-white	16	22	44	18
White-collar background	14	20	50	16
Blue-collar background	28	19	37	14
Both parents attended college	17	18	45	20
One parent attended college	17	20	45	18
Neither attended college	28	22	39	8
Above-average students	16	20	45	18
Average and below	27	23	40	8
East	19	13	47	19
Midwest	18	22	48	11
South	25	26	34	12
West	20	22	43	13
Large city	10	21	44	26
Suburb	21	20	43	12
Small town	21	22	42	12
Rural	26	19	43	12
Republican	23	20	42	13
Democrat	20	25	40	13
Independent	23	20	42	14
Protestant	23	23	41	12
Catholic	16	21	47	15
Church attender	17	23	43	5
Non-attender	24	20	42	14

GO 12869; Q. 26

3.13 School Discipline

Do you feel that discipline in your school is very strict, somewhat strict, not very strict, or not at all strict?

	September – October 1992			
	Very strict	**Somewhat strict**	**Not very strict**	**Not at all strict**
National	**32%**	**52%**	**11%**	**5%**
Male	29	56	8	7
Female	34	48	14	4
Ages 13 – 15	28	54	13	5
Ages 16 – 17	37	50	8	6
White	30	53	12	4
Non-white	35	48	5	13
White-collar background	27	57	12	4
Blue-collar background	36	47	10	7
Above-average students	31	54	9	5
Average and below	32	50	13	5
East	30	57	7	7
Midwest	26	54	14	6
South	35	50	9	4
West	34	48	13	5
Large city	34	50	11	4
Suburb	30	53	12	4
Small town	32	54	9	5
Rural	30	49	12	8
Republican	29	54	14	3
Democrat	33	51	12	5
Independent	36	45	11	7
Protestant	28	56	10	5
Catholic	38	46	9	6
Church attender	35	50	9	5
Non-attender	28	54	12	5

GO 12869; Q. 25

Cheating on Tests and Exams

In 1992, 46 percent of the teens said they had ever cheated on an exam or test at school. This proportion represents a 13 percentage-point decline since 1986 when six teens in 10 (59 percent) said they had cheated. As teens grow older, the proportion admitting they have cheated grows to 57 percent among those who are 16 years of age and older.

Also in 1992, 21 percent of the teens said there is a great deal of cheating going on at their school, and an additional 34 percent said there is a fair amount. Forty-four percent, however, believed there is not very much cheating.

Students whose academic achievements are above average are somewhat less likely to admit to cheating on tests or exams than those whose work is average or below average, by a margin of 42 percent to 51 percent.

Moral teaching may not have much influence on the decision of whether or not to cheat at school, since the number of cheaters who are recent church attenders is about as great as those who have not attended.

3.14 Cheating at School — Trend

	Great deal	Fair amount	Not very much	Have cheated
1992	21%	34%	44%	46%
1986	22	44	30	59
1981	37	39	24	66
1978	30	42	26	62
1959	22	60	18	NA

3.15 Cheating

At your school, how common is cheating on tests or exams? Would you say there is a great deal, a fair amount, or not very much cheating?
Have you, yourself, ever cheated on a test or exam?

	September – October 1992			
	Great deal	**Fair amount**	**Not very much**	**Have cheated**
National	**21%**	**34%**	**44%**	**46%**
Male	20	33	46	49
Female	22	34	43	43
Ages 13 – 15	19	31	49	39
Ages 16 – 17	24	38	37	57
White	22	35	42	47
Non-white	16	29	55	44
White-collar background	19	39	42	47
Blue-collar background	21	31	46	45
Above-average students	20	36	42	42
Average and below	21	30	47	51
East	27	27	44	46
Midwest	21	35	44	42
South	19	37	42	47
West	20	32	48	51
Large city	24	24	50	43
Suburb	26	40	33	58
Small town	19	36	44	44
Rural	17	33	48	42
Republican	17	37	44	49
Democrat	23	36	40	51
Independent	26	32	41	44
Protestant	19	33	47	39
Catholic	20	33	47	52
Church attender	20	34	46	48
Non-attender	21	34	43	44

Note: 1 percent of the teens gave no estimate of the amount of cheating at school.

GO 12869; Q. 27–28

Violence in the Schools

One student in four (24 percent) feared for his physical safety while at school in 1992. For 7 percent of the students, these fears became reality when they were physically assaulted or beaten up while attending school. Since 1977 there has been an increase in the number of teens who feared for their physical safety and who have been physically assaulted at school.

Also in 1992, 15 percent of students reported they had money stolen, and 14 percent that their personal property had been vandalized at school.

Most apprehensive about threat to their safety are non-whites (30 percent) and teens under age 16 (28 percent).

The fears and realities of victimization do not differ greatly according to region of the country or by urbanization factors.

3.16 Trends in School Violence

	1992	1985	1977
Been physically assaulted	7%	3%	4%
Had money stolen	15	13	12
Had property stolen	na	28	24
Had property vandalized	14	14	11
Ever fear for physical safety	24	21	18

Disturbances and Violence

Classroom disturbances are persistent problems in the nation's schools. In 1992, seven students in 10 (69 percent) reported that student disruptions were at least a fairly big problem in their schools.

A majority of 58 percent said fighting is a problem, and a very alarming 28 percent said that students bringing guns or knives into the schools are problems they face.

Although the 1992 survey was taken during a time of economic recession, no increase was reported in the incidence of theft at school. No increase was reported in the incidence of vandalism in the form of the destruction of school property or of the personal property of students.

Despite popular stereotypes of inner-city "blackboard jungles," these problems occur with about equal frequency in communities of all sizes.

3.17 1992 — Disturbances and Violence

September – October 1992		
Very big	**Fairly big**	**Not big at all**

	Very big	Fairly big	Not big at all
Classroom disturbances	30%	39%	31%
Fighting	23	35	42
Theft	14	31	55
Vandalism	14	27	59
Weapons	9	19	72

3.18 Disturbances and Violence Trend

	1992	1989	1985	1980
Classroom disturbances	30%	36%	26%	30%
Fighting	23	22	10	13
Theft	14	16	14	21
Vandalism	14	14	13	21
Weapons	9	9	6	8

3.19 School Disturbances and Violence

How big a problem would you say each of the following is in your school — very big, fairly big, or not big at all: Students creating disturbances which disrupt classroom work? Fighting? Theft of personal property? Vandalism, the destruction of personal or school property? Students bringing weapons such as guns or knives to school?

	September – October 1992				
	"Very Big Problem" in School				
	Disturbances	Fighting	Theft	Vandalism	Weapons
National	**30%**	**23%**	**14%**	**14%**	**9%**
Male	30	23	12	13	12
Female	29	24	16	15	6
Ages 13 – 15	32	24	10	12	8
Ages 16 – 17	27	22	19	17	11
White	28	20	14	12	8
Non-white	37	33	12	20	13
White-collar background	25	16	14	11	6
Blue-collar background	35	32	16	17	12
East	22	22	17	19	11
Midwest	29	20	14	5	7
South	34	29	12	16	10
West	29	18	15	17	9
Large city	26	27	15	22	9
Suburb	27	27	17	12	12
Small town	32	21	11	14	9
Rural	29	20	14	9	6

GO 12869: Q. 31a–e

3.20 Fear and Victimization at School

When you are at school, do you ever fear for your physical safety, or not?
During the past 12 months have any of the following happened to you at school: Have you been physically as-saulted or beaten up? Have you had money stolen? Have you had your personal property damaged or stolen?

	September – October 1992			
	Fear for safety	Physical assault	Money stolen	Property vandalized
National	**24%**	**7%**	**15%**	**14%**
Male	23	9	10	17
Female	25	5	19	10
Ages 13 – 15	28	8	16	14
Ages 16 – 17	19	4	13	13
White	23	7	15	14
Non-white	30	6	14	12
White-collar background	21	4	14	12
Blue-collar background	27	8	16	17
Above-average students	20	6	15	12
Average and below	30	8	15	17
East	20	9	12	15
Midwest	20	4	12	10
South	28	6	19	13
West	26	9	13	17
Large city	28	6	14	17
Suburb	27	9	16	18
Small town	23	6	11	12
Rural	22	5	21	12
Republican	24	8	16	11
Democrat	25	9	15	15
Independent	24	4	13	16
Protestant	25	6	16	12
Catholic	20	6	11	12
Church attender	26	6	15	13
Non-attender	23	8	15	15

GO 12869; Q. 29–30

Extracurricular Activities

Interscholastic sports head the list of extracurricular activities in which high school students are participating. Overall, nearly all teens (97 percent) have participated in some form of extracurricular activity during their school years. In 1989, about three teens in four (73 percent) said they were actively engaged in extracurricular activities.

The fitness craze that appears to have taken hold of many young people is reflected in the audit on extracurricular activities, which shows that nearly half of all teens (45 percent) participate in interscholastic sports. By comparison, in 1985, only 32 percent of teens reported membership on an interscholastic team. Much of the growth in interscholastic sports participation has come from young women (40 percent), who now are almost as likely as young men (50 percent) to be found on the interscholastic playing fields and courts. One teen in four (25 percent) is now participating in intramural sports, compared with 29 percent in 1985.

Young men (33 percent) are twice as likely as young women (16 percent) to report intramural athletic team membership.

Cheering on the student athletes are 5 percent of the student body on the cheerleading squad and 17 percent who play in the school band. Less than 1 percent of the cheerleaders are male, compared to 7 percent of young women.

The school choir does not appear to be the place for changing adolescent male voices, with young women choristers (22 percent) outnumbering the tenors, baritones, and basses (10 percent) by a margin of more than two to one.

Membership in a school science or math club is reported by 17 percent of the students. Most likely to belong to the clubs are above-average students (21 percent), those who are 16 or older (21 percent) and young men (19 percent).

School plays and student drama groups have captured the attention of 14 percent of the teens surveyed — young women (19 percent) more so than young men (9 percent).

One student in 10 reports working on either the school newspaper staff (10 percent) or the yearbook staff (10 percent). The debating team is the choice of only 4 percent of the teens.

3.21 Participation in Extracurricular Activities

For each of the following extracurricular activities, please say if you now participate in that activity, used to participate in it, or have never participated in it.

| | March 1989 | | | | |
| | Now Participating in Activity | | | | |
	National	Male	Female	Ages 13–15	Ages 16–17
Interscholastic sports	45%	50%	40%	48%	42%
Intramural sports	25	33	16	27	22
Cheerleading	5	*	10	7	3
Band or orchestra	17	15	19	20	12
Choir	16	10	22	17	15
Dramatics or school play	14	9	19	14	13
School newspaper	10	8	12	9	11
School yearbook	10	9	10	11	8
Debating team	4	4	5	5	4

*Less than one-half of 1 percent.

3.22 Extracurricular Activities Trend

	1989	1985
Interscholastic sports	45%	32%
Intramural sports	25	na
Cheerleading	5	7
Band or orchestra	17	17
Choir	16	15
Science or math club	17	14
Dramatics or school play	14	11
School newspaper	10	8
School yearbook	10	na
Debating team	4	3

Self-Grading

Despite repeated testing that suggests that America's teens often lag far behind their foreign counterparts in mathematics and the sciences, a majority of teens rate themselves as excellent or good in these subjects. The results seem to support some educators' views that American students are not lacking in ability, but rather are simply not being challenged sufficiently to be competitive with foreign students. Asked to disregard their grade-point average, a surprisingly high six teens in 10 rate their mathematical ability as excellent (33 percent) or good (28 percent). A majority of teens also say their abilities in science are excellent (24 percent) or good (31 percent).

Government and scientific leaders have long been concerned about the comparatively small numbers of women and non-whites who go on to careers in science and mathematics. It is generally believed that this is not due to any innate difference in ability, but because women and non-whites often have not been adequately encouraged or prepared in school in order to consider these subjects as careers.

According to the survey, 60 percent of young women say their mathematical abilities are excellent or good, compared to 64 percent of young men. Similarly, 51 percent of women rate themselves highly in science, compared to 58 percent of young men.

Among non-whites, 57 percent grade themselves highly in math, compared to 64 percent of the whites. Non-whites (53 percent) and whites (55 percent) show no statistically significant difference in rating themselves on scientific ability.

As would be expected, students who say their academic work in general is above average are the most likely to grade themselves highly for their mathematical (75 percent) and scientific (65 percent) abilities

Family background can also play an important role in determining teens' self-assessments: Those from white-collar families (69 percent) are more likely than teens from blue-collar households (59 percent) to say they are good at math. Scientists appear to be more likely to come from white-collar households (64 percent) than from blue-collar families (48 percent).

3.23a Self-Grading

Regardless of whatever grades you may have received at school, for each of the following please tell if you think your abilities are excellent, good, fair, or poor.

	March — April 1990		
	"Excellent" or "Good"		
	Math	Science	Geography
National	**61%**	**55%**	**50%**
Male	64	58	53
Female	60	51	47
Ages 13 – 15	65	58	52
Ages 16 – 17	58	50	48
White-collar background	69	59	59
Blue-collar background	59	48	43
Above-average students	75	65	63
Average and below	45	41	36

Despite test reports that from time to time suggest teens have poor knowledge of geography, teens themselves are divided on their self-ratings of geographical knowledge. Only 15 percent of the students rate themselves as excellent in studies of geography, but an additional 35 percent believe their abilities are good.

In reading, 87 percent of the young women interviewed say their abilities are excellent or good, compared to just 68 percent of the young men. Young women also regard their writing abilities more highly, by a margin of 80 percent to 66 percent over young men. Women maintain their lead in foreign languages as well, with 48 percent of young women grading themselves excellent or good, compared with 33 percent of the young men.

Sixty-four percent of young men and 62 percent of young women rate their historical knowledge positively

The gap in geographical knowledge is wider, with 53 percent of the young men giving themselves high marks compared with 47 percent of young women.

America's teens generally have a high degree of self-confidence in their ability to read and write, but they lack assurance in applying their reading skills to learn subjects such as history, geography, and foreign languages.

Three teens in four believe they possess excellent (42 percent) or good (35 percent) reading skills.

When it comes to writing, teens are also inclined to rate themselves highly. Thirty percent say they are excellent writers and 43 percent believe they have good writing talents.

A majority of teens do not believe they are very fluent in foreign languages. Twenty-six percent rate themselves as fair and 31 percent as poor. Only 14 percent of the teens claim excellent fluency in at least one language other than their own, and 25 percent rate themselves as good.

Many non-white students out-distance white teens with their confidence in bilingual abilities. Among non-whites, 22 percent say they have excellent abilities in a language other than English, and 25 percent rate themselves as having good fluency in a second language.

Many teens rate their abilities in studying history as excellent (25 percent) or good (38 percent). Only about one teen in three rates his knowledge of history as just fair (30 percent) or as poor (6 percent).

3.23b Self-Grading

| | March – April 1990 | | | |
| | "Excellent" or "Good" | | | |
	Reading	Writing	History	Foreign languages
National	**77%**	**73%**	**63%**	**39%**
Male	68	66	64	33
Female	87	80	62	48
Ages 13 – 15	78	69	64	40
Ages 16 – 17	77	77	62	38
White-collar background	78	76	65	45
Blue-collar background	77	71	60	37
Above-average students	87	79	74	48
Average and below	65	65	50	31

Post-secondary School

College preferences

Likely occupation

CAREER PLANS, COLLEGE

Post-Secondary School Plans

College classrooms were bulging at the seams in the autumn of 1992 as more and more young people, unable to find work or concerned about the need for higher education to obtain future job security, sought a college degree. The next few years may show an even greater influx of students, because there has been a dramatic increase in the number of teen-agers who hope to attend college full-time. At the same time, there has been a corresponding decrease in the number of teens who are seeking to combine part-time jobs and night school, or want full-time jobs, or plan to enlist in the armed services.

Two teen-agers in three in 1992 said they would like to attend college full time after they graduate from high school. This represents a 17 percentage-point increase over the previous five years. In 1987, only barely half of the nation's teens (51 percent) wanted to attend college full time.

Only one student in 20 in 1992 wanted to enter the labor force directly full time right after leaving high school. Another 5 percent said they would like to join the armed services. Twice as many teens in 1987 wanted to work full time (10 percent) or to join the armed services (9 percent).

A combination of part-time work and college attendance was the choice of 18 percent of the students in 1992, in comparison to 26 percent in 1987, who wanted to try a joint program.

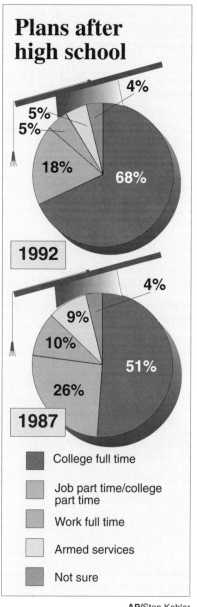

Plans after high school

4%
5%
5%
18%
68%
1992

4%
9%
10%
51%
26%
1987

- College full time
- Job part time/college part time
- Work full time
- Armed services
- Not sure

AP/Stan Kohler

In preparation for all of these plans, over nine teens in 10 who were interviewed in 1992 said it is either very likely they will graduate from high school (88 percent) or that they already had graduated (4 percent). Less confidence was shown by 6 percent who felt it was only somewhat likely they would complete their secondary schooling, while 2 percent showed little or no confidence at all that they would ever earn a high school diploma.

As would be expected, most students who say they are doing above-average work in high school are usually among those expecting to go to college. Even among those who say their current academic performance is just average or below average, however, many still hope to go to college full time or to take some college courses while holding down a part-time job. Fourteen percent of the academic underachievers in 1992 expected to enter the work force directly or to join the armed services. Among those who are doubtful about even finishing high school, a great proportion hope to gain a full-time job in the labor force or to enter the armed services.

Greater-than-average intentions of going to college are found among teens who come from households where both parents themselves had attended a college or university.

4.1 Post-High School Plans

	1992	1987
Attend college full-time	68%	51%
Find a job and go to college part-time	18	26
Work full-time	5	10
Join the armed services	5	9

4.2 Graduation Expectations

How likely is it that you will graduate from high school — very likely, somewhat likely, not too likely, or not at all likely?

| | June – July 1992 | | | |
	Very likely	Somewhat likely	Not too likely	Not at all likely
National	**88%**	**6%**	**1%**	**1%**
Male	86	7	*	1
Female	90	5	1	1
Ages 12 – 13	92	8	–	–
Ages 14 – 15	92	6	1	1
Ages 16 – 17	80	4	1	1
White	88	5	1	1
Non-white	85	7	–	*
Black	86	8	–	*
Hispanic	81	12	2	–
White-collar background	88	6	*	*
Blue-collar background	88	6	1	1
Above-average students	94	2	*	–
Average and below	84	11	1	1
East	86	6	1	1
Midwest	92	4	*	*
South	86	6	*	1
West	85	7	1	*
Large city	86	7	1	1
Suburb	88	6	1	1
Small town	89	6	*	1
Rural	89	5	1	–
Protestant	90	5	*	1
Catholic	87	7	1	–
Church attender	90	4	*	–
Non-attender	86	7	1	1

*Less than one-half of 1 percent.

Note: Does not include 4 percent who have already graduated. Among those who are 16 to 17 years of age, this is 12 percent of the age group.

GO 21505702; Q. Q. 7

4.3 Post-Secondary School Plans

What are you likely to do after high school — Attend college full time? Find a job and go to college part time? Join the armed services? Work full time?

	June – July 1992			
	Full-time college	Part-time college	Armed services	Full-time work
National	**68%**	**18%**	**5%**	**5%**
Male	66	17	7	5
Female	70	19	3	5
Ages 12 – 13	70	17	4	3
Ages 14 – 15	71	17	4	4
Ages 16 – 17	63	19	6	7
White	68	18	5	5
Non-white	67	18	5	5
Black	68	15	6	6
Hispanic	46	28	8	9
White-collar background	74	15	4	2
Blue-collar background	63	20	6	7
Above-average students	79	13	3	2
Average and below	57	24	7	8
East	74	13	3	4
Midwest	65	18	7	5
South	67	18	4	5
West	66	20	5	4
Large city	70	19	5	3
Suburb	71	17	2	5
Small town	66	18	7	5
Rural	69	17	4	5
Protestant	70	16	6	4
Catholic	67	21	6	2
Church attender	72	14	5	5
Non-attender	66	21	4	5

Note: 4 percent of had no plans.

GO 21505702; Q. 8

College Preferences

Most college bound teenagers are seeking to enter large universities and colleges, especially in their home states.

About two high school juniors and seniors in three (63 percent) say they hope to attend college in their home state. Expecting to travel to an out-of-state college are 36 percent of the students. Young women (67 percent) are more apt than young men (58 percent) to want to stay close to home when they go to college. Most likely to select an out-of-state location are young men (40 percent), students from the East (48 percent), those from families where both parents attended college (45 percent), and above-average students (40 percent).

A majority of students would prefer a state university (53 percent). Private colleges are the choice of 37 percent, while 7 percent say they would prefer a religious-affiliated institution of higher learning.

State universities are popular across the nation, but are somewhat less desirable in the eyes of college-bound students in the East (47 percent). Instead, private colleges show their greatest drawing power among eastern college applicants (48 percent). Church-affiliated colleges are most popular in the South and West (11 percent).

Colleges of all sizes attract applicants, but the edge usually goes to the larger universities. About six students in 10 (58 percent) say they would prefer to attend a large college with 5,000 or more students. Smaller colleges, with enrollments of less than 5,000, are attractive to four students in 10 (40 percent).

The larger college is most attractive to students from families in which both parents went to college (72 percent), among above-average students (63 percent), young men (63 percent), and in the South (61 percent) and West (72 percent). Smaller colleges more often attract young women (45 percent), students from the East (44 percent) and Midwest (46 percent), and those whose high school academic records are only average or even below average (48 percent).

Students who may be the first in their families to enter college usually want to go to a school that is smaller in size (54 percent) and is in their home state (66 percent). They also are the most likely to choose a private college (41 percent).

4.4 College Preferences

	1989			
	Home state	Out-of-state	Small	Large
National	**63%**	**36%**	**40%**	**58%**
Male	58	40	35	63
Female	67	33	45	54
Above-average students	59	40	36	63
Average and below	70	28	48	49
Both parents attended college	54	45	28	72
One parent attended college	69	31	32	64
East	52	48	44	52
Midwest	67	31	46	52
South	68	32	39	61
West	64	35	28	72

AIPO 810; Q. 408, 410

87

Expected Future Occupation

The great majority of teen-agers expect to pursue a career in business, the professions, or technology. Very few believe they will be working in skilled, semi-skilled, or service occupations.

If the teen predictions come true, over eight in 10 of today's young people will be executives, professionals, or highly trained technicians when they become adults.

The most frequently named expectation of young men is that they will become business executives. Their second choice is a career in computers or electronics. A career in law is in a three-way tie with professional athletics or the arts (fine arts, music, drama, etc.) as a leading occupation forecast by young men. In sixth place, is a career as a physician.

The next few occupational slots named by young men feature vocations that require use of the hands. A skilled craftsmanship position is seventh on their list, while engineering is eighth. Despite all the recent publicity about the decline of American automotive manufacturing, an automotive career is ninth on the list of young men. It is tied for this position with future expectations of becoming a law enforcement officer or an architect.

The need for a military presence may seem diminished now, but that has not deterred some young men from expecting to enter the country's armed services as a career. The list of occupational expectations by young men is rounded out by predictions that they will become scientists, teachers, or pursue a career in communications or journalism.

Nursing Now Top Choice of Young Women

Reports and forecasts about nationwide nursing shortages may not have gone unnoticed by young women, who now name it as their top occupational expectation. A career as a physician had been their previous first choice in recent years, but has slipped to third place.

Teaching is the second-most-frequently mentioned choice, regaining a level of popularity that had not been achieved since 1977, when it also placed second on their list.

A career in the arts is fourth among expected occupations of young women.

In fifth place is a business career in which women expect to take their place in the executive suite of the nation's offices. A secretarial or clerical career, which in the past had often been the number one expectation of young women, is now well down the list.

A legal career is sixth on the list of young women. Tied for sixth is a career in communications or electronic or print journalism.

Science ranks eighth on the list compiled by young women, while a career as a veterinarian is ninth.

As women pursue these careers and as many try to juggle them with raising a family, a new occupation, child care, appeared on the Gallup Youth Survey occupational audit for the first time in 1991.

Occupational expectations remain fairly constant throughout the teen years with two notable exceptions: forecasts about becoming physicians or professional athletes drop drastically as teens grow older and perhaps view their abilities and choices more realistically.

One of the more dramatic changes over the years recorded by the Gallup Youth Survey, has been the increasing tendency for young women to cite occupational expectations in fields formerly thought of as being appropriate for or restricted to men only.

Likely Occupation

As of right now what kind of work do you think you will do for a career?

4.5 Career Choices of Young Men

1991

1. Business.
2. Computers, electronics
3. Lawyer
   Pro athlete
   The arts
6. Physician
7. Skilled worker
8. Engineer
9. Auto mechanic
   Architect
   Law enforcement

1987

1. Computers, electronics
2. Business
3. Skilled worker
4. Physician
5. Engineering
6. Law
7. Military
8. Pro athlete
9. The arts
10. Auto mechanic

1984

1. Computers, electronics
2. Physician
3. Engineering
4. Skilled worker
5. Business
6. Law
7. Auto mechanic
8. Pro athlete
9. The arts
10. Architect

1980

1. Skilled worker
2. Physician
3. Engineering
4. Computer, electronics
5. Auto mechanic
6. Business
7. Architect
8. Law
9. Aviation
10. The arts

1977

1. Skilled worker
2. Engineering
3. Lawyer
4. Teaching
5. Athlete
6. Musician
7. Architect
8. Farmer
9. Physician
10. Military

Likely Occupation

4.6 Career Choices of Young Women

1991

1. Nursing
2. Teaching
3. Physician
4. The arts
5. Business
6. Law
   Communications
8. Scientist
9. Veterinarian
10. Child care

1987

1. Physician
2. Business
3. Law
4. Secretary
5. Teaching
6. Beautician
7. Nursing
8. Social worker
9. Scientist
10. Computers, electronics

1984

1 Physician
2 .Nursing
3. Teaching
4. Secretary
5. Computers, electronics
6. Business
7. Law
8. Beautician
9. Scientist
10. Social worker

1980

1. Medicine
2. Secretary
3. Nursing
4. Teaching
5. The arts
6. Computers, electronics
7. Law
8. Beautician
9. Business
10. Advertising

1977

1. Secretary
2. Teaching
3. Nursing
4. Medical technician
5. Veterinarian
6. Model
7. Physician
8. Social worker
9. Business
10. Beautician

Activism

School programs

Volunteers and contributors

Willingness to serve

National service

Environmental service

Military service

SERVICE

Activism

Communes and cults may encounter difficulty in the future in attracting apathetic or alienated young people who are fed up with society or actively seeking an alternative life style. Today's teens are far more likely instead to join a community action group to bring about changes in the society in which they live.

5.1 Teen Action or Apathy?

Here are some ways people use to show their support or opposition to the way things are done. When you are old enough to vote, how likely are you to do these things: very likely, somewhat likely, or not at all likely — Join a community action group? Join a group that believes in 'dropping out' of society and living a completely different life style? Do nothing, because you figure the system can't be changed?

	January 1991		
	Community action	Do nothing	Drop out
National	**82%**	**21%**	**13%**
Male	78	21	12
Female	86	20	14
Ages 13 to 15	83	19	10
Ages 16 to 17	81	23	16
White	84	19	13
Non-white	77	25	12
Above-average students	85	18	13
Average and below	77	22	12
White-collar background	81	19	13
Blue-collar background	80	21	7
East	81	21	14
Midwest	87	23	12
South	83	16	11
West	75	26	14

School Community Service Programs

Many schools across the nation now require their students to perform community service as an important part of the educational process. The size of the teen-age volunteer force that is available through school programs, however, could be doubled, according to the findings of the Gallup Youth Survey. The value of a larger teen volunteer force to local communities that have had to cut back on many services because of reduced tax revenues during the recession would be enormous.

Currently, one student in four is now required by the local school to perform some community service such as helping the poor, the sick or the elderly. Another one in three of the teens interviewed say that on their own they are performing similar services to the community that are not required or sponsored by their school.

When high school students who are not now required to participate in community programs are asked about their interest in them, an additional one in four say they would be very willing to volunteer to do these kinds of services if their schools would help them to find a way to put their youthful energy and charitable instincts to good use.

5.2 Teen Volunteers

Does your school require you to perform some community service such as helping the poor, the sick, or the elderly? Not including any school requirement, do you, yourself, happen to be involved in any charity or social service activities such as helping the poor, the sick, or the elderly? If your school helped you find a way to volunteer for community service, how likely would you be to volunteer: very likely, somewhat likely, not too likely, not at all likely?

	June – July 1991		
	School requires community service	Performing service not sponsored by school	Very likely to volunteer for service
National	**25%**	**34%**	**24%**
Male	22	29	13
Female	28	38	35
Ages 13 to 15	29	34	23
Ages 16 to 17	20	34	25
White	22	33	22
Non-white	37	37	23
Above-average students	27	41	25
Average and below	23	24	21

GO 224007; Q. 22–24

Volunteers and Contributors

Teens are a vital source of voluntary labor and charitable contributions. In a 1990 Gallup Organization study for the Independent Sector it was estimated that teen-agers donate an annual total of 1.6 billion hours in voluntary service. Even when such informal activities as babysitting for free or baking cookies for a school fair are eliminated, it is estimated that teens spend 1.2 billion hours as volunteers for non-profit organizations in their communities. These formal services by teens are considered the equivalent of having 766,000 employees. The annual value of the teen contribution in salaries if people had to be hired and paid to perform these voluntary services would be an estimated $4.4 billion.

Nearly six teens in 10 reported doing voluntary service during the 12-month period preceding the time of interview. When asked how they got involved in their volunteer activity, the majority of teens say it was either through the schools or through a church or synagogue.

The most frequently cited reasons by teens for first volunteering and for continuing to give service are that they want to do something useful in their lives and because they feel they would enjoy the work. In return, teens are most likely to cite that as a result of their service they have acquired such skills as getting along with and relating to other people; being kind, helpful and respectful; learning how to take care of children; and feeling better about themselves.

The great majority of teens (85 percent) rate their experience as volunteers as good or very good.
Schools and religious institutions can have great influence on voluntary activities by teens. Among the 61 percent of teens who report that their schools encourage community service, 69 percent actually volunteered. By comparison, only 48 percent of those attending schools where community service is not encouraged volunteered services during the previous year.

Among the three teens in four (75 percent) who are members of religious organizations such as churches or synagogues, 62 percent are volunteers and 56 percent make charitable contributions. Among the remaining 25 percent of teens who have no religious affiliation, 44 percent are volunteers and 25 percent are contributors.
Beyond church membership, active involvement in religious organizations appears to have a great impact on the proportion of teenagers who volunteer and give. The proportion of the teen population who were volunteers increased from 34 percent among the 16 percent of respondents who report never attending religious services to 73 percent among the 41 percent who attend weekly. Similarly, the proportion who made charitable monetary contributions increased from 17 percent among those never attending to 69 percent among those attending weekly.

Overall nearly half of the teens surveyed made charitable contributions the previous year. The annual average of all donations was $46 in 1990. Three in four of the teens channeled their contributions through a religious organization. In 1990, the average teen volunteer gave 2.3 hours of time during a typical week.

Willingness To Serve

Nine teens in 10 believe that doing charitable or voluntary work in the community is an important factor of being a good U.S. citizen, according to a Gallup Youth Survey conducted in 1991. This includes 51 percent who think it is very important, and 41 percent who consider it somewhat important.

Most likely to consider voluntarism very important are young women, non-white teens, and residents of the Midwest.

If teen volunteers are not always in evidence, their absence may be explained more by lack of opportunity to serve than by a lack of desire. Past surveys have indicated that those willing to serve a wide range of causes and issues far outnumber those who have already found an outlet for their instincts to volunteer.

5.3 Causes and Issues

In the past there have been certain issues which have captured young people's attention, or served as a rallying point, such as the Vietnam War. Please tell me which of the following issues or causes, if any, you are now actively involved in? . . . you would like to serve?

	1985	1982
Now serving		
Conserving natural resources	11%	7%
Racial harmony	9	5
Environment	9	6
World peace	7	6
Women's rights	7	6
Improved government	6	5
Would like to serve		
Conserving natural resources	56	62
Racial harmony	54	58
Environment	50	52
World peace	68	70
Women's rights	49	42
Improved government	63	68

AIPO 837 Q. 121 – 122

National Service

First there was the draft, then came calls for "universal military service," and then out of the Peace Corps, Vista, and similar programs came proposals for "national service." More recently, several bills have come before Congress to reward young people with tuition vouchers in return for national service, and the 1992 presidential candidates all included national service proposals in their appeals to voters. But what about young people, themselves? Do they still feel the need to serve in a nation reeling from recession and in a world that no longer requires a military draft or even a sizable peacetime army? The answer is a growing "yes," although the kinds of services that are seen as needed may have changed somewhat.

In 1992, 52 percent of teens approved of national service for all young men, and 47 percent believed all young women should also serve. Young men are somewhat more likely than young women to endorse national service programs for both sexes.

Interest in national service peaked in 1986, when 62 percent of young people approved of it for young men and 56 percent favored it for young women as well. By 1989, however, the number favoring service for young men dropped to 49 percent, and for young women to 44 percent.

On other past surveys when teens were asked if they would like to serve in return for college tuition or financial incentives, interest in national service rose dramatically.

Teens now say that if they had to choose they would prefer non-military over military service by a two-to-one margin. Young men far more often than young women choose military service.

Despite the recent lessening of world tensions, the proportion of teens preferring military service dropped only slightly, from 40 percent in 1989 to 32 percent in 1992.

A majority of teens (56 percent) say that if they were required to give non-military service, they would prefer to meet their obligations in their own communities. The desire to serve in one's home town is particularly strong among teen residents of large cities. An additional 6 percent of teens say they would like to be out of town, but still within their home state.

Service in another state would be the choice of 16 percent of the teens, and 20 percent would like to meet their service obligation by working in a developing foreign country.

Young men are somewhat more likely than young women to say they want to stay in their home communities. Young women would be about twice as likely as young men to volunteer for overseas duty in a developing country.

5.4 Favor National Service — Trend

	For young men	For young women
1992	52%	47%
1989	49	44
1986	62	56
1984	62	51
1977	47	38

5.5 Approval of National Service

Would you favor or oppose requiring all young men (women) to give one year of service to the nation, either in the military services or in non-military work here or abroad, such as work in hospitals or with elderly people?

	September – October 1992	
	Favor service for young men	**Favor service for young women**
National	**52%**	**47%**
Male	55	51
Female	49	42
Ages 13 – 15	56	48
Ages 16 – 17	48	45
White	49	43
Non-white	64	60
White-collar background	50	46
Blue-collar background	54	47
Above-average students	53	47
Average and below	51	46
East	60	56
Midwest	54	48
South	48	44
West	47	40
Large city	61	57
Suburb	46	35
Small town	55	51
Rural	44	40
Republican	59	50
Democrat	52	44
Independent	49	46
Protestant	54	48
Catholic	56	52
Church attender	57	51
Non-attender	47	42

GO 12869; Q. 32–33

5.6 Type of Service Preferred

If all young people were required to do this [give one year's national service] would you, yourself, prefer military or non-military service?

| | September – October 1992 | |
	Military	Non-military
National	**32%**	**67%**
Male	44	56
Female	21	78
Ages 13 – 15	29	69
Ages 16 – 17	37	63
White	34	65
Non-white	25	73
White-collar background	29	70
Blue-collar background	37	62
Above-average students	26	72
Average and below	40	59
East	28	72
Midwest	33	66
South	34	65
West	33	65
Large city	36	62
Suburb	30	68
Small town	32	67
Rural	32	66
Republican	35	64
Democrat	30	70
Independent	37	62
Protestant	31	68
Catholic	33	67
Church attender	31	68
Non-attender	33	66

Note: 1 percent of teens expressed no preference.

GO 12869: Q. 34

5.7 Where Teens Would Like To Serve

If all young people were required to give non-military service, where would you, yourself, most like to serve — in your local community, in another community in this state, somewhere else in the United States, or in a developing country?

	September – October 1992			
	Local community	Other community in state	Elsewhere in U.S.	Developing foreign country
National	**56%**	**6%**	**16%**	**20%**
Male	63	5	16	14
Female	51	7	15	24
Ages 13 – 15	53	8	15	22
Ages 16 – 17	61	4	17	16
White	55	7	17	19
Non-white	60	4	17	16
White-collar background	59	6	18	17
Blue-collar background	48	5	17	26
Above-average students	57	7	14	20
Average and below	55	5	19	20
East	56	12	13	17
Midwest	57	5	19	18
South	61	3	11	24
West	51	5	18	21
Large city	68	–	10	21
Suburb	58	11	12	19
Small town	51	6	22	19
Rural	59	4	14	22
Republican	58	5	14	20
Democrat	50	5	21	22
Independent	55	5	16	23
Protestant	57	6	15	22
Catholic	58	7	16	18
Church attender	59	6	16	18
Non-attender	54	7	15	22

Note: 2 percent of teens expressed no preference.

GO 12869; Q. 35

Preferred Service Applications

Teen-agers have the freedom of turning their attention now to a wide range of social and economic concerns. If broad programs of national service are enacted, should not lack for volunteers. Many teens in a 1992 survey expressed willingness to serve their country by helping the homeless, the elderly, and AIDS patients. Others would like to help rebuild cities, clean up migrant camps, serve in fire departments, or even go abroad to help the people of developing countries. Most of all, they would like to help young children in the nation's schools to get a good start in life.

5.8 Preferred National Service Duties

If you were told you had to serve one year in non-military service, how interested would be in doing these things [listed below] — very interested, somewhat interested, not too interested, or not at all interested?

	September – October 1992			
	Very interested	**Somewhat interested**	**Not too interested**	**Not at all interested**
Helping young children in school	70%	23%	3%	4%
Working with homeless people	52	32	11	5
Working in a hospital or clinic	47	34	8	11
Working with the elderly	45	38	10	7
Helping AIDS patients	43	36	12	8
Helping people in developing countries	34	39	14	12
Helping people in migrant work camps or Indian reservations	32	36	18	12
Helping to rebuild cities	31	47	13	9
Serving in a fire department or rescue squad	28	34	18	19

Less than one-half of 1 percent.

GO 12869; Q. 136a–i

National Service Incentives

Teens give very practical reasons for wanting to enroll in national service programs. Obtaining money for higher education and gaining work experience are the leading incentives to attract young people. Majorities of teens also say they are interested both in having the opportunity to help others and to earn money for themselves.

Comparatively fewer teens view national service as something exciting or simply as a way to get away from home.

5.9 Why National Service Interests Young People

How important is [statement below] as a reason why young people might be interested in military or non-military service — very important, somewhat important, not very important, or not at all important?

| | June – July 1989 | | | |
	Very important	Somewhat important	Not very important	Not at all important
To obtain money for future education	74%	21%	4%	1%
To gain work experience	65	30	4	1
An opportunity to help others	57	37	5	1
An opportunity to earn money	55	37	8	*
It would be exciting	39	44	11	4
To get away from home	22	41	29	8

*Less than one-half of I percent

AIPO 881; Q. 306

Some view national service as a way to give themselves a new start in life. Others see it as a means of leading drug offenders to a straighter life. It also is viewed as a way for dropouts to obtain high school equivalency diplomas.

Fortunately, not too many teens seem concerned that getting the "best jobs" would be a matter of knowing someone of influence.

There appears to be little support for limiting student loans solely to those who have done national service. (This attitude, however, probably would change if the programs became universal or at least more widespread beyond the current limited demonstration activities.)

5.10 National Service Features

For each of these statements about national service, please tell me if you agree very much, agree somewhat, disagree somewhat, or disagree very much.

	December 1989			
	Agree very much	Agree somewhat	Disagree somewhat	Disagree somewhat
It would give me a new start in life	48%	39%	10%	3%
Convicted young drug offenders should be given the opportunity to get straight through national service	47	41	7	4
High school dropouts should be given a chance to get their degree while doing national service	34	46	11	8
You probably would have to know somebody to get the good jobs	16	31	33	19
Government-backed student loans should be given only to those who have done national service	8	22	37	31

AIPO 881; Q. 306

Interest in national service is considerably enhanced when teens are exposed to proposals outlining weekly pay and voucher systems. Interest becomes even greater as the financial inducements rise.

Greater interest in military service is shown by young women when pay differentials are introduced.

5.11 Reaction to National Service Proposals

It has been proposed that young people be paid $100 a week while they serve, and at the end of their service receive $3,000 to be used for education or further training. How interested would you be in this plan: very interested, somewhat interested, or not very interested?

Another plan would also pay $100 a week, but at the end of service people would receive a voucher for $10,000 for non-military service or $12,000 for military service. The voucher could be used for education or a down-payment for a house. How interested. . .

Which would you prefer then, military or non-military service?

	November 1989		
	Total	**Male**	**Female**
$3,000 Voucher Plan			
Very interested	36%	31%	41%
Somewhat interested	46	48	45
Not very interested	18	21	14
$10,000 – $12,000 Voucher Plan			
Very interested	54	50	58
Somewhat interested	35	37	33
Not very interested	11	13	9
Would then prefer:			
Military service	45	54	35
Non-military service	49	39	59
Not sure	6	7	6

AIPO 881 Q. 308 – 310

If required to do national service, a slight majority of teens say they would prefer to put in their one year of duty before going to college. This is even more true of above-average students who undoubtedly are those most likely to enter college full time upon graduating from high school.

5.12 Best Time To Serve

If you were required to give one year's national service, when would you prefer to serve: before attending college, or after college?

	Total	Above-average students	Average or below-average students
Before attending college	52%	61%	42%
After college	39	36	42
Don't intend to go to college	8	2	14
Not sure	1	*	2

*Less than one-half of 1 percent

AIPO 881 Q. 307

Seven teens in 10 say they would approve of allowing young people to fulfill national service obligations by doing mission work for their church.

5.13 Substituting Mission Work for National Service

Would you approve or disapprove of allowing young people to fulfill their national service obligation by doing mission work for their church, provided they are paid by the church and not by the U.S. Government?

	Approve	Disapprove	Not sure
Total	70%	28%	2%
Protestant	73	25	2
Catholic	70	27	3

AIPO 881 Q. 312

5.14 Opinion of Environmental Service Corps

Would you favor or oppose requiring all young people in the U.S. to give one year of service protect and restore the world's environment?

	September – October 1992	
	Favor	**Oppose**
National	**82%**	**16%**
Male	80	16
Female	84	16
Ages 13 – 15	83	14
Ages 16 – 17	80	18
White	83	15
Non-white	78	19
White-collar background	83	16
Blue-collar background	81	17
Above-average students	83	14
Average and below	79	19
East	82	15
Midwest	82	15
South	83	16
West	79	18
Large city	82	14
Suburb	82	17
Small town	81	16
Rural	79	19
Republican	84	14
Democrat	86	12
Independent	76	22
Protestant	86	11
Catholic	78	20
Church attender	82	16
Non-attender	81	16

Note: 2 percent of teens had no opinion.

GO 12869; Q. 37

Military Service

In a Gallup Youth Survey taken shortly before the outbreak of hostilities in the Persian Gulf, nine teens in 10 said they believe it is important for American citizens to serve in the military during wartime when they become eligible. This included 69 percent who feel it is very important and 23 percent who think it is somewhat important. Only 5 percent say it is not too important, 3 and percent that it is not important at all.

In answer to a further question about "would you still be patriotic if you disagreed with United States policies," 46 percent believe it is very important to do this and 34 percent that it is somewhat important. Disagreeing with the philosophy of "my country, right or wrong" are 17 percent of the teens, while 3 percent are undecided.

The Draft

Most teen-agers in recent years have felt that a military draft is no longer necessary. If it were to become necessary, however, many would like to have women as well as men to be subject to the draft.

5.15 Opinion of the Draft

Do you think we should return to the military draft at this time, or not? If a draft were to become necessary, should young women be required to participate, as well as young men, or not?

	Approve of draft for young men	Approve of draft for young women
1989	9%	61%
1988	12	60
1986	12	60
1985	15	37
1980	38	41

AIPO 881 Q. 121

Armed Services Branch Preference

The U.S. Air Force has perennially been the military service branch that most teenagers would choose if they were required to give a one-year tour of duty to their nation. Preference for the Air Force grew from 35 percent to 47 percent between 1982 and 1989.

At the same time, preference for the Army dropped from 27 percent to 19 percent. The proportion of teens preferring the Navy has remained steady, but interest in the Marine Corps has dropped. Young men are more likely than young women to be attracted by the Marine Corps.

5.16 Preferred Branch Trend

If you had to serve a year in the military service, which would you prefer: The Army, Air Force, Navy, or Marines?

	1989	1986	1984	1982
Air Force	47%	43%	37%	35%
Army	19	19	24	27
Navy	19	18	17	18
Marines	13	17	18	17

AIPO 881; Q. 304

Teens show greater confidence in the U.S. military than in federal, state, or local government. Only about half of the teens surveyed on American institutions in 1991, expressed a great deal or quite a lot of confidence in the civilian branches of government. Three in four, however, gave top marks to the military.

NATIONAL AND POLITICAL AFFAIRS

Greatest Problem Facing America Today

Teen-agers for the first time in recent history have the luxury of spending less time worrying about international tensions, the economy, and even the war on drugs, and are able to turn their focus on a variety of social problems confronting the nation and their generation. Drug abuse still ranks first as the problem of greatest concern to teens, but its importance is diminished as it is joined by other social concerns

6.1 Most Important Problem Facing the Nation

	1992	1991	1989	1988	1986	1982	1978
Drug abuse	32%	31%	49%	13%	4%	*%	*%
AIDS	15	9	4	8	–	–	–
Economic issues	13	17	7	16	10	52	57
Environment, pollution	8	12	3	*	2	1	1
Poverty, hunger, homelessness	8	18	12	12	10	*	*
International tensions	6	11	10	33	57	23	23
Crime	6	9	5	1	2	2	2
Teen pregnancy	3	*	*	*	*	*	*
Education	3	3	*	1	1	*	*
Abortion	3	2	6	*	*	*	*
Racial discrimination	3	3	*	1	*	*	*
Political issues	2	2	1	*	*	4	1
Miscellaneous	4	11	9	6	5	3	2
Not sure	5	12	7	15	14	14	14

* Less than one-half of 1 percent.

Note: Columns add to more than 100% because some teens named more than one problem.

Confidence in the U.S.

Teens' confidence in their country has been on a roller coaster ride over the past decade.

In the 1970's teens rapidly lost confidence in the U.S. until by 1980 when the nation seemed at the mercy of hostage takers and oil merchants in the Middle East, only 23 percent said they were satisfied with the way things were going in the U.S. Under the Reagan administration, however, their confidence in the nation gradually recovered. By 1983, 41 percent of the teens said they were satisfied with affairs in the U.S. The momentum of confidence grew until it peaked in 1986 when seven teens in 10 expressed satisfaction.

Since that time the momentum has once again shifted downward, with satisfaction ratings dropping to 61 percent of all teens in 1987, to 59 percent in 1988, and finally to just 30 percent in 1992.

6.2 Trends in Satisfaction with the United States

1992	30%
1988	59
1987	61
1986	70
1985	67
1983	41
1980	23
1979	42

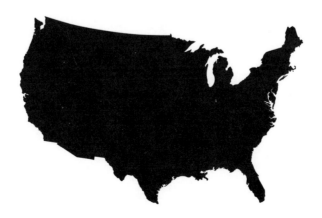

In general, are you satisfied or dissatisfied with the way things are going in the United States at this time?

	September – October 1992	
	Satisfied	**Dissatisfied**
National	**30%**	**66%**
Male	34	62
Female	27	70
Ages 13 – 15	31	64
Ages 16 – 17	30	68
White	25	67
Non-white	34	62
White-collar background	25	72
Blue-collar background	33	62
Above-average students	28	68
Average and below	33	63
East	27	70
Midwest	32	67
South	34	60
West	24	70
Large city	28	69
Suburb	21	76
Small town	30	66
Rural	36	59
Republican	36	60
Democrat	25	75
Independent	23	75
Protestant	37	60
Catholic	25	72
Church attender	34	60
Non-attender	26	69

Note: 4 percent of teens had no opinion.

GO 12869; Q. 14

Presidential Approval Ratings

Both George Bush and Ronald Reagan received their highest approval ratings at time when they were achieving military victories and foreign policy success. Their lowest ratings occurred when the nation was in the midst of deep economic recessions.

6.4 Presidential Approval Ratings

	Approve	Disapprove	Not sure
George Bush			
September – October 1992	38%	51%	11%
June – July 1992	48	45	7
June – July 1991	69	18	13
March 1989	70	14	16
Ronald Reagan			
1988	56	32	12
1987	50	38	12
1986	67	24	9
1985	71	21	8
1984	59	30	11
1983	49	39	12
1982	43	47	10
1981	58	52	10

In a 1985 Gallup Youth Survey, teens named Abraham Lincoln, George Washington, and John Kennedy as the three best Presidents of the United States.

Do you approve or disapprove of the way George Bush is handling his job as President?

	September – October 1992		
	Approve	**Disapprove**	**Not sure**
National	**38%**	**51%**	**11%**
Male	36	57	7
Female	40	45	15
Ages 13 to 15	38	52	10
Ages 16 to 17	38	49	13
White	38	49	13
Non-white	39	56	5
White-collar background	36	52	12
Blue-collar background	37	55	8
Above-average students	38	52	10
Average and below	38	50	12
East	43	50	7
Midwest	32	55	13
South	42	50	8
West	35	48	17
Large city	32	64	4
Suburb	41	48	11
Small town	38	51	11
Rural	36	49	15
Republican	59	30	11
Democrat	21	71	8
Independent	30	60	10
Protestant	44	43	13
Catholic	35	60	5
Church attender	43	47	10
Non-attender	33	55	12

GO 12869: Q. 12

Clinton vs. Bush

If the nation's teen-agers could have voted in 1992, they would have chosen Bill Clinton over George Bush, by a margin of 54 percent to 40 percent. On the survey which began before H. Ross Perot announced he was reentering the race, only 1 percent volunteered they would prefer Perot. Just one teen in 20 (5 percent) was undecided.

Earlier in the year before the conventions, George Bush held a commanding lead of 43 percent to 29 percent for the yet-to-be-named Democratic candidate and 21 percent for Perot.

Bush clearly lost the confidence of teens, as only 38 percent by September 1992 still said they approved of the job he was doing in handling his job as president, while 51 percent disapproved. A year before in the afterglow of the success of the War in the Gulf, Bush got positive ratings from 69 percent.

"TEEN ELECTIONS"

1992

Clinton	54%
Bush	40

1988

Bush	52%
Dukakis	48

1984

Reagan	52%
Mondale	40

1980

Reagan	39%
Carter	38
Anderson	11

The size of the Clinton lead was all the more impressive when it is considered that an incumbent president normally enjoys a tremendous advantage among teens because he may be the only president who is familiar to them, and so they have no basis for comparison. When teens gave their opinions in 1980, Ronald Reagan led Carter by only one percentage point. Reagan as an incumbent then gained a 12 percentage-point advantage over Walter Mondale in 1984. Teens gave Bush just a 4 percentage-point lead over Michael Dukakis in 1988.

Bush carried a majority vote only from teen Republicans, but even among the party faithful 26 percent deserted him for Clinton. By comparison, only 9 percent of teen Democrats said they would switch over to Bush, while 90 percent backed Clinton. Among the important future independent voters, Clinton outpolled Bush, by a margin of 56 percent to 37 percent.

Bill Clinton received a majority of the vote from teens from all walks of life and from all sections of the country. His strongest regional showings were in the Midwest and South.

Black and Hispanic teens were among Clinton's strongest supporters.

Bush was not able to attract blue-collar youngsters in 1992 the way he and Ronald Reagan did in the past. Clinton commanded a 58-percent-to-35-percent point lead among teens who come from blue-collar family backgrounds.

6.6 Clinton vs. Bush

Suppose the presidential election were being held today. If George Bush were the Republican candidate, and Bill Clinton were Democratic candidate, who would you vote for? Those who were undecided were asked: As of today, do you lean more to Bush, the Republican, or to Clinton, the Democrat? [In the earlier survey, respondents were asked: "Would you be more likely to vote for George Bush or for the Democratic Party's candidate, or for an independent candidate such as Ross Perot in 1992?"]

	Sept. – Oct. 1992		April 1992		
	Clinton	Bush	Clinton	Bush	Perot
National	**54%**	**40%**	**29%**	**43%**	**21%**
Male	56	37	29	43	21
Female	52	44	28	42	21
Ages 13 – 15	55	40	27	47	20
Ages 16 – 17	51	42	32	37	22
White	54	43	26	48	20
Non-white	62	32	40	26	26
White-collar background	57	41	30	41	23
Blue-collar background	58	35	25	47	20
Above-average students	55	40	32	39	22
Average and below	54	41	26	47	20
East	51	40	33	42	20
Midwest	58	37	32	41	16
South	57	40	27	46	21
West	50	48	26	42	27
Large city	57	41	na	na	na
Suburb	58	39	na	na	na
Small town	53	42	na	na	na
Rural	54	38	na	na	na
Republican	26	73	72	7	18
Democrat	90	9	17	66	14
Independent	56	37	24	39	28
Protestant	52	45	25	50	20
Catholic	58	36	38	38	14
Church attender	48	39	26	47	20
Non-attender	60	33	32	38	22

GO 12869: Q. 9–10

6.7 Bush vs. Dukakis

Suppose the 1988 elections were being held today: If George Bush were the Republican candidate and Michael Dukakis were the Democratic candidate, which would you like to see win? As of today, do you lean more toward Bush, the Republican, or to Dukakis, the Democrat?

	September 1988		June – July 1988	
	Bush	Dukakis	Bush	Dukakis
NATIONAL	**52%**	**42%**	**47%**	**47%**
Male	55	39	53	47
Female	49	44	42	46
Ages 13 – 15	53	42	49	47
Ages 16 – 17	51	41	46	46
White collar background	55	40	42	52
Blue collar background	49	43	50	45
Above-average students	52	44	43	51
Average and below	53	39	53	40
East	56	42	44	47
Midwest	45	49	49	49
South	53	38	51	43
West	55	37	43	49
Large city	49	45	45	43
Suburb	56	39	44	51
Non-metropolitan	51	42	51	45
Republican	78	17	76	22
Democrat	19	76	17	81
Protestant	53	41	46	50
Catholic	53	41	50	45

AIPO 1866, Q 104 – 105, AIPO1865 Q. 114-115

6.8 Reagan vs. Mondale

Suppose the 1984 elections were being held today: If Ronald Reagan were the Republican candidate and Walter Mondale were the Democratic candidate, which would you like to see win? As of today, do you lean more toward Reagan the Republican, or to Mondale the Democrat?

	July – September 1984	
	Reagan	**Mondale**
NATIONAL	**52%**	**40%**
Male	54	40
Female	51	40
Ages 13 – 15	50	40
Ages 16 – 18	55	39
White collar background	56	35
Blue collar background	51	44
Above-average students	56	36
Average and below	49	43
East	51	50
Midwest	47	43
South	57	37
West	55	31
Large city	45	53
Suburb	54	38
Non-metropolitan	56	35
Protestants	53	41
Catholics	52	37

AI 822; Q. 104ab

6.9 Reagan vs. Carter

In the presidential election on November 4th, who did you, yourself, want to see win?

	November 1980		
	Reagan	**Carter**	**Anderson**
NATIONAL	**39%**	**38%**	**11%**
Male	41	37	12
Female	38	39	11
Ages 13 – 15	44	37	10
Ages 16 – 18	35	39	13
White-collar background	43	31	16
Blue-collar background	37	43	8
Above-average students	39	36	14
Average and below	39	41	8
East	35	38	18
Midwest	44	34	9
South	39	44	6
West	39	32	6

AI 755, Q. 21a

Presidential Candidates Teens Would Avoid

Heavy drinkers, check bouncers, and those who have trouble making up their minds about major issues, would have gotten little support in 1992 from the nation's teens as presidential candidates. Teen Republicans in particular are likely to take a dim view of moral lapses among candidates.

Leading the parade of candidates teens would avoid are heavy drinkers, with nine teens in 10 saying a tipsy candidate would be a matter of concern to them. Only one teen in three, however, would be concerned if a candidate smoked marijuana once or twice in college — whether or not he inhaled. (A Gallup Youth Survey in 1992, found that 15 percent of teen marijuana users also said they did not inhale.)

A candidate who keeps changing his mind about major issues would be a matter of concern to eight teens in 10. Those who are 16 and older and soon nearing the time when they will be able to vote in elections, are most likely to take dim views of candidates who show inconsistent records on the issues.

A past history of bouncing checks would put a candidate in political hot water with three teens in four.

Military service history touched all of the major candidates in 1992 because of Bill Clinton's avoidance of the Vietnam draft, questions about Dan Quayle's National Guard privileges, and Ross Perot's seeming inability to keep his stories straight about just why did he seek to get released from his naval obligations prematurely. A majority of teens said they found possible draft avoidance a matter of concern.

Allegations of past affairs knocked Gary Hart out of the running in 1988, and President Clinton had his hands full with the steamy headlines from the nation's tabloids in the '92 campaign, but this would matter to only one teen in three.

Few teens say it would matter to them if a candidate came from a very rich family.

Religion may have been an important factor in past presidential races, but just one teen in eight says a candidate's religion is now a matter of concern. The level of concern rises to 20 percent among those who are frequent church attenders.

Jerry Brown is about as close as we have come in recent years to having a bachelor seek the White House, but the fact that a candidate has never married would matter to only one teen in 20.

Matters of concern to teens in presidential candidates

	Total	GOP	DEM	Indep.
Heavy drinking	91%	94%	92%	88%
Changing stands on issues	80	85	79	77
Check bouncing	75	83	70	71
Draft avoidance	53	61	59	44
Affairs	33	45	28	27
Marijuana experimentation	32	37	25	34
Inherited wealth	14	12	16	15
Religion	12	19	13	6
Being single	6	8	4	7

AP/Stan Kohler

Political Parties and the Issues

When teens are asked to choose between the major parties on their abilities to deal with the campaign issues of 1992, Republicans are given the edge on national defense and foreign affairs, but Democrats more often are seen as better able to cope with the nation's growing domestic problems.

George Bush received his highest confidence ratings ever in the aftermath of the highly successful Operation Desert Storm campaign, but while the president's ratings declined precipitously to less than half their previous level afterwards, the Republican party still was viewed by a majority of teens as best able to govern the nation's defense and conduct its foreign affairs. Only one teen in three in 1992 gave a similar vote of confidence to the Democrats.

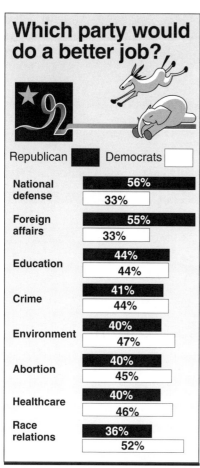

AP/Stan Kohler

While the Republican edge in these matters was impressive, it may have been outweighed by the confidence Democrats were given for dealing with domestic issues.

George Bush tried to position himself as the "education president", but teens rated the parties as equal in their expected abilities to deal with the nation's academic problems.

Republicans once had the "law and order" image pretty much to themselves, but teens saw the parties as about equal in their abilities to deal with the crime issue The crime issue is especially important to teens, who in recent years have consistently identified drug abuse and associated crime as the leading problem facing both the country and their generation.

Prior to President Bush's trip to Rio de Janeiro to attend the Earth Summit on the Environment, teens gave Democrats the edge over Republicans on being able to handle environmental issues.

Democrats also were given the edge over Republicans on their ability to solve the highly emotional issue of abortion, and to deal with health care issues.

A majority of teens felt the Democrats would do a better job than Republicans in dealing with the nation's often tense race relations. Non-white teens expressed confidence in the Democrats over Republicans to handle race relations by a two-to-one margin.

Political Parties and the Economy

In 1992 the majority of America's teen-agers believed the Democratic Party could do a better job than the Republican party in dealing with the country's problems of poverty, homelessness, and unemployment. Overall, the parties were seen as nearly equal for coping with general economic conditions and managing the federal budget deficit, but Democrats are given a slight edge.

These findings spelled trouble for the G.O.P., since teens tend to be far more optimistic (some would say "naive") than their parents or college-age youth about the economy. As teens grow older and near the age when they, themselves, will be able to vote, their tendency is to turn away from Republicans and towards the Democrats to provide solutions for the country's economy.

When economic issues are mixed with those who are hurting in our society, Democrats take a clear lead over Republicans in being seen as the party best able to solve the problems.

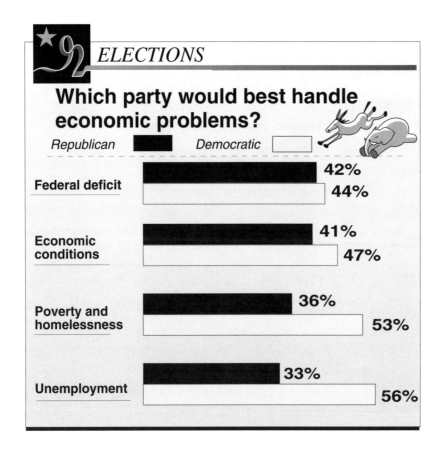

6.10a Partisan Issues

Which political party, the Republican or the Democratic, do you think would do a better job of dealing with each of the following —

> . . . *national defense?*
> . . . *foreign affairs*
> . . . *education?*
> . . . *economic conditions?*

	April 1992							
	Defense		*Foreign affairs*		*Education*		*Economy*	
	GOP	Dem	GOP	Dem	GOP	Dem	GOP	Dem
National	**56%**	**33%**	**55%**	**33%**	**44%**	**44%**	**41%**	**47%**
Male	59	31	56	36	44	44	41	50
Female	54	35	54	31	44	44	41	44
Ages 13 – 15	52	34	53	31	46	39	42	44
Ages 16 – 17	62	31	56	37	41	50	40	51
White	60	29	56	32	47	35	45	44
Non-white	47	44	52	36	41	50	40	51
White-collar background	60	30	58	31	46	44	46	43
Blue-collar background	53	36	53	35	45	41	35	54
Above-average students	61	31	62	29	45	47	40	52
Average and below	50	35	43	40	43	40	43	40
East	54	33	60	28	41	48	39	48
Midwest	52	40	53	35	45	38	39	46
South	57	32	49	39	51	40	43	48
West	63	25	60	29	35	52	43	46
Republican	72	20	70	22	75	23	67	25
Democrat	48	51	49	48	24	73	27	70
Independent	52	35	51	36	38	48	36	52
Protestant	59	33	60	31	50	39	48	43
Catholic	51	37	51	40	49	41	36	53
Church attender	61	30	59	30	47	40	47	43
Non-attender	52	36	50	37	40	47	35	51

GO 224007; Q. 14

6.10b Partisan Issues

. . . Federal budget deficit?
. . . Crime?
. . . Environmental issues?
. . . Healthcare policy?

| | April 1992 | | | | | | | |
| | Federal deficit | | Crime | | Environment | | Healthcare | |
	GOP	Dem	GOP	Dem	GOP	Dem	GOP	Dem
National	**42%**	**44%**	**41%**	**45%**	**40%**	**47%**	**40%**	**46%**
Male	44	47	41	46	38	49	40	48
Female	40	42	42	43	41	44	40	44
Ages 13 – 15	42	42	40	45	45	40	42	42
Ages 16 – 17	41	48	44	44	32	57	37	52
White	43	43	44	42	45	40	43	42
Non-white	39	49	36	51	39	49	32	57
White-collar background	45	42	45	41	41	46	43	46
Blue-collar background	39	49	34	52	37	51	36	50
Above-average students	40	49	44	45	42	48	43	48
Average and below	44	38	38	43	36	45	36	43
East	40	47	43	40	35	50	42	44
Midwest	38	46	43	44	49	38	36	48
South	47	41	43	44	37	51	44	45
West	41	45	36	52	37	48	37	46
Republican	68	24	63	27	64	27	61	28
Democrat	25	68	24	69	23	74	23	72
Independent	35	49	40	45	35	48	39	46
Protestant	47	42	46	41	46	42	46	44
Catholic	37	49	37	49	44	44	38	51
Church attender	48	39	49	37	46	41	44	43
Non-attender	35	50	34	52	32	53	36	49

GO 224007; Q. 14

6.10c Partisan Issues

. . . Abortion?
. . . Race relations?
. . . Poverty and homelessness?
. . . Unemployment?

	April 1992							
	Abortion		*Race relations*		*Poverty*		*Unem- ployment*	
	GOP	Dem	GOP	Dem	GOP	Dem	GOP	Dem
National	**40%**	**45%**	**37%**	**48%**	**36%**	**52%**	**33%**	**56%**
Male	43	43	38	49	35	56	37	54
Female	38	47	37	47	36	49	29	58
Ages 13 – 15	41	42	41	42	39	46	28	65
Ages 16 – 17	40	49	33	57	46	61	28	65
White	44	40	40	46	26	62	37	52
Non-white	30	59	29	56	26	62	21	68
White-collar background	42	46	39	48	35	40	31	57
Blue-collar background	44	42	41	45	40	51	37	52
Above-average students	42	47	36	52	34	57	31	62
Average and below	38	41	38	42	38	47	37	46
East	32	52	38	42	39	50	36	48
Midwest	39	43	36	46	36	52	33	58
South	47	39	40	49	33	55	33	58
West	42	46	34	56	36	52	30	58
Republican	66	22	61	28	68	35	54	36
Democrat	21	74	16	77	12	86	11	86
Independent	38	45	38	47	38	49	36	54
Protestant	48	40	36	50	44	49	39	53
Catholic	34	49	42	47	35	53	33	57
Church attender	46	39	44	44	39	49	38	51
Non-attender	34	50	31	53	33	56	28	60

GO 224007; Q. 14

Party Preference

"None of the above" is becoming an increasingly popular political choice for America's teens. Republicans and Democrats still attract teens in large numbers, but the ranks of those who say they are "independents" or who have no political party preference are growing.

The growth in the number of teen independents appears to have come more at the expense of the Republicans than of the Democrats. As recently as in 1990, the Republicans could count upon nearly half (48 percent) of the "teen vote," compared to 38 percent for the Democrats. While both parties have lost young followers since that time, the Republicans suffered an 18-percentage point decline, compared to a drop of 12 percentage points for the Democrats.

The Republicans enjoyed a plurality of teen followers for most of the Reagan-Bush years. The high-water mark for the Republicans occurred in 1986 when they held a commanding lead over the Democrats of 51 percent to 31 percent in attracting the future teen vote. The Democrats have not held the lead since 1982, when Ronald Reagan's popularity ratings were still low. In 1982, teens declaring themselves to be Democrats were more numerous than Republicans, by a margin of 45 percent to 33 percent.

6.11 Political Party Preference

	Republicans	Democrats	Independent/ No preference/ No opinion
1992	30%	26%	44%
1990	48	38	14
1989	52	32	16
1988	44	36	20
1987	45	35	20
1986	51	31	18
1985	52	28	20
1984	41	38	21
1983	38	39	23
1982	33	45	22
1977	21	32	47

6.12 Political Party Preference

When you are old enough to vote, do you think you will be a Republican, a Democrat, or an Independent?

| | September – October 1992 | | |
	GOP	Democrat	Independent
National	**27%**	**25%**	**30%**
Male	28	26	31
Female	26	24	30
Ages 13 – 15	28	23	29
Ages 16 – 17	26	28	33
White	30	22	33
Non-white	15	36	24
White-collar family background	29	24	32
Blue-collar family background	22	26	32
Above-average students	27	30	30
Average and below	27	19	32
East	30	20	34
Midwest	25	26	34
South	25	30	26
West	31	22	30
Large city	24	26	36
Suburb	31	26	32
Small town	23	28	34
Rural	32	23	25
Protestant	30	25	26
Catholic	29	25	33
Church attender	31	23	30
Non-attender	23	27	31

Note: 18 percent expressed no party preference.

GO 12869; Q. 11

Congress

Teens may start out favoring Republican congressional candidates, but as they grow older and near the age when they can cast ballots for the first time, the balance of power slowly shifts to the Democrats. The Democrats draw their greatest strength because of a gender gap in political preferences among teens that increases rapidly as they grow older.

Overall, Republican congressional candidates in 1992 held a 46-percent to 40-percent lead in the "teen vote" over their Democratic rivals, but that margin may have been illusory, because Republicans draw their greatest strength from younger teens, ages 13 to 15, who give them the nod over Democratic congressional aspirants by a margin of 50 percent to 36 percent. Among those who are 16 and 17, however, the balance of power switches, with the Democrats commanding a 47-percent to 41-percent lead.

It may of course be only natural that younger teens started out heavily favoring Republican candidates since the party had held the presidency and nation's leadership ever since they could remember. As teens grow older, they become exposed to alternatives to the incumbent party and may begin to follow the voting preferences of their parents and other adults in selecting congressional candidates.

Knowledge of Congress is not very high among teens. A 1978 Gallup Youth survey found only 27 percent could name their congressman. Even in 1980, at the height of that year's presidential election when presumably political awareness would be at a peak, the ability to name the incumbent congressman actually fell to 25 percent of the teen population. Also that year, while one teen in three was able to state how many members there are in the U.S. Senate, only 15 percent knew how many members there are in the U.S. House of Representatives.

The image of congressmen suffers further indignity in terms of the compensation they receive, with 69 percent of teens stating in a 1982 survey that they are overpaid.

Vice Presidents of the United States may serve as President of the U.S. Senate, but that distinction does not necessarily bring much attention or recognition from America's teens.

In 1981, three teens in four were able to identify Robin Williams as the actor who played "Mork" in the popular TV comedy series *Mork and Mindy*. Only 66 percent, however, knew that George Bush at that time was Vice President of the United States.

His successor fared only slightly better in 1990. Seventy-four percent of teens were able to identify Dan Quayle as Vice President, but 94 percent were able to identify "Bart Simpson" as the animated star of TV's *The Simpsons*.

6.13 Congressional Candidate Choices

In general, would you be more likely to vote for a Republican or for a Democrat as a congressman to represent your district?

	April 1992	
	GOP	**Democrats**
National	**46%**	**40%**
Male	45	42
Female	47	39
Ages 13 – 15	50	36
Ages 16 – 17	41	47
White	50	36
Non-white	41	47
White-collar background	46	37
Blue-collar background	47	41
Above-average students	48	42
Average and below	43	39
East	39	45
Midwest	47	40
South	48	41
West	50	36
Republican	88	6
Democrat	9	87
Independent	41	40
Protestant	51	37
Catholic	43	41
Church attender	54	32
Non-attender	37	49

GO Q. 13

Political Participation Intentions

Until 1992, voting turnouts among the young in recent years had been very low, but Gallup Youth Survey results show that teens usually start out in life intending to be politically active. Furthermore, many teens not only expect to vote regularly, but some day hope to join a political party, work for its candidates, and maybe even consider running for office themselves.

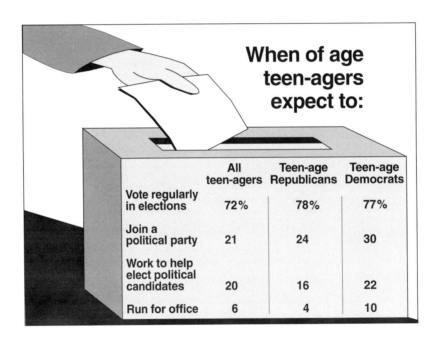

When of age teen-agers expect to:

	All teen-agers	Teen-age Republicans	Teen-age Democrats
Vote regularly in elections	72%	78%	77%
Join a political party	21	24	30
Work to help elect political candidates	20	16	22
Run for office	6	4	10

6.14 Future Political Activism

	Join party	Work for candidates	Run for office
1992	21%	20%	6%
1990	23	20	8

Voting Rights and Reforms

Most of America's teen-agers apparently believe that one way to increase citizen participation in government is to extend the privilege of voting to as many people as possible.

Many young people favor greater use of foreign-language ballots to help citizens for whom English is a second language, but proposals to require future voters to pass a test on U.S. government before they can register fail to gain approval from a majority of teens. Teens also adamantly oppose any attempt to deny voting rights to those who may be on welfare. When it comes to their own time to vote, few would like to wait longer by reinstituting 21 as the minimum voting age.

6.15 Teen Approval of Voting Reforms
(Percent of teens approving of each reform)

Please tell me if you agree or disagree with these statements about voting in this country — People should be required to take a test on U.S. government and pass it before being allowed to register. The legal voting age should be raised to 21. People on welfare should not be allowed to vote. Voting ballots should be printed in foreign languages for those who do not speak English very well

	January 1991			
	Foreign language ballots	Require voting exam	Raise voting age to 21	No vote for those on welfare
National	**75%**	**39%**	**17%**	**6%**
Male	74	40	16	8
Female	77	38	18	4
Ages 13 – 15	79	44	18	6
Ages 16 – 17	71	33	16	6
White	74	39	16	6
Non-white	79	41	20	8
Above-average students	77	41	18	5
Average and below	72	36	16	8
White-collar background	73	37	16	6
Blue-collar background	79	44	17	6
East	74	37	19	5
Midwest	74	37	13	7
South	74	44	19	7
West	75	39	18	6
Republicans	78	43	18	6
Democrats	75	38	17	6

GO 224007

Young Voter Apathy

A generation ago the mood of apathetic young voters during the late 1960s was captured by protest song writers Mick Jagger and Keith Richard who urged people to think of the stay-at-home voter, "faced with a choice of cancer or polio." Most teens reject this approach, but some echo these sentiments of past protests and say that if you do not like any of the candidates then there is no point to showing up at the polling place. Others are more selective and say they do not feel that local elections matter, and so there is no real reason to choose among those running for local office. Still others may be interested in voting, but rather than study the candidates and their views on the issues, feel it is best to vote a "straight ticket" by always casting ballots for people of the same party.

6.16 Negative Voting Attitudes

Please tell me if you agree or disagree with these statements about voting in this country: People should only vote for the candidates of the same party. It really doesn't matter much to me who wins local elections. There is no reason to vote if you do not like any of the candidates.

	January 1991		
	Don't vote if you don't like the candidates	Local elections don't matter	Always vote for the same party
National	**28%**	**20%**	**14%**
Male	30	20	16
Female	27	19	12
Ages 13 – 15	28	18	11
Ages 16 – 17	29	22	18
White	24	20	14
Non-white	42	19	14
Above-average students	26	16	14
Average and below	32	25	13
White-collar background	26	17	12
Blue-collar background	31	19	13
East	33	22	14
Midwest	28	16	13
South	22	15	14
West	34	28	14
Republican	23	20	14
Democrat	34	20	15

GO 224007

Nuclear War

U.S. peace efforts

United Nations

The Third World

INTERNATIONAL AFFAIRS

Concern About Nuclear War

Despite the enormous decrease in international tensions in recent years, America's teens are no less likely now than in the past to fear there will be a nuclear war in their lifetime. At the same time, however, they say this possibility has less influence on how they think about and plan their future.

This suggests that although many young people may still think nuclear conflict is likely, they do not feel that their own country will become involved in the conflagration. That is very important since a previous study by the Gallup Youth Survey found that few teens thought that they personally (8 percent) or the United States (10 percent) stood a good chance of surviving a nuclear war.

Teens in this country are divided in their opinion of the possibility of future nuclear war, with half believing it is very likely (10 percent) or somewhat likely (40 percent), and half saying it would be somewhat (25 percent) or very (24 percent) unlikely event. Opinion about the possibility of nuclear war is unchanged since 1988.

Less than half of the teens now say that the possibility of nuclear war has a serious influence (16 percent) or some influence (27 percent) on how they think or plan about their future. A majority of young people dismiss this possibility as having little (34 percent) or no influence (22 percent) on their future plans.

There has been a steady decrease in the number of teens who report anxieties about the possibility of nuclear war since 1983, when six in 10 said they had serious concerns (31 percent) or at least some concerns (30 percent) about it.

Somewhat less likely than average to foresee nuclear conflict in their lifetime are teens who are 16 and older (48 percent), young men (44 percent), and students who are doing above-average work at school (47 percent).

Those most likely to fear future nuclear war are younger teens (52 percent), young women (56 percent), and students doing average or below-average work at school (54 percent). Almost two teens in three living in large cities, which presumably would be prime targets in a nuclear war, show the greatest level of concern about the possibility of a nuclear strike (63 percent).

7.1 Influence of Threat of Nuclear War

	Serious influence	Some influence	Little or no influence
1992	16%	27%	56%
1988	21	35	42
1986	27	34	38
1984	25	24	47
1983	31	30	37

"No opinion" (1 to 4 percent) is not shown.

7.2 Influence of the Threat of Nuclear War

Does the possibility of nuclear war have a serious influence, some influence, little, or no influence on the way you think or plan about the future?

	September – October 1992			
	Serious influence	Some influence	Little influence	No influence
National	**16%**	**27%**	**34%**	**22%**
Male	18	23	32	25
Female	14	31	36	18
Ages 13 – 15	18	26	32	22
Ages 16 – 17	13	29	35	22
White	15	29	33	21
Non-white	17	21	36	22
White-collar background	14	28	34	22
Blue-collar background	18	29	29	23
Above-average students	14	26	37	23
Average and below	18	30	30	19
East	20	28	32	18
Midwest	12	30	34	24
South	17	23	40	19
West	16	30	24	27
Large city	17	25	39	19
Suburb	16	26	34	23
Small town	18	24	33	24
Rural	11	38	33	24
Republican	17	29	33	21
Democrat	17	27	39	16
Independent	17	25	31	26
Protestant	12	31	35	20
Catholic	18	28	33	21
Church attender	14	27	35	23
Non-attender	18	28	33	21

Note: 1 percent of teens had no opinion.

GO 12869; Q. 39

7.3 Likelihood of Nuclear War in Lifetime

How likely do you feel it is that there will be a nuclear war in your lifetime — very likely, somewhat likely, somewhat unlikely, or very unlikely?

| | September – October 1992 | | | |
	Very likely	Somewhat likely	Somewhat unlikely	Very unlikely
National	**10%**	**40%**	**25%**	**24%**
Male	12	32	26	28
Female	9	48	23	20
Ages 13 – 15	12	39	22	26
Ages 16 – 17	8	40	29	23
White	10	39	22	26
Non-white	11	44	23	22
White-collar background	8	39	29	24
Blue-collar background	13	43	17	27
Above-average students	9	38	26	26
Average and below	11	43	23	21
East	12	42	24	21
Midwest	11	39	26	24
South	10	39	25	25
West	9	40	23	27
Large city	8	55	11	26
Suburb	13	32	30	26
Small town	10	37	28	24
Rural	10	42	27	21
Republican	11	38	25	26
Democrat	12	42	29	17
Independent	11	41	20	28
Protestant	12	38	29	20
Catholic	7	39	24	30
Church attender	7	39	24	29
Non-attender	13	40	26	20

Note: 1 percent of teens gave no estimate.

GO 12869; Q. 40

U.S. Peacekeeping Efforts

Teen-agers are evenly divided between those who believe the U.S. is doing all it can to preserve peace in the world, and those who feel it could do more (49 percent, each).

Most likely to believe the U.S. is doing its best are young men (56 percent), suburbanites (60 percent), and teen-age Republicans.

Most dissatisfied with U.S. efforts to achieve world peace are young women (56 percent), residents of large cities (61 percent), and teen Democrats.

There has been little change in recent years in the proportion of teens who believe their country is doing all it can to gain peace. The high mark in regard for the U.S. occurred in 1986 when 57 percent viewed American actions positively. By contrast, in past years few American teens felt the Soviet Union was doing all it could to achieve world peace. Opinion of Soviet peace efforts, however, became somewhat more positive in recent years.

7.4 Opinion of U.S. and Soviet Peace Efforts

(Percent believing each country doing all it can)

	U.S.	Soviet Union
1992	48%	na
1988	49	29
1986	57	22
1984	55	15
1982	52	13

When cold war tensions ran high, few American teens thought their own country would be a likely nuclear aggressor. In the early 1980s as many as two teens in three felt the Soviet Union might initiate a nuclear war, but fears of Soviet nuclear aggression abated as the years passed and nuclear disarmament efforts increased.

7.5 Likely Nuclear Aggressor

	U.S.	Soviet Union
1988	10%	39%
1986	6	44
1984	5	68
1982	9	63

7.6 U.S. Peace Efforts

Do you think the U.S. is doing all it can to keep peace in the world?

	September – October 1992	
	Yes	No
National	**49%**	**49%**
Male	56	43
Female	42	56
Ages 13 – 15	48	50
Ages 16 – 17	50	48
White	50	48
Non-white	44	53
White-collar background	50	50
Blue-collar background	44	53
Above-average students	50	49
Average and below	47	51
East	47	53
Midwest	48	49
South	53	45
West	46	54
Large city	39	61
Suburb	60	40
Small town	47	52
Rural	49	46
Republican	56	44
Democrat	41	59
Independent	51	47
Protestant	52	45
Catholic	46	54
Church attender	53	47
Non-attender	45	52

Note: 2 percent of the teens had no opinion.

GO 12869; Q. 41

138

United Nations

Six teens in 10 in 1992 felt the United Nations is doing a good job in trying to solve the problems it has had to face. Its performance has been poor according to 36 percent of the teens, and 5 percent are undecided about the U.N.

Teen Republicans, perhaps recalling George Bush's performance as leader of the U.N. coalition in the Persian Gulf conflict, are the teens most likely to endorse the international body's performance. A majority of teens from all other political persuasions and walks of life rate the U.N. job as good.

In 1986, overall teen opinion of the United Nations was somewhat higher, with 70 percent saying they thought it was doing a good job. Just 23 percent felt it was doing a poor job, and 7 percent had no opinion. Also that year, most teens (92 percent) held the view that the U.S. should not leave the U.N., with only 5 percent believing the U.S. should give up its membership.

Only a small proportion of American teen-agers (8 percent) have ever visited U.N. headquarters in New York City. Those from the East, however, are more than three times as likely to have visited the U.N. (19 percent) than teens from the Midwest (3 percent), South (6 percent), or West (4 percent).

7.7 United Nations Performance

In general, do you think the United Nations is doing a good job or a poor job in trying to solve the problems it has had to face?

	September – October 1992		
	Good job	Poor job	Not sure
National	**59%**	**36%**	**5%**
Male	60	34	5
Female	57	37	6
Ages 13 – 15	62	33	5
Ages 16 – 17	54	40	6
White	61	33	6
Non-white	50	47	3
White-collar background	60	33	7
Blue-collar background	55	41	4
Above-average students	62	33	5
Average and below	55	39	6
East	63	30	7
Midwest	56	40	4
South	56	39	5
West			
Large city	64	30	6
Suburb	64	36	–
Small town	60	34	6
Rural	48	43	9
Republican	68	28	4
Democrat	52	43	5
Independent	52	42	6
Protestant	61	36	3
Catholic	58	35	7
Church attender	59	36	5
Non-attender	59	34	7

GO 12869; Q. 42

Interest in the Third World

Europe and the Middle East may grab the headlines now, but as American teen-agers approach the 21st Century, they want to learn more about the third world. In the opinion of high school students, too little attention is being given to Africa, Latin America, and Asia.

Two teens in three believe that their schools, teachers, and textbooks now present too little information about Africa.

A majority of high school students look south of the border and say they would like to see greater coverage at school of Mexico and Latin America.

Nearly half of the teens, perhaps recognizing the growing importance of "the Pacific Rim," would like to see more presentation at school about Asian cultures and people.

The dramatic events in Eastern Europe in recent years undoubtedly have led about four teens in 10 to wish they knew more about the seemingly ever-growing number of countries and ethnic groups that populate the area.

The Persian Gulf War and continuing turmoil in the Mideast probably have played a part in leading four students in 10 to ask their schools to devote more attention to the area.

Some students appear to agree with modern educational reformers who say that history and literature courses have been too "Eurocentric." The reformers use this term to describe instruction that places primary emphasis on the history and culture of Western Europeans and the United States. The term usually also is generally understood to mean this history is further restricted to the study of the deeds of elite white males. The teens in the survey were least likely to say they wanted the schools to place greater emphasis in the future on studies of Western Europe or the United States.

7.8 Coverage Given in School to Places of the World

	Too little	About right	Too much
Africa	65%	28%	6%
Mexico/Latin America	56	37	6
Asia	47	43	9
Eastern Europe	42	47	11
Middle East	41	45	14
Western Europe	37	49	13
United States	15	55	30

Note: 1 percent of teens had no opinion

VALUES AND RELIGION

Material vs. Non-Material Values

Today's teens grew up during the 1980s, a time that now is largely regarded as a "decade of greed." Despite the signs of affluence of those times, and despite the current pressures of economic recession in the early 1990s, the majority of teens say they very much place personal happiness over being rich, and want to help those less fortunate than themselves. They fail, however, to completely reject the assertion that "making money and living well are what it's all about."

8.1 Teen Economic Values

Now, I'm going to read a list of statements. For each of them, tell me whether you agree very much, agree somewhat, disagree somewhat, or disagree very much. If you neither agree nor disagree with a statement, you can tell me that.

	July 1991		
	Agree "very much"		
	Personal happiness more important than being rich	**Want to help those less fortunate than myself**	**Making money is what it's all about**
National	67%	58%	25%
Male	60	48	28
Female	75	68	22
Ages 13 to 15	64	58	26
Ages 16 to 17	72	58	24
White	69	56	21
Non-white	61	64	42
Above-average students	68	60	21
Average and below	66	54	30
East	69	58	17
Midwest	71	57	26
South	68	63	28
West	60	49	24

GO 224007; Q. 25

Educational Values

It seems unlikely that there has ever been a student who at some point has not asked his teachers or parents, "Why do I have to learn all of this stuff?"

Traditionally, they have been told in response that knowledge is either necessary to get ahead in life, to reach the top, or can be important in its own right. According to the Gallup Youth Survey, all of these answers have become an important part of teens' motivations to study. Most want to achieve excellence in their chosen career, many see their schooling as the key to a good job, and as they grow older, there is growing awareness that knowledge can be important for its own sake.

8.2 Teen Education and Career Goals

Now, I'm going to read a list of statements. For each of them, tell me whether you agree very much, agree somewhat, disagree somewhat, or disagree very much. If you neither agree nor disagree with a statement, you can tell me that.

	July 1991		
	Agree "very much"		
	Want to reach top of chosen career	Main purpose of education is to get a good job	Knowledge is important for its own sake
National	**78%**	**55%**	**46%**
Male	79	52	41
Female	78	58	51
Ages 13 to 15	80	61	42
Ages 16 to 17	75	48	50
White	77	53	44
Non-white	83	64	52
Above-average students	82	50	50
Average and below	74	62	40
White-collar background	83	50	46
Blue-collar background	72	60	45
Both parents attended college	84	48	49
One attended	77	56	47
Neither attended	76	59	44

GO 224007; Q. 25

Relationships

"To thine own self be true" is a maxim that most of today's teen-agers appear to have taken to heart, while also frequently rejecting the pressure to go along with what most of their friends are doing. At the same time, however, many teens still feel very close to their families, according to the findings of the most recent Gallup Youth Survey.

While struggling to establish their individual identities within the framework and pressures of family ties and friendships with their peers, young people place greatest emphasis upon being true to themselves. Seven in 10 agree very much that how they feel about themselves is more important than what other people may think of them.

The emphasis in recent years to instill pride in their heritage and to enhance their sense of self-esteem among non-white Americans may be paying dividends. According to the survey evidence, non-white teens are more likely than whites to agree very much that how they feel about themselves is more important than what others have to say, by a margin of 80 percent to 67 percent.

Family relationships are given great emphasis, with 65 percent of teens agreeing very much that they have a very close relationship with their family.

The old slogan that "the family that prays together, stays together" appears to be holding true in the present-day teen world. Three teens in four who attended church during the week preceding the time of interview, also report that they have a very close relationship with their family.

Just one teen in 10 reports he is very much inclined to go along usually with what his friends are doing.

8.3 Self, Family, and Peers

| | July 1991 | | |
| | Agree "very much" | | |
	How I feel about myself is more important than what others think	I have a very close relationship with my family	I usually go along with what my friends are doing
National	70%	65%	10%
Male	65	65	13
Female	75	64	8
Ages 13 to 15	69	66	11
Ages 16 to 17	71	63	9
White	67	64	11
Non-whites	80	68	5
Above-average students	69	70	12
Average and below	71	57	7
White-collar background	73	65	8
Blue-collar background	68	60	11
Attended church last week	69	74	9
Did not attend	71	56	11

GO 224007; Q. 25

146

World Values

Being well educated and achieving personal peace and happiness are top priorities for teenagers nowadays. A majority view helping people in their community and working toward world peace as being very important. However, becoming deeply religious fails to capture majority interest among teens.

More than nine teens in 10 (92 percent) say that having personal peace of mind and happiness is very important to them. An additional 7 percent think that achieving these goals is somewhat important.

Similarly, nine teen-age students in 10 (91 percent) believe it is very important to become well educated. A good education is regarded as somewhat important by 7 percent, and only 2 percent are not interested in becoming better educated.

Two teens in three (66 percent) report it is very important to them to help people in their communities. This is considered somewhat important by 31 percent, and only 3 percent do not feel an obligation to assist others in their local areas.

The proportion of teens considering community work to be very important rises to three in four among young women (75 percent), compared to only 57 percent of the young men who were interviewed for the survey. Above-average interest in community work also is displayed among non-whites and teens from blue-collar family backgrounds (both 72 percent).

Only slightly fewer teens (60 percent) believe it is very important for them to work for peace in the world. Contributing toward world peace is somewhat important to 34 percent of the teenagers. But 6 percent feel it is not something they consider important enough to merit their effort. Young women also are more likely than young men to consider the goal of world peace to be very important, by a margin of 65 percent to 54 percent. Non-white teens (67 percent) are more likely than whites (57 percent) to want to work for world peace.

Having strong religious faith is very important to four teens in 10 (43 percent). It is somewhat important to 33 percent, but 23 percent of the teens show no interest in being devoutly religious. Those who attended church during the seven-day period preceding the interviews are more likely than non-attenders to consider a deep religious faith to be very important by a ratio of 58 percent to 29 percent. Protestants are more apt than Catholic youths to rate religious faith very important, by a margin of 50 percent to 39 percent.

To have a deep religious faith is very important to more young women (49 percent) than young men (38 percent). Regionally, teens seeking a deep religious faith are more likely to be found in the South (58 percent) and West (46 percent) than in the Midwest (38 percent) and East (28 percent). Non-whites more often than whites say they are seriously seeking religious faith a margin of 51 percent to 41 percent.

8.4 World Values

For each of the following please tell me if it is very important, somewhat important, or not very important to you — Having a deep religious faith? Being well educated? Working for peace in the world? Having personal peace and happiness? Helping people in the community?

	March – April 1990				
	Consider "very important"				
	Personal peace	Education	Community work	World peace	Religious faith
National	**92%**	**91%**	**66%**	**60%**	**43%**
Male	91	89	57	54	38
Female	94	94	75	65	49
Ages 13 – 15	92	93	68	62	44
Ages 16 – 17	94	94	75	65	49
White	93	90	63	57	41
Non-white	90	94	72	67	51
White-collar background	92	91	61	57	42
Blue-collar background	92	92	72	61	46
Above-average students	95	95	66	61	43
Average and below	89	88	67	58	45

	Very important	Somewhat important	Not important
Personal peace	92%	7%	1%
Being well educated	91	7	2
Helping people in the community	66	31	3
Working for peace in the world	60	34	6
Having a deep religious faith	43	33	23

Personal Qualities

Responsibility, honesty, self-respect and hard work head the list of qualities that teens consider important for people their age to learn.

Nearly all teens (93 percent) believe it is important for their contemporaries to acquire a sense of responsibility. This represents a 4 percentage point increase since 1987, when 89 percent of teens held similar beliefs. Currently, only 7 percent of teens believe it is only fairly important to learn a sense of responsibility.

Honesty is considered a very important trait by 89 percent of teens. An additional 10 percent say it is fairly important to be honest.

Self-respect is important according to 88 percent of teens; and 11 percent say it is fairly important, and 1 percent not so important. Young women are slightly more likely than young men to value self-respect very much, by a margin of 91 percent to 86 percent.

Hard work appears to have become a youthful virtue once again, with eight teens in 10 (81 percent) rating it very, important as a quality for their generation. An additional 18 percent consider it fairly important.

Teens who come from blue-collar family backgrounds (86 percent) are more likely than those from white-collar families to rate hard work as very important for young people. In comparison to the 81 percent who now rate hard work as very important, in 1987, only 70 percent saw much virtue in the quality.

Obedience is considered a very important trait by 68 percent of teens and fairly important by 29 percent. Most likely to consider obedience very important are teens from blue-collar families (76 percent), those who attend church regularly (73 percent), and those who live in the South (74 percent).

Independence is highly valued by two teens in three (67 percent), while 27 percent say it is somewhat important. Young women (75 percent) are far more likely than young men (59 percent) to consider a sense of independence to be a very important trait.

Patience is not a virtue usually associated with teens, but 64 percent of them consider it very important. It is deemed fairly important by 33 percent.

Half the teens (49 percent) consider religious faith an important quality for people their age to learn. It is considered fairly important by 36 percent, but 15 percent do not consider it an important quality. Protestant teens (58 percent) are more likely than Catholics (42 percent) to say that developing religious faith is important. Sentiment for considering religious faith to be very important is strongest in the South (62 percent) and weakest in the East (36 percent).

8.5 Personal Qualities Trend

Of the following personal qualities, how important do you feel each one is for a person your age to learn — very important, fairly important, or not so important?

Consider "very important"	1989	1987
Responsibility	93%	89%
Honesty	89	89
Self-respect	88	87
Hard work	81	70
Obedience	68	60
Independence	67	65
Patience	64	61
Religious faith	49	44

Traits

In choosing their values, teens often reject materialism, and instead focus upon having a good family life, a good self-image, and sound physical health.

Nine teens in 10 believe it is very important to have an harmonious family life (89 percent) and to possess a good self-image or self-respect (88 percent). Especially likely to emphasize the importance of a good family life are young women (93 percent), non-whites (96 percent), Southern teens (96 percent), and those who live in small towns and rural areas (92 percent).

Being in good physical health is considered very important by 84 percent of the teens, and an additional 16 percent consider it to be somewhat important.

Three teenagers in four (74 percent) say it is very important to have a sense of accomplishment and lasting contribution. This is considered a somewhat important attribute by 23 percent of the teens. The drive to achieve this value may be a key to academic performance, with 80 percent of students who are doing above-average work in school saying it is very important, compared to only 68 percent of those who report their work is just average or below average. The desire for accomplishment is also much higher among teens from households where both parents attended college (80 percent) than it is in households in which neither parent attended (69 percent).

Two teens in three (63 percent) consider having an exciting, stimulating life to be very important, but 32 percent consider it only somewhat important, and 4 percent say it is very unimportant to them. Young men (68 percent) more often say it is important for them to seek excitement in their lives than do young women (58 percent).

A slim majority, of teens consider it very important to work for the betterment of American society (54 percent). Such work is believed to be somewhat important by *37* percent, but 6 percent say it is very unimportant. The above-average student is far more likely than other students to consider working for the betterment of our society very important, by a margin of 61 percent to 46 percent.

About half of the teens (53 percent) believe following a strict moral code is very important. It is considered a somewhat important trait by 37 percent of teens, but 9 percent reject the concept. Most likely to want to follow a strict code of behavior are teens who attend church regularly (61 percent).

Only four teens in 10 (43 percent) consider it very important to have a nice home, car and other expensive items. Material possessions are considered somewhat important by 46 percent of the teens, but 11 percent believe they are very unimportant. Most likely to consider material goods to be very important are students who are doing only average or below-average work at school (51 percent).

8.6 Very Important Traits

	June – July 1989		
	National	Male	Female
Having a good family life	89%	86%	93%
Having a good self-image or self-respect	88	87	89
Being in good physical health	84	83	84
Having a sense of accomplishment and lasting contribution	74	72	76
Having an exciting, stimulating life	63	68	58
Working for betterment of American society	54	55	54
Following a strict moral code	53	48	57
Having a nice home, car, and other belongings	43	48	39

AIPO 881; Q. 110

Prep School Student Values

In a study of 404 graduating seniors from five prominent preparatory schools in May 1991, 80 percent listed being happy as their leading priority. Next came having a good family life (64 percent), making lasting friendships (55 percent) and living life as they see fit and standing up for their own rights (both 53 percent.)

Only 10 percent consider making large amounts of money as essential.

And comparatively few report it is important for them to be of service to others (7 percent), to be truthful even if it hurts the feelings of other people (10 percent), or to have deep religious faith (7 percent).

Relations between racial and ethnic groups is the subject that most prep school students say "bothers them very much" (38 percent). About three in 10 are most concerned about school rules and regulations (32 percent), the pressure to maintain good grades (29 percent), and being accepted by a prestigious college (26 percent). World problems are of great concern to 29 percent of the students.

One student in four discloses having the traditional adolescent problem of acquiring a sense of identity (25 percent) or in relationships with members of the opposite sex (24 percent). Few of the students (13 percent) say they are bothered a great deal by parental pressures.

Only 3 percent acknowledge they are concerned about drugs. Most disapprove of crack (94 percent), heroin (91 percent), LSD (71 percent) and non-prescription use of barbiturates (75 percent) or stimulants (70 percent). Far fewer disapprove of the use of potentially addictive substances such as marijuana (34 percent), tobacco (22 percent), or liquor (10 percent).

Alcohol abuse (37 percent) and drug abuse (22 percent) are viewed by students as very serious problems on prep school campuses. Similar concern is expressed about lying (29 percent), stealing (28 percent), sexual promiscuity (18 percent), and cheating (17 percent).

Asked how they would like to be remembered 50 years from now, most prep school students reply: being caring, honest, fun-loving, helpful to others, happy, and a good friend. About two in three said it is very important for them to have a reputation of being honest (71 percent), broad-minded (70 percent), loyal (70 percent), loving (70 percent), responsible (66 percent), and independent (65 percent). Few attach as much importance to being clean (17 percent), obedient (16 percent), and religious (12 percent).

In viewing the traits of others, preparatory school students say they most often admire honesty, self-confidence, sensitivity to others, caring, having a sense of humor and open-mindedness. When asked to describe people their own age, however, most view their peers as confused or insecure, fun-loving, self-centered, and ambitious. But few characterize their peers as rebellious, lazy, power-hungry, or narrow-minded.

Law or medicine are the careers most prep school students speculate they will pursue. Some show interest in teaching, psychological counseling and science. But fewer say they will seek careers in protecting the environment, in international relations, and in social work.

A majority of prep school students (52 percent) report they believe that "any kind of sexual activity is OK so long as nobody gets hurt."

Prep School Student Religion and Values

A majority of preparatory school students say they believe in God (57 percent). This is far lower than the level of belief found in general teen-age population in the United States (95 percent).

Sixty-five percent of all teen-agers believe there is life after death, compared to only 42 percent of prep school students. Additionally, only 17 percent of prep school students contend that the wicked are punished by "going to hell. "

Despite images of prep school students attending weekly, if not daily chapel services, only one student in four (26 percent) reported attending religious services during the seven-day period preceding the survey. Among the general teen-age population, 57 percent attend church or a synagogue during a typical week.

Prep school students credit their own abilities to reason (74 percent), the opinions of their parents (70 percent) and classmates (60 percent) in developing their ethical, moral and spiritual values. Far fewer identify their teachers (30 percent) or members of the clergy (6 percent) as molders of their values.

If faced with a most serious problem, more than four students in 10 (45 percent) say they would rely on the opinions of close friends to help them. About one in four (27 percent) would turn to their parents, 10 percent to an adult affiliated with his or her school and less than one percent would consult a member of the clergy.

Three students in four feel what is important to them is very similar (25 percent) or somewhat similar (49 percent) to their parents' values. About two prep students in three (64 percent) reject the contention that "parents' ideals are hopelessly old-fashioned."

Almost half of the students (45 percent) believe they spend more time than others of their own age thinking about the values that are most important to them. Only 6 percent feel they put in less time, while 46 percent say the amount is about the same.

A majority of the "preps" (56 percent) speculate that their values are much different from prep students 20 years ago. Current students say they are more aware and concerned about international issues, problems caused by the environment, AIDS and equal rights. It was also determined that more young women than men (50 percent to 37 percent) are likely to pursue a set of rules connected with their sexual behavior.

The preceding findings were taken from a study conducted in May 1991 by The George H. Gallup International Institute for the Institute on Values at St. Paul's School.

8.7 Basic Teen-age Religious Beliefs and Practices

	All teens
Believe in God or universal spirit	95%
Believe God loves them	93
Believe Jesus Christ is God or son of God	86
Personally experienced presence of God	29
Believe there is a heaven	91
Believe there is a hell	76
Believe in life after death	67
Pray alone frequently	42
Go to Sunday school	41
Belong to church-sponsored youth group	36
Read Bible at least weekly	36
Listened to religious program on radio or TV last month	35
Have confidence in organized religion	52
Believe religion is increasing its influence on American life	40
Consider own religious beliefs very important	39
Consider religion more important than parents do	27
Believe religion can answer today's problems	25

Religious Preference

The religious map of teen-age America shows concentrations of Protestants in the South and Midwest and of Catholics in the East. In the West, where religious participation usually is lowest, the Mormon Church appears to be gaining many teen adherents.

While elders may worry about teens joining cults, being lured by exotic religions of the East, or even flirting with Satanism, Gallup Youth Surveys show teen religious preferences and practices usually closely mirror those of their parents and other adults. Teens even are slightly more likely than adults to be found in church!

Nearly half of America's teens name a Protestant denomination as their religious preference. The highest concentrations of teen Protestants are found in the South and Midwest

Three teens in 10 say they are Roman Catholics by preference. The greatest concentration of teen Catholics is found in the East (30 percent), where they are the dominant denomination. Many teen Catholics also are found in the Midwest where one in three professes faith in the Roman Catholic Church.

Among adults the comparable figures are 56 percent who are Protestants and 25 percent Roman Catholics. The greater number of teen Catholics than adult Catholics can be illusory, because, historically in this country, preference for the Protestant faiths usually has grown as people grow older, while the ranks of those preferring Catholicism has declined.

The Jewish faith is stated as a preference by 2 percent of the teens, nationwide.

Another 2 percent of teens say their preference is the Church of Jesus Christ of Latter-day Saints, more popularly known as "Mormons." The Mormon presence is particularly strong in the West where 13 percent of the teens say it is their religious preference.

There are few teen adherents of other Middle Eastern or Eastern religions such as Islam, Buddhism, or Hinduism. Each of these faiths is given as a religious preference by well less than one-half percent of the teens interviewed.

About one teen in eight (13 percent) has no religious preference, about the same proportion of adults who have no preference (11 percent). This figure should not be interpreted as meaning that many teens are atheists or agnostics, because past Gallup Youth Surveys have shown few teens are non-believers. Instead, it probably is a reflection of households where the parents have no preference and teens have not ventured out on their own yet to establish a religious identity and affiliation.

In a typical week, nearly half of the teens attend religious services at least once.

Teen attendance is slightly greater than adult attendance which was 42 percent during the past year. Younger teens, ages 13 to 15, are slightly more likely than those who are 16 and older to be church attenders, by a margin of 48 percent to 43 percent.

Black teens are far more likely to be Protestants than Catholics. They are also one of the groups most likely to be found in church, with close to a majority reporting attendance during the previous week.

Hispanic teens are about three times likely to be Catholics to say one of the Protestant denominations is their preference. Church attendance by Hispanic teens is lower than the national average.

Among white teens, 46 percent are Protestants, 31 percent are Roman Catholics, and 45 percent attended church during the previous week.

8.8 Religious Preference

	Teens	Adults
Protestant	47%	56%
Roman Catholic	30	25
Latter-day Saints (Mormons)	3	2
Jewish	2	2
Other	5	6
None	13	11

8.9 Religious Faith Profile

What is your religious preference?
Did you, yourself, happen to attend church or synagogue in last seven days?

| | June – July 1992 | | | |
	Protestant	Catholic	Attended church	Did not attend
National	**48%**	**31%**	**45%**	**54%**
Male	46	33	43	56
Female	51	29	46	53
Ages 12 – 13	47	31	50	49
Ages 14 – 15	49	31	42	57
Ages 16 – 17	48	31	43	56
White	46	33	44	56
Non-white	58	21	49	49
Black	69	18	49	49
Hispanic	22	63	37	62
White-collar background	45	33	43	56
Blue-collar background	51	30	48	52
Above-average students	50	32	49	51
Average and below	47	30	41	58
East	32	47	39	60
Midwest	47	35	44	56
South	64	22	52	47
West	40	24	39	60
Large city	46	33	42	58
Suburb	36	39	39	60
Small town	55	29	50	50
Rural	54	26	45	54
Protestant	100	–	51	49
Catholic	–	100	44	56
Church attender	56	30	100	–
Non-attender	43	32	–	100

GO21505702; Q. 5, 6

Belief in the Supernatural and Paranormal

Three teens in four (76 percent) now say they believe in angels. Teen belief in the heavenly messengers and guardians has increased steadily over the years since 1978 when 64 percent of young people believed in them. Most likely to believe in angels are recent church attenders (82 percent), Catholic teens (81 percent), and young women (80 percent).

Belief in ghosts rose in 1992, with three teens in 10 (31 percent) claiming they exist. Only about two teens in 10 believed in the spirits of the departed in past years.

A slim majority of 54 percent of teens say they believe in astrology. This represents a 4 percentage-point drop since 1988 in the number who feel that their lives may be influenced by the movement of the stars and planets. Young women are probably more likely than young men to use the line of "what sign are you?" by a margin of 57 percent to 51 percent. The highest level of belief is found among Hispanic teens, with 71 percent showing interest in their horoscopes.

Belief in extrasensory perception (ESP), the belief that one can communicate or perceive events without use of normal physical senses, has declined to 43 percent of the teen population. Back in 1978, two teens in three (67 percent) believed ESP was possible.

The level of teen belief in clairvoyance—the ability to see into the future or beyond normal sensory range—has held steady. Currently, one teen in five (21 percent) believes in clairvoyance, the same percent who believed in it in 1988. The high point of teen belief in clairvoyance occurred in 1984 when 28 percent of teens thought it was possible.

Witches, after hitting a high point of 29 percent teen belief in 1988, have fewer followers now, with just 19 percent teens thinking they exist. Belief in witches increases somewhat as teens grow older. Among those who are 13 to 15 years of age, just 15 percent believe in witchcraft, compared to 24 percent who are 16 and older.

The supermarket tabloids are probably going to have to come up with a new pantheon of gigantic creatures that stalk our earth, if they hope to capture new teen readers. Both "Bigfoot" and "Nessie," the Loch Ness monster whose breathlessly reported sightings have entertained tabloid readers for many years, now have few teen believers.

"Bigfoot" currently is believed in by only 12 percent of teens. Belief in the humanoid creature who supposedly stalks the Pacific Northwest forests along with the ever elusive spotted owl has dropped from a high level of 40 percent among teens in 1978.

As for "Nessie," just 11 percent of teens still believe the prehistoric aquatic dinosaur plies the depths of Loch Ness in Scotland or elsewhere. The monster's highest level of teen belief occurred in 1978 when 31 percent of teens hoped it had still managed to survive the ages.

Only one teen in 20 (5 percent) does not believe in any of the supernatural characters or forces tested on the survey. The highest level of skepticism is found among black teens (9 percent).

8.10 Supernatural Belief Trend

	1992	1988	1986	1984	1978
Angels	76%	74%	67%	69%	64%
Astrology	54	58	52	55	40
ESP	43	50	46	59	67
Witchcraft	19	29	19	22	25
Bigfoot	12	22	16	24	40
Ghosts	31	22	15	20	20
Clairvoyance	21	21	19	28	25
Loch Ness Monster	11	16	13	18	31

8.11 Belief in the Paranormal and Supernatural

Which of the following do you believe in?

	Angels	Astrology	ESP	Ghosts	Clair-voyance	Witch-craft
September – October 1992						
National	**76%**	**54%**	**43%**	**31%**	**21%**	**19%**
Male	73	52	39	29	20	17
Female	80	57	46	34	22	20
Ages 13 – 15	78	56	38	30	19	15
Ages 16 – 17	75	52	49	33	24	24
White	76	54	45	34	22	20
Non-white	77	56	31	19	15	14
White-collar background	71	52	46	30	24	18
Blue-collar background	80	61	39	32	15	20
Above-average students	76	52	39	28	24	16
Average and below	76	57	47	37	16	22
East	78	57	53	38	25	19
Midwest	73	54	42	30	26	22
South	83	51	38	24	18	16
West	68	59	41	39	17	20
Large city	79	52	44	28	22	18
Suburb	77	51	43	33	24	21
Small town	72	59	42	31	19	19
Rural	78	50	43	34	21	17
Republican	82	46	38	26	19	16
Democrat	71	56	43	31	25	22
Independent	75	58	46	34	24	18
Protestant	78	49	34	27	16	15
Catholic	81	58	46	34	24	18
Church attender	82	48	38	25	18	17
Non-attender	71	61	47	38	24	20

Note: 5 percent of teens do not believe in any of the above.

GO 12869; Q. 43

HEROES AND
ROLE MODELS

Most Admired Man

Earvin "Magic" Johnson, riding on the crest of publicity surrounding his dramatic announcement that he was infected with the AIDS virus, was the most admired man to America's teens in 1991. George Bush was second on the teen list, while another basketball player, Michael Jordan, placed third.

These lists often are strongly influenced by people who figure prominently in the headlines. Two weeks later after the Gallup Youth Survey was taken, for example, adults were asked the same question when the release of the hostages in Lebanon was the big story in the news, with the result that Terry Anderson ranked second on their list. Magic Johnson by that time, however, was able to get only a fifth-place standing in the opinion of the adults.

Teens in 1991 named George Bush second, while adults placed him in number one on their list.

9.1 Most Admired Man in 1991

(Choices of teens)

1. Earvin "Magic" Johnson
2. George Bush
3. Michael Jordan
4. Norman Schwarzkopf
5. Mikhail Gorbachev
6. Patrick Swayzee
7. Arnold Schwarzenegger
8. Nelson Mandela
9. Luke Perry
10. Michael Jackson

(Choices of adults)

1. Bush
2. Terry Anderson
3. Schwartzkopf
4. Gorbachev
5. Johnson
6. Pope John Paul II
7. Billy Graham
8. Ronald Reagan
9. Mandela
10. Jesse Jackson (tie)
    Michael Jordan

9.2 Most Admired Man

What one man that you have heard or read about, alive today in any part of the world, do you admire the most — not including any of your relatives or personal friends? And who would be your second choice?

1991

1. Magic Johnson
2. George Bush
3. Michael Jordan

1989

1. George Bush
2. Jesse Jackson
3. Ronald Reagan

1988

1. Ronald Reagan
2. Jesse Jackson
3. Mikhail Gorbachev

1987

1. Ronald Reagan
2. Jesse Jackson
3. George Bush

1986

1. Ronald Reagan
2. Jesse Jackson
3. Don Johnson

1985

1. Ronald Reagan
2. Jesse Jackson
3. Pope John-Paul II

1983

1. Ronald Reagan
2. Pope John Paul II
3. Jesse Jackson

1981

1. Ronald Reagan
2. Jimmy Carter
3. Pope John Paul II

1980

1. Jimmy Carter
2. Ronald Reagan
3. Burt Reynolds

1979

1. Pope John Paul II
2. Jimmy Carter
3. Edward Kennedy

1978

1. Jimmy Carter
2. Anwar Sadat
3. Gerald Ford

1959

1. John Kennedy
2. Dwight Eisenhower
3. Winston Churchill

Most Admired Woman

Women in politics generally have dominated the leadership of the most-admired woman polls among teens, but there are exceptions. In 1991, actress Julia Roberts was at the head of the list, and in 1978, actress, Farrah Fawcett-Majors took the top position. In between those years, Nancy Reagan most often was named first in the teen ratings, challenged by Geraldine Ferraro and Margaret Thatcher. Barbara Bush was never ranked higher than second by teens.

Other women who have been rated highly by teens during the past decade include Supreme Court Justice Sandra Day O'Connor, who was first in 1981, former first lady, Rosalyn Carter who was first in 1979, and astronaut Sally Ride, who placed third in 1983.

Prominent figures from the entertainment world who have received high rankings from teens have included Paula Abdul, Oprah Winfrey, Madonna, and Jane Fonda.

9.3 Most Admired Woman in 1991

(Choices of teens)

1. Julia Roberts
2. Barbara Bush
3. Paula Abdul
4. Madonna
5. Oprah Winfrey
6. Margaret Thatcher
7. Janet Jackson
8. Anita Baker
9. Nancy Reagan
10. Christie Brinkley

(Choices of adults)

1. Barbara Bush
2. Mother Teresa
3. Margaret Thatcher
4. Nancy Reagan
5. Oprah Winfrey
6. Jacqueline Kennedy Onassis
7. Elizabeth Taylor
8. Queen Elizabeth II
9. Sandra Day O'Connor
10. Betty Ford

9.4 Most Admired Woman

Now, what woman do you admire the most—again not including any of your relatives or personal friends? And who would be your second choice?

1991

1. Julia Roberts
2. Barbara Bush
3. Paula Abdul

1989

1. Nancy Reagan
2. Barbara Bush
3. Oprah Winfrey

1988

1. Nancy Reagan
2. Margaret Thatcher
3. Geraldine Ferraro

1987

1. Nancy Reagan
2. Geraldine Ferraro
3. Margaret Thatcher

1986

1. Nancy Reagan
2. Geraldine Ferraro
3. Madonna

1985

1. Geraldine Ferraro
2. Margaret Thatcher
3. Nancy Reagan

1983

1. Nancy Reagan
2. Margaret Thatcher
3. Sally Ride

1981

1. Sandra Day O'Connor
2. Nancy Reagan
3. Margaret Thatcher

1979

1. Rosalyn Carter
2. Jane Fonda
3. Farrah Fawcett-Majors
   Cheryl Ladd

1978

1. Farrah Fawcett-Majors
2. Rosalyn Carter
3. Betty Ford

1959

1. Jacqueline Kennedy
2. Eleanor Roosevelt
3. Helen Keller

Favorite Movie Stars

Arnold Schwarzenegger and Eddie Murphy have been battling in recent years for top honors as teens' favorite male movie stars. Until 1988, however, Tom Cruise reigned for three years at the top of the teen lists. From 1978 to 1984, Burt Reynolds was the teen favorite.

Julia Roberts is the current favorite female movie actress. Before she captured the top spot, it was occupied for several years by Molly Ringwald. Barbra Streisand was considered the favorite in the late 1970s and early 1980s.

Increasingly, "favorite movie star" has come to include anybody who appears on the screen, whether or not that happens to be a motion picture projection screen. As a result of cross-overs, people from other media such as Don Johnson from television, and Madonna from rock videos, increasingly are showing up on the movie lists.

9.5 Favorite Male Movie Actor — 1991

1. Arnold Schwarzenegger
2. Kevin Costner
3. Tom Cruise
4. Mel Gibson
5. Patrick Swayzee
6. Jean Claude VanDamme
7. Eddie Murphy
8. Steven Segal
9. Christian Slater
10. Luke Perry

Honorable mention:

Kenu Reeves
Richard Gere
Robert DeNiro
Sylvester Stallone
Clint Eastwood

9.6 Favorite Female Movie Actress — 1991

1. Julia Roberts
2. Whoopi Goldberg
3. Demi Moore
4. Bette Midler
5. Goldie Hawn
6. Jodie Foster
7. Signourney Weaver
8. Kim Basinger
9. Winona Ryder
10. Michelle Pfeiffer

Honorable mention:

Mary Elizabeth Mastrantonio
Meryl Streep
Kirstie Alley
Melanie Griffith

9.7 Favorite Male Movie Star

Who is your favorite male movie star? And who would be your second choice?

1991

1. Arnold Schwarzenegger
2. Kevin Costner
3. Tom Cruise

1989

1. Eddie Murphy
2. Tom Cruise
3. Arnold Schwarzenegger

1988

1. Tom Cruise
2. Eddie Murphy
3. Patrick Swazee

1987

1. Tom Cruise
2. Rob Lowe
3. Michael J. Fox

1986

1. Tom Cruise
2. Rob Lowe
3. Tom Selleck

1985

1. Sylvester Stallone
2. Clint Eastwood
3. Burt Reynolds

1984

1. Burt Reynolds
2. Clint Eastwood
3. Tom Selleck

1983

1. Burt Reynolds
2. Eddie Murphy
3. Tom Selleck

1981

1. Burt Reynolds
2. Clint Eastwood
3. Robert Redford

1980

1. Burt Reynolds
2. Clint Eastwood
3. Robert Redford

1979

1. Burt Reynolds
2. Clint Eastwood
3. Robert Redford

1978

1. Burt Reynolds
2. John Travolta
3. Robert Redford

1977

1. Robert Redford
2. John Wayne
3. Clint Eastwood

9.8 Favorite Female Movie Star

Now, who is your favorite female movie star? And who would be your second choice?

1991

1. Julia Roberts
2. Whoopi Goldberg
3. Demi Moore

1989

1. Kim Basinger
2. Bette Midler
3. Cher

1988

1. Molly Ringwald
2. Cher
3. Alyssa Milano

1987

1. Molly Ringwald
2. Cybill Shepherd
3. Meryl Streep

1986

1. Molly Ringwald
2. Cybill Shepherd
3. Meryl Streep

1985

1. Madonna
2. Sally Field
3. Brooke Shields

1984

1. Bo Derek
2. Jane Fonda
3. Sally Field

1983

1. Sally Field
2. Brooke Shields
3. Goldie Hawn

1981

1. Brooke Shields
2. Bo Derek
3. Barbra Streisand

1980

1. Barbra Streisand
2. Sally Field
3. Jane Fonda

1979

1. Barbra Streisand
2. Sally Field
3. Farrah Fawcett-Majors

1978

1. Barbra Streisand
2. Farrah Fawcett-Majors
3. Olivia Newton-John

1977

1. Barbra Streisand
2. Farrah Fawcett-Majors
3. Jane Fonda

Favorite Vocalists

Perhaps nothing in the world changes faster than teen musical tastes. A hit song or music video one week, is forgotten the next. The singer or group at the top of the charts this month often is somewhere near the bottom of the "top 100" a week or a month later. Fan magazine columns about "whatever happened to . . ." have become a cliché.

After some experimentation at the Gallup Youth Survey, we gave up the idea of asking about favorite rock groups because too often by the time the results came out, the winning group had either disbanded or had been deserted by its fickle fans. Individual vocalists have demonstrated longer staying power, and recognition. But even in the case of individuals, a single year's top-10 list too often produces some names that are dimly if at all recalled.

A compilation of Gallup Youth Survey results taken over an entire decade does, however, produce lists of the individual vocalists who have lasted the longest, and even older readers will probably recognize most of the names.

9.9 Favorite Male Vocalists of the 1980s

1. Michael Jackson
2. Lionel Richie
3. Kenny Rogers
4. Rick Springfield
5. Bruce Springsteen
6. Phil Collins
7. Billy Joel
8. Barry Manilow
9. George Michael
10. Prince

9.10 Favorite Female Vocalists of the 1980s

1. Pat Benatar
2. Madonna
3. Diana Ross
4. Whitney Huston
5. Olivia Newton-John
6. Barbra Streisand
7. Stevie Nicks
8. Janet Jackson
9. Debbie Gibson
10. Donna Summer

Local Community Services and Workers

All local service workers who were tested on on a 1991 survey received above-average grades from teen-agers in their community. About two teens in three or more gave top grades to firefighters, local librarians, the clergy, welfare workers, those who run drug prevention programs.

By comparison, teachers in the local schools have been receiving an A or B for their efforts from about seven students in 10 in recent years.

9.11 Opinion of Community Services and Workers

Students are most often given grades A, B, C, D, and FAIL for the quality of their work. Suppose services in your own community were graded this way, what mark would you give each of the following [listed below]?

	1991				
	A	B	C	D	FAIL
Firefighters	61%	30%	5%	1%	1%
Local library	52	32	12	2%	1
Clergy	52	29	9	2	1
People who help the poor	38	31	19	7	3
Drug prevention programs	37	27	19	5	5
People who run youth and recreation programs	36	37	18	3	2
Sanitation workers and garbage collectors	27	46	19	5	2
Police	20	48	18	5	2
Mayor	20	41	19	4	2

Note: "No opinion" (1% – 14%) is not shown.

Opinion of Pay Levels

No matter how much teen-agers may idolize them, two in three believe that both rock superstars (67 percent) and professional athletes (66 percent) are paid too much for what they do.

When teens focus their attention upon the nation's capital, a narrow majority (52 percent) cast their votes in favor of reducing the pay levels of U.S. senators and representatives.

Physicians and business executives often are perceived as earning high salaries and fees, but more than half of the teens consider their compensation to be just. The earnings of physicians are about right, according to 52 percent of the teens, but more think they are paid too much (36 percent) than believe they are receiving too little (11 percent). Executive pay levels are believed to be about right by 55 percent of the teens. Disagreeing are 35 percent who say they are paid too much, and 6 percent who think compensation in the executive suite should be even higher.

Half of the teens (51 percent) believe that priests, ministers and rabbis are now paid too little. Only 33 percent say their compensation is about right, and just 9 percent that their compensation is too high.

A majority believe the police in their community are paid too little (55 percent), while 34 percent hold the view they are being paid the right amount for what they do. In contrast, a slight majority of teens (53 percent) think members of the armed services are receiving the right pay, and only 38 percent think they should receive more.

Two teens in three think that people who work in factories should be paid more (66 percent). Teens in the same proportions from both white-collar and blue-collar households share this view that factory workers are underpaid.

Perhaps the nicest compliment high school students could give to their teachers is that they are singled out as being the most underpaid of the professions and occupations tested. Eight teens in 10 (82 percent) say they deserve more pay.

9.12 Pay Levels

I am going to read you a list of professions or occupations. For each one, please tell me whether you think people in that profession or occupation are being paid too much, about the right amount of money, or too little for what they do.

	June – July 1989		
	Too much	About right	Not enough
Rock superstars	67%	28%	4%
Professional Athletes	66	29	3
U.S. Senators and Congressmen	52	38	7
Physicians	36	52	11
Business executives	35	55	6
Clergy	9	33	51
Policemen	6	34	55
Armed Forces	3	53	38
Factory Workers	3	28	66
Your teachers	3	15	82

AIPO 881; Q. 108

Note: "No opinion" (1% – 7%) is not shown.

SUBSTANCE ABUSE

Dangerous Substances

Nearly all teens recognize that crack and cocaine are very dangerous substances. The Gallup Youth Survey in recent years has found only about 1 percent or less of the teen population who report they are current users of either substance. Marijuana also is an illicit substance, and while 83 percent of teens consider it very dangerous, 14 percent say it is only somewhat dangerous, and 3 percent feel it is not dangerous at all.

Far fewer teens consider either alcohol or tobacco to be very dangerous, although most recognize the substances can be at least somewhat dangerous.

As teens grow older, opinion that marijuana, alcohol, and tobacco products are dangerous substances often decreases.

10.1 Degree of Danger Associated with Substances

	June – July 1992		
	Very dangerous	Somewhat dangerous	Not very dangerous
Crack	99%	1%	*%
Cocaine	98	1	*
Marijuana	83	14	3
Alcohol	65	32	3
Cigarettes	61	36	3
Snuff	60	29	3
Chewing tobacco	63	42	4

Note: "No opinion" (1 – 8 percent) is not shown.

*Less than one-half of 1 percent.

GOGO21505702; Q. 3

10.2 Substances Considered Very Dangerous

How dangerous do you think the use of each of these substances is — very dangerous, somewhat dangerous, or not very dangerous?

	June – July 1992 Consider "Very Dangerous"				
	Marijuana	Alcohol	Cigarettes	Snuff	Chewing tobacco
National	**83%**	**65%**	**60%**	**60%**	**53%**
Male	80	60	58	55	50
Female	86	71	63	66	56
Ages 12 – 13	93	75	72	71	60
Ages 14 – 15	85	65	57	63	56
Ages 16 – 17	71	56	53	48	45
White	82	64	60	60	52
Non-white	85	69	64	65	60
Black	84	71	68	65	63
Hispanic	80	61	58	61	55
White-collar background	85	64	60	62	51
Blue-collar background	86	67	59	59	55
Above-average students	86	67	64	62	54
Average and below	82	65	59	60	54
East	80	62	63	62	53
Midwest	85	67	60	62	52
South	85	64	58	55	50
West	79	68	63	65	60
Large city	84	62	58	59	52
Suburb	81	64	61	58	49
Small town	83	69	63	62	57
Rural	85	64	60	61	54
Protestant	85	69	63	60	53
Catholic	80	59	57	58	50
Church attender	88	70	63	64	55
Non-attender	79	61	59	57	52

GO 21505702; Q. 3

Addiction Problems

In 1992 a record 29 percent of all teens reported that drinking had ever been a cause of trouble in their family. By comparison, fewer teens reported that either drugs (11 percent) or gambling (6 percent) had ever been causes of domestic trouble.

Reports of family drinking and drug problems increase as teens grow older, suggesting either that they become more aware of the problems, or that in some cases, that they, themselves, have become the source of the problem through substance abuse.

Reports of addictive problems come more frequently from teens who are doing only average or below-average work at school and from those who have blue-collar family backgrounds.

Drinking problems more often are reported in the East and West, than in the Midwest or South where abstention historically has been higher than average.

10.3 Family Addiction Trends

	Liquor problems	Drug problems	Gambling problems
1992	29%	11%	6%
1989	16	7	6
1987	19	na	na
1985	16	na	na
1982	22	na	na
1979	20	na	na
1977	18	na	na

10.4 Family Addiction Problems

Have any of the following ever been a cause of trouble in your family — Drugs? Gambling? Liquor?

| | September – October 1992 | | |
	Liquor	Drugs	Gambling
National	**29%**	**11%**	**6%**
Male	28	8	7
Female	30	14	6
Ages 13 – 15	27	9	7
Ages 16 – 17	32	13	7
White	31	11	5
Non-white	22	12	11
Black	24	13	14
Hispanic	33	10	12
White-collar background	26	9	4
Blue-collar background	37	16	8
Above-average students	22	9	4
Average and below	39	13	8
East	28	7	8
Midwest	35	11	5
South	24	12	7
West	30	12	4
Large city	24	8	7
Suburb	26	13	6
Small town	31	10	5
Rural	31	13	5
Republican	27	10	5
Democrat	30	14	6
Independent	34	11	8
Protestant	26	10	3
Catholic	30	11	9
Church attender	26	12	8
Non-attender	33	10	4

GO 12869; Q. 43

Marijuana

America's teen-agers appear to be winning their own war against drugs. They long identified drug abuse as the leading problem facing their generation, and as a result have led the opposition to legalizing its use. In 1992, about three teens in four (77 percent) said they were opposed to legalizing marijuana.

Similarly, three in four (74 percent) also believe it would be wrong to decriminalize possession of small amounts of marijuana.

In recent years only about one teen in 10 has reported ever using marijuana, and a scant 4 percent reported use in the 30-day period preceding the interview.

When this series of questions was first asked by the Gallup Youth Survey in 1978, 39 percent of the teens reported they had tried marijuana, and 27 percent said they had used it in the previous month. Not surprisingly then, only 42 percent of the teens in 1978 opposed decriminalization of marijuana and just 62 percent were against its legalization.

As teens grow older, however, levels of experimentation rise and attitudes against marijuana soften slightly. Among those who are 16 or 17 years old, 18 percent of the teens in 1992 said they had experimented with marijuana, and 8 percent reported use in the past month. Among the older teens, opposition to decriminalization of marijuana dropped to 65 percent and of legalization to 73 percent.

10.5 Trends in Acceptance and Use of Marijuana

	Oppose Legalization	Oppose Decriminalization	Ever Used	Used In Past Month
1992	77%	74%	11%	4%
1989	83	80	12	4
1988	89	77	11	2
1987	88	76	16	5
1986	82	70	24	6
1985	87	73	23	8
1983	80	70	19	8
1982	74	60	37	13
1981	74	57	37	13
1980	68	46	40	na
1979	65	44	41	27
1978	62	42	39	27

10.6 Marijuana Use

Have you, yourself, ever happened to try marijuana?
About how long ago did you last try marijuana?
Do you think the use of marijuana should be made legal, or not?
Do you think the possession of small amounts of marijuana should or should not be treated as a criminal offense?

	September – October 1992			
	Oppose legal- izing	Oppose decriminal- izing	Ever used	Used last month
National	**77%**	**74%**	**11%**	**4%**
Male	74	72	12	6
Female	80	77	10	3
Ages 13 – 15	80	81	6	2
Ages 16 – 17	73	65	18	8
White	78	78	11	4
Non-white	74	63	13	5
White-collar background	77	77	10	4
Blue-collar background	76	72	13	4
Above-average students	80	77	9	4
Average and below	73	72	13	5
East	76	68	12	9
Midwest	72	72	12	4
South	82	84	8	2
West	75	68	14	7
Large city	67	73	14	8
Suburb	75	72	15	8
Small town	76	74	10	3
Rural	84	80	9	4
Republican	81	78	8	4
Democrat	70	67	15	6
Independent	74	77	14	6
Protestant	79	79	8	3
Catholic	78	74	13	5
Church attender	83	76	9	4
Non-attender	71	74	13	6

GO 12869; Q. 44, 46–48

Alcohol Now Drug of Choice Among Teens

While substances such as marijuana and cocaine are still being abused by some teens, alcohol clearly has become the drug of choice of the young people of America. According to the findings of the most recent Gallup Youth Survey, teen drinking and substance abuse now are more likely to occur in affluent white suburbs than in minority neighborhoods of the inner city.

In 1992, nearly one teen in five reported drinking alcoholic beverages at least once during the past month. By comparison, only 4 percent reported using marijuana, and less than 1 percent used cocaine during the same period.

Despite the fact that the sale of alcoholic beverages to teen-agers is now illegal in all 50 states, even among those who are 12 to 13 years old, 3 percent reported having had a drink during the 30-day period preceding the time of interview. The proportion of underage drinkers rises to 16 percent in the middle teen years of 14 to 15. By age 16, one teen in three is an alcohol user.

These high levels of teen alcohol use are found in all regions of the country Use is most prevalent in the East where one young person in five is a drinker of alcoholic beverages.

Drinking is highest in the suburbs where 22 percent of teens used alcohol in the past month.

By comparison, marijuana usage is also highest in the suburbs (5 percent) and is somewhat lower in the small towns (4 percent) and rural areas (3 percent) of America.

Only 2 percent of the teens in large cities report use of marijuana during the past month, but the metropolises have the dubious distinction of leading the nation in teen-age abuse of cocaine (1 percent). Cocaine use is reported by only one-half of 1 percent of suburban teens, and use is almost unknown and unreported in small towns and rural areas.

The survey evidence suggests that some teens may be using alcohol to compensate for their failures at school. Teens doing just average or below-average work at school are slightly more likely than above-average students to be drinkers. The proportion of drinkers rises to one in four among those who have doubts about graduating from high school, compared to 16 percent of those who feel it is very likely they will graduate. Even higher drinking rates are found among young people who do not intend to attend college (36 percent). That is about double the rate for those who hope to go to college part-time or full-time.

For some teens drinking may be a matter of morality since recent church attenders (12 percent) are far less likely than those who have not been in church recently (23 percent) to be alcohol users.

Alcohol use is higher among white and Hispanic teens than among non-whites. White and Hispanic teens also are slightly more likely than non-whites to report use of marijuana. Young men are only slightly more likely than young women (17 percent) to be alcohol users.

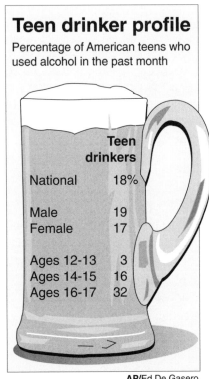

Teen drinker profile

Percentage of American teens who used alcohol in the past month

Teen drinkers

National	18%
Male	19
Female	17
Ages 12-13	3
Ages 14-15	16
Ages 16-17	32

AP/Ed De Gasero

Availability and Use of Alcohol

All states have raised their minimum drinking age to 21, but teen drinkers across the nation said in 1989 that it was still fairly easy to get alcoholic beverages whenever they wanted to do so.

Overall, one teenager in five (25 percent) classified himself as a drinker of alcoholic beverages. Among those who drink, beer (65 percent) and wine or wine coolers (38 percent) are more often consumed than liquor (14 percent).

Ready access to alcoholic beverages usually is not limited according to teen drinkers. Little difficulty is reported by them in getting drinks,with 40 percent saying it is very easy to obtain alcoholic beverages whenever they wanted to do so, and an additional 40 percent claimed it is fairly easy in their communities.

10.7 Type of Alcohol Consumed

	November 1989			
	Drink	Beer	Wine	Liquor
1989	21%	14%	8%	3%
1988	25	18	11	4
1987	22	16	9	7
1982	41	32	15	14
1979	38	26	16	10
1977	37	29	13	10
1959	22	14	6	2

10.8 Drinking in the Past Month

We are trying to find out what teens like yourself are currently doing in several areas. Please tell me if you personally have or have not done each of the following activities in the past 30 days. Have you drank alcohol such as beer, wine, or liquor?

	June – July 1992	
	Yes	No
National	**18%**	**82%**
Male	21	79
Female	15	85
Ages 12 – 13	3	97
Ages 14 – 15	16	84
Ages 16 – 17	34	66
White	20	80
Non-white	12	88
Black	11	89
Hispanic	17	83
White-collar background	22	78
Blue-collar background	16	84
Above-average students	16	84
Average and below	18	82
East	20	80
Midwest	18	82
South	18	82
West	16	84
Large city	18	82
Suburb	20	80
Small town	18	82
Rural	20	80
Protestant	20	80
Catholic	20	80
Church attender	12	88
Non-attender	23	77

GO 21505702; Q. 4

Driving Under the Influence

The number of teens driving under the influence of alcohol, or riding in a car driven by someone who is, has held steady in recent years.

Teen drinking and driving was one of the major influences that led to the current nationwide ban on drinking by those who are under 21 years of age. It was thought that by raising the minimum drinking age, the number of teen-age drivers who drive "under the influence" would be reduced, and so would the number of accidents and fatalities that they cause. Teens who drive under the influence still are present in large numbers, but their ranks have been thinned. In 1984, twice as many teens (14 percent) of the teens surveyed admitted driving shortly after they had been drinking. The proportion who did so dropped 6 percentage points in 1985, and since 1988 has stood at 7 percent of all teens.

Over one teen in three (36 percent) in 1984 reported being a passenger in a car driven by someone their own age who had just had a drink. Since 1988 the proportion of teens who put themselves at risk this way has dropped to about one in five.

Once teens reach driving age, the number who potentially place themselves at risk by driving or being in a car driven by teen-ager under the influence grows dramatically. Sixteen percent say they have themselves driven after drinking, and 39 percent have been passengers.

10.9 Teen Drinking and Driving Trend

	Driven under the influence	Passenger with driver Under the influence
1992	7%	21%
1988	7	22
1985	8	28
1984	14	36
1978	10	na

10.10 Teen Drinking and Driving

Have you, yourself, ever driven a car shortly after drinking alcoholic beverages?
Have you ever been a passenger in a car when a driver about your own age was under the influence of alcohol?

	September – October 1992		
	Drove after drinking	Passenger of teen drinker	Driver or passenger
National	**7%**	**21%**	**23%**
Male	8	20	21
Female	7	22	24
Ages 13 – 15	1	11	11
Ages 16 – 17	16	39	43
White	9	24	26
Non-white	2	10	11
White-collar background	7	24	25
Blue-collar background	7	20	20
Above-average students	4	18	18
Average and below	11	26	28
East	10	16	21
Midwest	7	26	26
South	8	21	22
West	5	20	20
Large city	5	17	17
Suburb	11	23	27
Small town	6	24	25
Rural	7	19	20
Republican	8	18	18
Democrat	6	25	25
Independent	9	25	29
Protestant	8	19	21
Catholic	7	23	25
Church attender	6	17	19
Non-attender	8	25	26

GO 12869; Q. 53–54

Recognizing the Dangers of Alcoholism

About three teenagers in four (78 percent) believe that the drinking of alcoholic beverages is having a very serious impact on our society. An additional 17 percent think drinking is a fairly serious societal problem, while only 5 percent see little or no danger.

In their schools, six teens in 10 (60 percent) say there is a very serious drinking problem by fellow students and 21 percent assess student drinking as fairly serious. Only 19 percent dismiss student drinking as being of little or no consequence.

Four teens in 10 (41 percent) believe drinking by at least one of their friends may be a very serious problem. It is termed a fairly serious danger by 21 percent. For 37 percent of the teens, the report was that there is no problem involving drinking among their acquaintances.

One-third of the teens (33 percent) say there may be a serious problem of drinking by family members, and an additional 16 percent see fairly serious difficulties. These figures far exceed those that show only 16 percent of the teens believe that drinking is causing difficulties in their families.

Similarly, 28 percent of the teens view their own drinking as being a potentially serious danger and 10 percent think it is fairly serious. This, too, is more than the number who report having used alcoholic beverages recently.

Younger teens show about twice as much concern about their own and their family members' drinking as those who are 16 and older. Among younger teens, 40 percent are concerned about family members' drinking, compared to 24 percent of the older teens. Thirty-five percent of the younger teens rate the dangers of their own drinking as very serious, compared to 18 percent of the older teens. Younger teens (47 percent) more often than older teens (33 percent) also express serious concern about drinking by their friends.

Awareness of Dangers

Nearly all teens (99 percent) know that the consumption of alcohol by pregnant women can cause birth defects.

Most teens (95 percent) believe one can become addicted to alcohol. Somewhat fewer teens (85 percent) believe that alcoholism is a disease, while 15 percent think otherwise. Least likely to consider alcohol a disease are younger teens (80 percent). By age 16, 91 percent classify alcoholism as a disease.

Only 7 percent are of the opinion that "a person who drinks only beer or wine cannot become an alcoholic." The statement is labeled false by 92 percent of the teenagers and 1 percent were uncertain.

Particular emphasis has been put in recent years on educating young people and adults about the hazards of being drunk while driving. Now, only 2 percent of the teens believe that "some people become better drivers after having a drink or two." Ninety-eight percent think otherwise.

Many teenagers may not be aware that recent research disclosed that women can assimilate alcohol only about half as quickly as men. About one teen in four (27 percent) believes that the impact of alcohol on both sexes are similar, assuming the men and women weigh about the same and are of similar ages. About 72 percent of the teens correctly disagree.

Alcohol has been termed a "gateway drug" because it can lead users to try more dangerous drugs such as cocaine, crack and heroin. About 16 percent of the teen-agers falsely agree that people who drink alcoholic beverages are less likely to try other drugs. This assumption may stem from the 1960s when many young people were persuaded to use more dangerous drugs than alcohol.

The frequent role alcohol plays in increasing the number of criminals is recognized by 82 percent of the teens who agree that "many people in prison had drinking problems that led to crime."

10.11 Concerns About Alcohol

How serious a problem would you say each of the following is — very serious, fairly serious, not too serious, or not at all serious: The impact of drinking alcoholic beverages in our society? Students drinking at your school? Drinking by your friends? Drinking by members of your family? Your own drinking?

	March — April 1990				
	Society	**School**	**Friends**	**Family**	**Self**
National	**78%**	**60%**	**41%**	**33%**	**28%**
Male	75	56	38	29	26
Female	81	64	44	37	30
Ages 13 – 15	78	59	47	40	35
Ages 16 – 17	78	60	33	24	18
White	75	57	38	30	26
Non-white	85	68	52	43	32
White-collar family	76	63	44	30	29
Blue-collar family	50	60	39	35	28
East	79	58	37	31	25
Midwest	75	53	38	32	23
South	82	69	52	39	36
North	73	55	33	26	23

Here are some statements about alcoholism. For each, please tell me if you think the statement is true or false?

	March — April 1990		
	True	**False**	**No Opinion**
The use of alcohol by pregnant women can cause birth defects	99%	1%	*%
Alcoholism is an addiction	95	4	*
Alcoholism is an disease	85	1	*
Many people in prison had drinking problems that led to crime	82	16	2
There is no difference in the amount of alcohol women and men can handle if they are the same weight and age	27	72	1
People who drink are less likely to try drugs	16	84	*
A person who drinks only wine or beer cannot become an alcoholic	7	92	1
Some people become better drivers after having a drink or two	2	98	—

Peer Pressures

The tobacco industry has long contended that the primary cause of teen-age smoking is peer pressure, but only about one teen in 10 feels any peer pressure to smoke cigarettes, including just 3 percent who say they are under are a great deal of pressure to do so.

By comparison somewhat more teens (20 percent) report pressure to consume alcoholic beverages, while slightly fewer (8 percent) say they feel peer pressure to use drugs.

10.12 Peer Pressures To Use Substances

	June – July 1992		
	Alcohol	**Drugs**	**Cigarettes**
Great deal	5%	4%	3%
Some	15	4	9
Hardly any	13	11	11
None at all	67	81	77

The pressure to use the substances has decreased substantially since 1988 when 36 percent said they felt at least some peer pressure to drink alcoholic beverages, 23 percent to smoke cigarettes, and 19 percent to use marijuana.

Only 1 percent of teens say they would be more likely to be interested in a person of the opposite sex who smokes. Among teens who are non-smokers, two in three (67 percent) say they would be less likely to be attracted to a smoker.

Teen smokers are more likely than non-smokers to live in a household where someone else smokes, by a margin of 65 percent to 45 percent. Four in 10 teen smokers report that their father (40 percent) or mother

The findings on tobacco on this and the following seven pages are taken from an in-depth study on teen-age attitudes and behavior concerning tobacco. The study was conducted among 1,125 young people, ages 12 to 17, in the Summer of 1991 by The George H. Gallup International Institute. Major funding for the study was provided by The Robert Wood Johnson Foundation.

Tobacco Use

An alarming number of America's teen-agers continue to use tobacco. Cigarettes are the form preferred by most teens, but use of "smokeless tobacco" and even pipes and cigars is also reported.

Health experts have long identified tobacco use, particularly cigarette smoking, as the leading preventable cause of premature death. It is currently estimated that over 400,000 people in the U.S. annually die from diseases caused by cigarette smoking. While it has been hoped that by cutting off the adoption of tobacco at early ages this grim statistic could be reduced, current findings that about one teen in 8 (13 percent) is experimenting or using tobacco regularly are not very encouraging.

Use and experimentation with tobacco escalates rapidly as teens grow older. Just 2 percent of those who are 12 to 13 years old report any use of tobacco during the week preceding the time of the interview. By the middle teen years of 14 to 15, use grows to 13 percent of the age group. By age 16, one teen in four (24 percent) reports tobacco use during the preceding week. The level of tobacco use among older teen users approaches that of the latest Gallup Poll results which found in late 1991 that 28 percent of the adult population are cigarette smokers.

In addition to cigarettes, 2 percent of the teens said last week they smoked cigars and 1 percent lit up a pipe. So-called "smokeless tobacco," which has been identified as the cause of several disfiguring and life-threatening forms of cancer, was used by a net 3 percent of the teens, with 2 percent saying they used either chewing tobacco or snuff last week.

Young men are slightly more likely than young women to be tobacco users, by a margin of 15 percent to 12 percent. While the sexes are about equal when it comes to smoking cigarettes, the findings for greater overall tobacco use among young men are accounted for by their more frequent use of alternate forms such as pipes, cigars, chewing tobacco, and snuff.

Whites (14 percent) are more likely than non-whites (5 percent) to be tobacco users. About one Hispanic teen in 10 (9 percent) is a tobacco user.

Tobacco use by teens is fairly evenly spread throughout the country, with the highest incidence occurring in the West (15 percent) and lowest in the Midwest (12 percent). Teens living in small towns and rural areas are more than likely than those from large metropolitan areas and the suburbs to be tobacco users, by a margin of 16 percent to 11 percent.

Students who do well at school also often are too smart to use tobacco. Academic underachievers (18 percent) are more than twice as likely as those teens doing above-average work at school (8 percent) to be tobacco users. Tobacco use skyrockets among teens who say they are likely to become high school dropouts.

The teen socio-economic tobacco use patterns resemble adult tobacco user profiles which increasingly are becoming dominated by blue-collar workers with little or no formal education after high school. Teens from blue-collar households (15 percent) are only slightly more likely than those from white-collar families to be tobacco users (13 percent), but teens who do not expect to receive any further training after high school (25 percent) are three times as likely as those planning to go to college full time (8 percent) to be tobacco users.

Teen cigarette smoking

21%
Ages 16-17

28%
Ages 18 and over

10%
Ages 14-15

1%
Ages 12-13

AP/Stan Kohler

10.13 Cigarette Smoker Profile

We are trying to find out what teens like yourself are currently doing in several areas. Please tell me if you personally have or have not done each of the following activities in the past 30 days. In the past 30 days have you smoked a cigarette?

	June – July 1992	
	Yes	No
National	**14%**	**86%**
Male	14	86
Female	13	87
Ages 12 – 13	3	97
Ages 14 – 15	14	86
Ages 16 – 17	25	75
White	15	85
Non-white	6	94
Black	4	96
Hispanic	11	89
White-collar background	14	86
Blue-collar background	13	87
Above-average students	8	92
Average and below	18	82
East	14	86
Midwest	13	87
South	14	86
West	14	86
Large city	13	87
Suburb	12	88
Small town	15	85
Rural	15	85
Parents smoke	18	82
Very likely to graduate from high school	12	88
Somewhat likely to graduate	22	78
Not likely to graduate	60	40
Protestant	14	86
Catholic	13	87
Church attender	10	90
Non-attender	17	83

GO 21505702; Q. 4A

Concerns About Smoking

Nearly all teens (99 percent) recognize that smoking can be harmful to their health, and most (96 percent) also realize that breathing smoke from other people's cigarettes is harmful. Nine teens in 10 (90 percent) believe the use of "smokeless tobacco" such as chewing tobacco or snuff is one of the causes of cancer.

Teens are more likely than adults to believe that cigarette smoking is a cause of lung cancer (99 percent), heart disease (86 percent), and birth defects (1 percent).

Non-smoking teens are more likely than smokers to express concern about the impacts of smoking.

10.14 Concerns About Smoking

	June – July 1992	
	Smokers	Non-smokers
It is bad for your health	87%	98%
Tobacco stains on your teeth	74	84
Smoking gives you bad breath	80	84
It is expensive	68	63
Your smoke can harm other people	78	92
You are afraid of becoming addicted to tobacco	62	86
Your parents disapprove	52	87
Your friends disapprove	23	58
You don't like the smell of cigarettes	na	85

GO 21505702; Q. 33, 39

Why Teens Smoke

Relieving stress and enjoying smoking when they go out to have a good time are the leading answers given by teens as the reasons why they smoke. Some say they enjoy the taste, but one in four confesses "I can't help it, I just have to keep smoking."

10.15 Reasons for Smoking

	June – July 1992		
	Very true	Somewhat true	Not at all true
It helps to calm you when you feel a lot of stress	54%	32%	14%
You enjoy smoking when you go out to have a good time	46	32	22
You enjoy the taste	28	43	28
You can't help it, you just have to keep smoking	25	28	47
It helps you to concentrate	14	28	57
It helps you to wake up in the morning	12	15	72
It helps you to control your weight	7	16	76
It is part of growing up and makes you feel older	5	20	75
You like the way you look when you smoke	2	15	82

GO 21505702; Q. 26

Tobacco Addiction

Seven teen smokers in 10 (69 percent) report they have smoked at least 100 cigarettes in their life.

Six in 10 (61 percent) have smoked at least one cigarette every day for at least a month. Nearly half (48 percent) smoked every day last month. By age 16, half of teen smokers (56 percent) are smoking daily.

The average teen smoker has eight cigarettes a day. Eighteen percent of teen smokers are smoking a pack or more a day.

Age 13 is when the average teen has had his or her first whole cigarette. By age 14, half have started to inhale. By 15, half have bought their first pack of cigarettes.

Four teen smokers in 10 (40 percent) have their first cigarette within an hour after waking up in the morning. One teen smoker in four (26 percent) finds it difficult to refrain from smoking in places such as school, church, libraries, or the movies where smoking normally is forbidden.

Only one teen in four (25 percent) reports any difficulty in purchasing cigarettes in the local community. Two teen smokers in three (65 percent) say they are rarely or never turned away from the counter when attempting to buy cigarettes.

Many teens already say that if they had to do it over again, they would not start smoking and add that they would like to give up smoking. Most feel they would be able to quit if they decided to do so. Many have tried, and have failed. In these respects their attitudes and behavior begin to mirror the experience of adult smokers.

10.16 Ability To Quit Smoking

	June – July 1992	
	Teens	Adults
If had to do it over again, would not start smoking	70%	83%
Would be able to quit smoking, if made the decision to do so	81	78
Would like to give up smoking	68	74
Have already made a really serious effort to stop smoking	51	67

GO 21505702; Q. 29–32

Alcohol and Tobacco Bans

A majority of America's teen-agers now say they would support a nationwide ban on all tobacco products. Even teen smokers, themselves, often say they would support national laws that would prohibit tobacco sales to anyone under age 18.

Six teens in 10 (62 percent) say they would endorse a total national ban on all tobacco sales. Support for a ban on sales to people under age 21 is given by three teens in four (76 percent). Even greater support is found for laws that would prohibit tobacco sales to people like themselves who are under age 18, with 85 percent approving of the proposed ban.

The level of support from teens for tobacco prohibition has grown greatly since 1987 when just 47 percent said they would endorse a total nationwide ban on all sales and 64 percent would go along with a ban on sales to people under age 21.

Teen smokers give far less support to proposals for prohibitions of tobacco sales. Only 22 percent of teen smokers say they would endorse a total national ban, and just one in three (34 percent) approves of limiting sales to people 21 and over. A majority of 58 percent of teen smokers, however, say they would favor a law that would directly most affect them by prohibiting sales to anyone under age 18.

Among non-smokers the support for the bans is overwhelming, with 68 percent favoring a total nationwide ban on the sale of all tobacco products. Bans on sales to those under 21 gain support from 83 percent of teen non-smokers, and 89 percent say that they would endorse a ban on sales to people under age 18.

A slim majority of teens also say they now would favor nationwide prohibition of sales of wine, beer, and liquor. By comparison in 1987, just 28 percent of teens endorsed the idea of a total ban on alcohol sales.

Three teens in four endorse a "smoke free" school policy that would completely ban all smoking in all areas of the school and school grounds by both students and teachers. Overall, only 16 percent of the students would oppose such a move.

Three teens in four report that their school already has a complete or limited smoke-free policy for students. This includes 62 percent who say that both the school building and grounds are smoke free, 9 percent who report there is a policy for the building only, and 3 percent who say smoking is banned only on the school grounds.

Smoke apparently may often still be seen billowing out of many high school faculty lounges, however, because far fewer students believe that their teachers are facing similar restrictions. Only one teen in three (34 percent) reports that teachers cannot smoke within the school building or on school grounds. Additionally, 8 percent say there is a ban against teacher smoking within the building, and another 8 percent say their teachers may not be seen smoking on the school grounds.

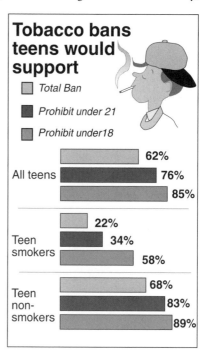

Tobacco bans teens would support

- Total Ban
- Prohibit under 21
- Prohibit under 18

All teens		62%
		76%
		85%
Teen smokers	22%	
	34%	
		58%
Teen non-smokers		68%
		83%
		89%

AP/Stan Kohler

10.17 Prohibition Trends

	National ban on tobacco	National ban on alcohol
1992	62%	51%
1987	47	28
1986	49	31
1984	42	28

10.18 Support for Prohibition

Would you favor or oppose a law forbidding the sale of all tobacco throughout the nation? . . . to people under 21 years of age? . . . to people under 18 years of age?
Would you favor or oppose a law forbidding the sale of all beer, wine and liquor throughout the nation?

| | June – July 1992 | | | |
| | Favor Tobacco Ban | | | |
	Total	Under age 21	Under age 18	Alcohol ban
National	**62%**	**14%**	**9%**	**51%**
Male	59	15	10	49
Female	65	13	7	54
Ages 12 – 13	74	11	4	64
Ages 14 – 15	63	15	8	51
Ages 16 – 17	50	17	13	41
White	62	14	9	50
Non-white	58	16	8	59
Black	58	17	7	59
Hispanic	54	15	8	50
White-collar background	63	13	9	48
Blue-collar background	62	15	7	54
Above-average students	66	15	7	52
Average and below	59	13	10	52
East	65	11	9	51
Midwest	67	14	7	54
South	54	18	10	51
West	65	12	8	49
Large city	66	12	7	50
Suburb	62	14	10	49
Small town	63	15	9	54
Rural	59	15	9	53
Protestant	60	16	7	51
Catholic	66	12	10	50
Church attender	68	14	6	58
Non-attender	57	15	11	46

GO 21505702; Q. 53–56

Substance Abuse by Student Athletes

Many of the nation's high school athletic coaches report that drug use among student athletes is a serious problem at their schools. Marijuana, cocaine, crack, and steroids may get the headlines, but alcohol and tobacco abuse are far more prevalent problems among high school student athletes.

Over one-third of the nation's coaches say that drug use among student athletes at their school is either a very big (4 percent) or fairly big (33 percent) problem. Less concerned are 42 percent who feel drug use by athletes is not too big, and 21 percent who say it is not big at all.

Follow-up questioning on specific substances, however, shows that student athlete substance abuse may be far greater than these responses suggest. The number of coaches who feel the use of marijuana (18 percent), cocaine (3 percent), or crack (3 percent) is a fairly big problem among student athletes, pales by comparison to those who give similar ratings to alcohol (79 percent) and tobacco (66 percent) abuse at their schools. In addition, one coach in 20 reports that there are problems with student athletes who use steroids (6 percent) or amphetamines (5 percent), perhaps in an attempt to improve their athletic performance.

Backing up these opinions, seven coaches in 10 report these figures are not just hearsay, but that they personally know student athletes who are abusing the substances. Specifically, 69 percent know of alcohol users, 55 percent of tobacco users, and 20 percent of marijuana users. One in 10 knows at least one athlete who already by high school age is on steroids. Personal knowledge of amphetamine (4 percent), cocaine (3 percent), and crack (1 percent) use are less often reported.

Most coaches took the youthful offenders aside and spoke to them about their substance abuse problem. Most also recommended that the students seek counseling. A majority of the coaches spoke with parents or guardians about the problem.

Six coaches in 10 (63 percent) reported abuse problems to school authorities when it came to their attention and suspended students from the team because of their substance abuse problems.

Three coaches in four report their schools have programs in place to deal with substance abuse problems. In addition, 28 percent of the coaches say they, themselves, have initiated special programs of their own to help address the issue. Beyond the stereotype of the high school gym teacher who just shows films in health classes, these coaches are actively engaged in counseling student athletes, meeting with their parents or guardians, and conducting special classes for students or their fellow coaches. Also, two coaches in three say they specifically discuss the problems of substance abuse at pre-season meetings with student team members, and sometimes with their parents.

For the future, nearly half of the coaches say they would like to receive special training to deal with the drug problem. Many also would like special education programs for the students, their fellow teachers, counseling programs for the students, and more meetings with students and parents

Most coaches say they or their schools have a uniform, written, code on the subject of drugs, but only 4 percent say their school now does drug testing.

10.19 Coach Reports on Drug Use by High School Student Athletes

	Big or fairly big problem	Know students who use substance
Alcohol	79%	69%
Tobacco	66	55
Marijuana	18	20
Steroids	6	10
Amphetamines	5	4
Cocaine	3	3
Crack	3	1

LAW AND ORDER

Fear and Incidence of Crime

Half of the teens interviewed in 1992 (51 percent) said there was more crime in their area than a year ago. Fewer teens (34 percent) believed there was less crime. The crime rate remained about the same according to 11 percent of the teens, and 4 percent were uncertain about whether there was more crime or less in their area.

Also in 1992, 41 percent of the teens said there was an area within a mile of where they lived in which they would not want to walk alone at night. The level of fear has remained fairly constant over the past decade.

Young women (49 percent) were more likely than young men (34 percent) to have reservations about walking alone at night in their own neighborhood.

Three teens in 10 (30 percent) reported that crimes were committed against their property or person in 1987. Most crimes were against property and were not personal assaults. One teen in four (24 percent) had property or money stolen that year. Destruction of personal property was reported by 13 percent of the teens. By comparison, in 1985 the incidence of theft was slightly lower (22 percent), but vandalization was much higher (19 percent).

Only 3 percent of the teens said they were personally assaulted or mugged in 1987. This was a statistically non-significant improvement over 1985 reports when 4 percent of the teens said they were victims of crimes against their person.

11.1 Crime Trends

	1992	1987	1985	1983	1981
More crime in area than a year ago	51%	42%	47%	35%	65%
Afraid to walk alone at night	41	37	38	41	46
Money or property stolen	na	24	22	24	32
Property vandalized	na	13	19	18	24
Personally assaulted	na	3	4	3	5

11.2 Fear of Crime

Is there more or less crime in your area than there was a year ago?
Is there any area within a mile of your home where you would be afraid to walk alone at night?

| | September – October 1992 | | | | |
| | Crime in Area | | | Fear | |
	More	**Same**	**Less**	**Yes**	**No**
National	**51%**	**11%**	**34%**	**41%**	**58%**
Male	50	9	35	34	65
Female	52	12	33	49	51
Ages 13 – 15	47	10	39	41	59
Ages 16 – 17	58	12	26	42	57
White	54	12	29	41	59
Non-white	44	4	51	44	56
White-collar background	53	12	31	43	57
Blue-collar background	53	9	35	38	62
Above-average students	53	12	33	45	55
Average and below	49	10	35	36	63
East	54	14	25	45	54
Midwest	52	11	37	35	65
South	50	10	36	43	57
West	49	10	35	44	56
Large city	51	6	39	53	46
Suburb	67	10	21	54	46
Small town	48	10	38	36	64
Rural	45	17	34	35	65
Republican	56	8	30	39	61
Democrat	50	11	36	41	58
Independent	52	10	34	44	56
Protestant	53	11	34	42	58
Catholic	55	10	33	42	58
Church attender	51	11	35	42	58
Non-attender	51	11	32	40	59

GO 12869; Q. 55–56

Guns

Nearly half of the nation's teens (46 percent) reported in 1992 that there was a gun in their house. This represented a 9 percentage-point decrease in gun ownership since 1988 when 55 percent of the teens said there was at least one gun in their house.

Seven teens in 10 (69 percent) favor the registration of all firearms. Opposed to such a measure are 28 percent of the teens, and 3 percent are undecided.

A majority of teens (52 percent) believe there should be a law prohibiting possession of pistols and revolvers except by police and other authorized persons. Opposed to a handgun ban are 47 percent of the teens, and 1 percent held no opinion.

Reports of guns in teen households are more likely to be made in small towns and rural areas than in large cities and the suburbs. The reports more often come from white teen households, and where there is a male teen in the family.

11.3 Gun Trends

	Guns In Home	Favor Registration	Favor Handgun Ban
1992	46%	69%	52%
1988	55	56	55
1986	51	59	58
1983	53	59	53
1981	55	66	56
1980	52	59	59
1978	55	67	50

11.4 Teens and Guns

Are there any guns in your home?
Now, here is a question about pistols and revolvers: Do you think there should be a law which forbids the possession of this type of gun except by police and other authorized persons?
Do you favor or oppose the registration of all firearms?

	September – October 1992		
	Guns in home	Favor handgun ban	Favor registration
National	**46%**	**52%**	**70%**
Male	49	45	73
Female	39	59	65
Ages 13 – 15	44	55	66
Ages 16 – 17	47	48	74
White	52	50	72
Non-white	22	60	59
White-collar background	44	56	72
Blue-collar background	54	47	73
Above-average students	42	55	74
Average and below	50	49	65
East	36	51	77
Midwest	51	49	65
South	47	56	68
West	45	51	70
Large city	35	47	70
Suburb	38	56	69
Small town	47	53	70
Rural	58	51	70
Republican	51	51	71
Democrat	46	54	75
Independent	45	49	69
Protestant	53	50	67
Catholic	39	63	68
Church attender	42	57	72
Non-attender	50	48	68

GO 12869; Q. 57–59

The Death Penalty

A majority of teenagers favor use of the death penalty for those convicted of murder, attempting to assassinate the President of the United States, or rape.

Overall, 84 percent of the teenagers whose opinion was solicited, said they favor use of the death penalty for at least one of the crimes listed in the interview.

Two teens in three (67 percent) favor the execution of those who are convicted of murder. Almost as many teens approve of the death penalty for those who are guilty of attempting to assassinate the president. Opposed to applying the death penalty in murder cases are 27 percent of the teens, while 35 percent oppose its use in attempted presidential assassinations.

Convicted rapists should forfeit their lives in the opinion of 54 percent of the teens. Young women are more likely than young men to approve of the death penalty for rapists, by a margin of 59 percent to 50 percent. Among young women who are 16 or older, 63 percent would seek the death penalty for rapists. Opposing death sentences for rapists are 44 percent of the young men and 39 percent of the young women.

Hijacking an airplane should result in the death penalty according to 40 percent of the teens, but a majority of 55 percent oppose its use in this case. Similarly, only 38 percent of the teens approve of executing those who are spying for foreign nations in times of peace, while 57 percent oppose such stringent measures.

In the current climate of public opinion support for harsh measures against drug peddlers is running high, but comparatively few teens (35 percent) will go so far as to endorse the death penalty for drug dealers who have not also been convicted of murder. Opposed to such sanctions against dealers are 64 percent of teens.

Teen Republicans are somewhat more likely than Democrats to approve of the death penalty for all of the crimes tested in the survey. Overall, 86 percent of those teens who identify themselves as Republicans approve of the death penalty for at least one crime, compared to 81 percent of the teen Democrats.

Also showing an above-average tendency to favor the death penalty in at least some cases are teens from small towns and rural areas (90 percent), southern teens (88 percent), those who are doing only average or below average work in school (89 percent), and teens from blue-collar family backgrounds (86 percent).

11.5 Opinion of the Death Penalty

Do you favor or opposed the death penalty for . . .

	Favor	Oppose	Not sure
Murder	67%	27%	6%
Attempting to assassinate the president	63	35	2
Rape	54	41	5
Hijacking an airplane	40	55	5
Spying for a foreign nation during peacetime	38	57	5
Drug dealers not convicted of murder	35	62	3

AIPO 881; Q. 109

Opinion of U.S. Legal System

The majority of America's teen-agers are of the opinion that the United States has the fairest legal system in the world, but many believe there still is plenty of room for improving the system.

A majority of teens feel the system contains serious inequities that enable the rich and even criminals often to get away scot free. At the same time it is felt by teens that too often the rights of victims are abused, and that under our system of justice blacks usually have difficulty in getting a fair trial. The solution to these problems in the view of some teens may be to reduce rather than to increase the number of lawyers in the country.

The flaw in the legal system most frequently stated by teens is that rich people are perceived as being able to hire smart lawyers who make it highly unlikely that they will ever see the inside of a jail cell because of their crimes. Fifty-eight percent think that affluent people receive preferential treatment in the courts.

Half of the teens believe that current laws in the U.S. do more to give rights to criminals than to protect their victims.

Nearly four teens in 10 (38 percent) believe our litigious society may have too many lawyers.

One third of the teen-agers (34 percent) believe that blacks do not get fair trials in the U.S. Among non-white teens, almost half (45 percent) believe the courts are biased against blacks.

Overall, six teens in 10 (62 percent), despite these criticisms, still believe that U.S. legal system is the fairest in the world.

11.6 The U.S. Legal System

	October 1990		
	Agree	Disagree	No opinion
The U.S. probably has the fairest legal system in the world	62%	34%	4%
Rich people almost never go to jail because they can hire smart lawyers	58	41	1
The laws usually do more to give rights to criminals than to protect their victims	51	45	4
There are too many lawyers in the U.S.	38	59	3
A black person usually cannot get a fair trial in this country	34	64	2

GO 124033

201

11.7 Opinion of the U.S. Legal System

Here are some statements about the legal system in this country. For each, please tell me if you agree or disagree with it — Rich people almost never go to jail because they can hire smart lawyers. The laws usually do more to give rights to criminals than to protect their victims. A black person cannot usually get a fair trial in this country. There are too many lawyers in the U.S. The U.S. probably has the fairest legal system in the world.

	October 1990				
	U.S. has fairest system	Rich never convicted	Too many criminal rights	Too many lawyers	No fair trials for blacks
National	**62%**	**58%**	**51%**	**38%**	**34%**
Male	68	59	50	46	35
Female	57	57	52	31	34
Ages 13 – 15	63	54	46	39	36
Ages 16 – 17	61	64	57	37	32
White	66	56	50	40	31
Non-white	52	64	51	32	45
Above-average students	66	57	52	43	32
Average and below	58	59	48	32	36
White-collar background	62	58	51	42	32
Blue-collar background	63	57	52	31	43
East	70	62	49	37	37
Midwest	64	54	50	39	37
South	60	54	53	42	31
West	56	64	53	42	31
Republicans	65	50	54	37	28
Democrats	62	64	46	39	42

GO 124033

Legal Rights

Maybe it is because of all of those arrest scenes in the detective stories they have been watching on television and at the movies, but teen-agers show a firmer grasp of their "Miranda" rights than of the basic principles of law. Most teens (95 percent), for example, know that a person accused of a serious crime is entitled to a court-appointed lawyer if they cannot afford one. The great majority (70 percent) also are aware that they may remain silent and refuse to answer questions if they are accused of a crime.

Many teens, however, seem confused about their most fundamental right: that in this country a person is presumed innocent until proven guilty. Less than half (44 percent) know that this is true.

11.8 Knowledge of Legal Rights

Here are some statements about the law in this country. For each, please tell me if you think it is true or false: People charged with crimes are considered guilty unless they can prove they are innocent. People charged with very serious crimes are guaranteed a lawyer even if they can't afford one. If you are accused of a crime, you can refuse to answer all questions.

	October 1990		
	Accused entitled to count-appointed lawyer	Accused can refuse to answer questions	People are guilty until proven innocent
National	**95%**	**70%**	**44%**
Male	97	71	41
Female	93	69	48
Ages 13 to 15	93	68	50
Ages 16 to 17	97	73	36
White	95	69	42
Non-white	95	73	52
Above-average students	97	71	40
Average and below	92	67	50
East	99	71	47
Midwest	93	71	44
South	94	70	38
West	94	67	50

Knowledge of the Court System

A large majority of teens mistakenly believe that only registered voters are eligible to serve on juries. Many teens also tend to overestimate the power of the nation's mayors and governors in judicial matters, and to believe that presidents can set aside the U.S. Constitution and over-turn the decisions of the highest court of the land whenever they choose to do so.

Seven teens in 10 (70 percent) believe that only registered voters can now serve on juries. Voting registration lists of course are frequently used as one of the sources for summoning people to jury duty, but in recent years court officials increasingly have turned to alternative sources such as motor vehicle department license records and local tax rolls to locate additional prospective jurors. The use of these supplemental lists is believed to be very important because it is felt that some people deliberately fail to become registered voters so that they can avoid jury duty. By using the alternative recruiting methods and publicizing their use it is hoped that more people would be encouraged to register to vote.

Students doing above-average work at school are more likely to hold this false impression than are academic underachievers, by a margin of 77 percent to 60 percent. White teens (74 percent) are far more likely than non-whites (56 percent) to believe jury duty is determined by voter registration. Also showing higher-than-average ignorance on the matter are younger teens who are 13 to 15 years of age (73 percent), compared to 67 percent of those who are 16 or older and nearing the time when they will be eligible to register to vote.

Pictures of people protesting for or against a trial in front of city hall or the state house are fairly common on the front pages of newspapers and on the local evening television news. The survey results suggest that many of the protesters may be there because they have the mistaken notion that the nation's mayors and governors have the legal power to dictate the outcome of a trial. This erroneous belief is shared by about four teen-agers in 10 (42 percent).

Teens from blue-collar family backgrounds (57 percent) are more likely than those from white-collar households (40 percent) to overestimate the power that mayors and governors have over the judiciary. Also believing that city and state leaders can dictate the outcome trials are nearly half of students who say they are doing just average or below-average work at school (49 percent) and 47 percent of non-white teens.

Many, if not most, past presidents undoubtedly have wished from time to time that they had the power to over-turn decisions of the U.S. Supreme Court. Attempts by presidents to alter the court's decisions, including Franklin Delano Roosevelt's effort to "pack the court," have always failed, but 38 percent of the country's teens mistakenly believe presidents do have this power. Disagreeing with the assertion and probably recognizing the constitutional principle of separate powers between the presidency and the judiciary are 61 percent of the teens.

Most often failing to recognize presidential limitations in dealing with the Supreme Court are those who are not doing well in school (43 percent), teens from blue-collar households (42 percent), non-whites (41 percent), younger teens (40 percent), and young women (40 percent). By comparison, fewer incorrect answers on the question were given by above-average students (34 percent), teens from white-collar households (35 percent), older teens (35 percent), white teens (37 percent), and young men (36 percent).

11.9 Knowledge of the Courts

Here are some statements about the law in this country. For each, please tell me if you think it is true or false: Only registered voters can serve on juries. A mayor governor can order a court to find that someone is innocent or guilty. The President of the United States can overrule the Supreme Court.

	October 1990		
	Only voters can serve on juries	**Mayors and governors can over-rule courts**	**Presidents can over-rule the Supreme Court**
National	**70%**	**42%**	**38%**
Male	69	41	36
Female	72	44	40
Ages 13 – 15	73	44	40
Ages 16 – 17	67	40	35
White	74	42	37
Non-white	56	47	41
Above-average students	77	38	34
Average and below	60	49	43
White-collar background	70	40	35
Blue-collar background	67	57	42
East	64	44	32
Midwest	77	43	44
South	70	44	33
West	69	38	44
Republican	69	45	37
Democrat	67	43	33

GO 124033

School programs

Emotional well-being

Suicide prevention

Seat belt use

HEALTH, WELFARE, AND SAFETY

School Prevention Programs

Less than half of America's teens say that their schools require medical examinations. Even among those that do, few appear to be offering teens professional health advice and help on such vital problems as drug and alcohol abuse, and suicide prevention.

Reports of medical examinations are given by less than half of the nation's teen-agers. Teens attending private schools, however, are far more likely than public school students to receive medical exams, by a margin of 67 percent to 45 percent.

The incidence of medical exams at school decreases as students grow older. A slight majority (53 percent) of junior high school, grades 6 through 9, report they receive medical check-ups. By senior high school, grades 10 through 12, the frequency of medical exams drop to 44 percent. The number of college students receiving required medical exams at college (42 percent) is even lower.

Medical and health examinations are ideal times to expose students to proper advice on avoiding risky behavior, to diagnose those who are at risk, and to provide professional help to those who are in need. Unfortunately, even among those now receiving required medical examinations, many are not getting this kind of help as a part of their health review.

Teens have long identified drug abuse as the leading problem confronting their generation, but, nationally, only one student in five now receives any information about drug abuse as a part of a medical examination procedure. Similarly, although alcohol increasingly is being identified as the drug of choice among young people, only 19 percent of those interviewed say they were given the opportunity to discuss alcohol-related problems during a school health examination. It should be pointed out that many schools include discussion and instruction on these matters in mandatory health courses.

12.1 School Prevention Programs

	Medical exams	Drug prevention	Alcohol prevention	Suicide prevention
National	**47%**	**20%**	**19%**	**8%**
Public school students	45	20	19	8
Private school students	67	24	23	8
Junior high	53	21	20	6
Senior high	44	19	19	8
College	42	17	16	4

Emotional Well-Being

Youthful optimism is not just a theory but may very well be a fact. Most teens in this country say they are excited about the future, feel very close to their families, and are generally happy persons. Many also consider themselves to be religious persons. Comparatively few teen-agers feel deeply depressed, but as they grow older, they increasingly feel the stresses and tensions of life.

Over nine teens in 10 say they are excited about the future, including 42 percent who strongly agree that this is true. About the only teens who do not view the future with enthusiasm are those who are doing so poorly at school that they feel their chances of graduating from high school are dim or non-existent.

Despite tales of youthful rebelliousness, most teens feel very close to their families. Nine teens in 10 say this is true. Family closeness cuts across all socio-economic lines, and diminishes only very slightly as teens grow older.

Given this background, it is not surprising then that nearly all teens (94 percent) say they are generally happy persons. When their attitudes towards themselves are probed, however, some admit that they often get depressed or feel sad. Just 7 percent strongly agree that depression and sadness are constant companions in their lives, but an additional 31 percent somewhat agree that this is true.

Non-white teens are somewhat more likely than white teen-agers to report frequent bouts with depression and sadness, by a margin of 46 percent to 36 percent. Nearly two in three potential high school dropouts (63 percent) report they often get depressed or feel sad.

Four teens in 10 report a lot of stress in their lives. Stress in the lives of the young appears to be very strongly correlated with the process of growing up. Among the youngest teens interviewed, ages 12 and 13, just one in three (35 percent) reported a lot of stress. By age 14, reports of a lot of stress rise slightly to 39 percent in the age group, but by age 16 high stress levels jump up to 50 percent of the teen population. Young women are somewhat more likely than young men to report a lot of stress in their lives, by a margin of 46 percent to 37 percent.

A surprisingly high proportion of teens say that religion is important in their lives. Half of the teens (50 percent) regard themselves as religious persons, and an additional 19 percent strongly agree that they are religious people. Only a scant 5 percent strongly disagree that they could be characterized as being religious. This is about the same percent who in past surveys have said they are agnostics or atheists, doubting or denying the existence of God.

Protestant teens are more likely than Catholic youth to strongly agree that they are religious persons, by a margin of 22 percent to 14 percent. As would be expected, most teens who attended church last week (86 percent) consider themselves religious persons, but so also do a majority of those who did not attend (55 percent). Religious feelings run highest in the South, where over three teens in four (77 percent) describe themselves as religious persons.

12.2 Emotional Well-Being

Please tell me whether you strongly agree, agree, disagree, or strongly disagree with the following statements — You feel very close to your family. You are generally a happy person. You often get depressed or feel sad. You have a lot of stress in your life. You are excited about the future. You are a religious person.

	June – July 1992					
	Generally happy	Excited about future	Very close to family	Religious person	Feel stress	Often sad
National	**94%**	**93%**	**90%**	**69%**	**41%**	**38%**
Male	96	93	92	69	37	33
Female	93	94	88	69	46	43
Ages 12 – 13	97	95	97	77	35	40
Ages 14 – 15	94	92	88	63	39	36
Ages 16 – 17	93	93	94	68	50	37
White	95	94	90	68	42	36
Non-white	92	90	89	73	40	46
Black	91	92	89	75	40	50
Hispanic	88	87	83	57	41	43
White-collar background	95	93	90	71	43	35
Blue-collar background	94	94	90	70	38	38
Above-average students	97	95	93	73	41	34
Average and below	92	91	87	65	41	43
East	95	92	87	63	41	35
Midwest	96	96	92	71	38	32
South	94	93	92	77	39	42
West	94	92	88	61	49	40
Large city	96	93	89	67	39	37
Suburb	93	93	89	68	44	34
Small town	96	93	91	71	45	40
Rural	94	95	87	72	34	37
Protestant	94	95	91	76	39	40
Catholic	96	93	90	72	43	35
Church attender	96	95	93	86	38	38
Non-attender	93	91	88	55	44	38

GO 21505702; Q. 2

Teen Suicide

A majority of teens believe that most (27 percent) or some (35 percent) young people their own age have thought about committing suicide. Among the remaining teenagers, 23 percent believe that only a few have thought about it, and 15 percent think virtually none have contemplated taking their own lives.

Drug and alcohol abuse head the list of reasons that young people feel can lead to suicide. Drug abuse is singled out as the most important cause by 20 percent, and 7 percent believe alcohol abuse is paramount.

Parental arguments and the numerous problems developing as the teens mature are frequently mentioned as leading causes.

Satanic cults and the morbid lyrics of heavy metal rock groups featuring self destruction are often named as potential contributing causes of teen suicides. Few young people, however, believe they are a leading cause.

Problems in school can lead to thoughts of suicide in the opinion of two teens in three . Career uncertainties are mentioned by 21 percent of the young people as a possible cause, and financing a college education is named by 12 percent. General economic pressures are cited by 36 percent of the teens and failure to obtain employment by 19 percent.

Teen pregnancy can result in suicidal behavior, according to 64 percent of the teens. AIDS is a cause in the opinion of 44 percent.

The pattern of some communities where one teen suicide leads to multiple teen suicides is a major problem in the opinion of 40 percent of the young people interviewed.

12.3 Opinion of Causes of Teen Suicide

Which of the following reasons [shown below] do you think causes teen-agers to think about committing suicide? Of the possible reasons, which the major or number one reason?

	November 1990 – January 1991	
	Causes	Most important Cause
Drug abuse	88%	20%
Trouble with parents	86	14
Problems in growing up	83	22
Peer pressures	83	16
Satanic cults	71	7
Alcohol abuse	68	3
School problems	65	3
Teen-age pregnancy	64	3
AIDS	44	3
Gangs	44	*
Other teens talking about or committing suicide	40	1
Economic problems	36	1
Heavy metal music	35	1
Career uncertainties	21	*
Unemployment	19	*
Playing Dungeons & Dragons	15	*
Financing college	12	*
Other	8	4
Don't know	*	2

Signs of Suicide

Teens believe the most obvious sign of suicidal contemplation is when one discusses or writes about it (94 percent). Almost as ominous, in the opinion of teens, are depression (91 percent), expressions that one is "worthless" (86 percent), having had personal problems for a long period of time (85 percent), or being a loner (83 percent).

Many teens say they would become concerned if a friend showed a sudden negative change in attitude or behavior (77 percent), or appeared to be confused (66 percent). Someone who suddenly started to give away his personal possessions could be inclined to commit suicide, according to 63 percent.

It would be of concern to 56 percent if young persons often became extremely angry, were not at all on the same wavelength with their parents (49 percent), were getting into trouble at school (36 percent), or were beginning to act wildly (31 percent).

Experience with Suicide

Many American teens became aware of the mushrooming teen-age suicide problem because friends or relatives have either taken or attempted to take their own lives. Six teenagers in 10 say they know someone who either attempted and failed (45 percent) or succeeded (15 percent) in committing suicide. In approximately one in three instances, the depressed teen was either a relative or a close friend.

Fifty percent among those who know someone who had tried to kill him or herself said they noticed early suicidal warning signs. These included discussing death, experiencing repeated personal problems, acting confused, sudden changes in attitude and behavior, withdrawing from friends, or being constantly depressed.

In addition, one teen in five (20 percent) reports that someone in his family had discussed suicide. Twelve percent revealed that a family member had tried to commit suicide, and five percent disclosed that a relative had succeeded in taking his or her own life.

Reported causes

A majority of the teens believe that most (27 percent) or at least some (35 percent) people their own age have considered committing suicide. Among the remaining teens interviewed, 23 percent said they feel that only a few people their age have thought about it, and 15 percent suspect virtually none have contemplated suicide.

Slightly more than half (52 percent) report they have discussed suicide with friends or others. Fifteen percent say they have come close to attempting suicide and 6 percent confessed they had attempted to take their own lives.

Family tensions headed the list of reasons that prompted teens to consider or attempt to take their own lives. Depression, peer pressures, low self-esteem, and problems developing because of relationships with boy or girl friends also were mentioned as contributing factors to the consideration of suicide.

Among those who had thought about or had attempted suicide, they were now most likely to point out: Suicide is not the answer to any of their problems (14 percent), there is no logical reason to kill oneself (12 percent), there is the possibility that they will escape from their gloomy predicaments (also 12 percent), life is too valuable (11 percent), and that they were loved by family and friends (9 percent).

When asked what advice they would give other teens who may be considering suicide, those who had had similar intentions said nothing is worth taking one's life (32 percent) and that the gloomy situations they find themselves in will improve (12 percent).

Providing Help

Some schools, religious organizations, and local communities offer a wide range of programs to cut down on the number of teen-age suicides. Four teenagers in 10 (41 percent) report their local schools are aware of the problem and are taking preventive measures. Actions most frequently cited are counseling programs (15 percent), seminars and meetings (8 percent), peer counseling (7 percent), classroom instruction and awareness programs (6 percent), and support groups (5 percent). Many students who do not have access to these programs say they would welcome them if they were introduced by their schools.

The large majority of the teens endorse suggestions about additional or new prevention measures taken by their schools. About nine in 10 (91 percent) favor special programs for troubled teens, courses for their parents on the problem (89 percent), and information about prevention programs outside of their schools (88 percent).

School assistance which many students also would endorse includes programs about emotional stress which can result in suicides (79 percent), courses on how young people can cope with their personal problems (78 percent), and family counseling services (75 percent).

One teen in five (21 percent) is aware of programs in their community designed to help prevent teen-age suicides. "Telephone Hot Lines" head the list of community programs (11 percent). Local counseling programs are reported by 4 percent, and another 4 percent say their community conducts awareness programs and meetings on the subject. More than nine teens in 10 (92 percent) believe their local communities should have a "Hot Line" program to help prevent teen suicide. Teens also respond favorably to suggestions that local communities should provide counseling services to those teens who need them, and centers where support groups would be available.

Many teens also feel local communities should make more of an effort to offer activities that would help young people get their minds off their problems and develop self-confidence (83 percent) or provide family counseling services (80 percent).

Local church suicide prevention programs are reported by more than one teen in four (28 percent). Most frequently mentioned as prevention offerings by local religious organizations are discussions on the topic (6 percent) and counseling services (also 6 percent).

Centers in which teens of the same or similar ages can discuss their problems with a qualified adult and other troubled young people (84 percent), counseling services (83 percent), and alternative programs in which teenagers can develop more self-esteem (82 percent) are most frequently endorsed as programs religious organizations can undertake to help reduce the number of youngsters taking their own lives. Almost as many teen-agers suggest that local houses of worship should provide family counseling services (79 percent) or offer hot line phone calls to those threatening to kill themselves (77 percent).

Seat Belt Use

Teen use of seat belts has been steadily increasing over the years. Currently, about eight teens in 10 (79 percent) report they used a seat belt the last time they rode in a car. By comparison, in 1977 only 23 percent of teens used a seat belt, and use actually dropped to 20 percent of all teens in 1982. The first noticeable improvement in seat belt use by teens was recorded in 1985, when about half the teens (49 percent) reported their use.

Most importantly, this high level of use is reported by teens of all ages, including those of driving age. In past years, older teens often showed less-than-average use of seat belts.

Undoubtedly, the steady increase in the number of states mandating use of the safety devices has played a part in the increased use, but education and training may also be important influences in encouraging teens to believe that using seat belts is the smart thing to do. Highest incidence of seat belt use is found among teens come from households where both parents went to college (90 percent). Use is still high among those from families where only one parent attended college (87 percent), but drops sharply in households where neither parent attended (69 percent). Teens, who themselves are doing above-average work in school are more likely than those doing average or below work, to report use, by a margin of 86 percent to 70 percent.

Highest use is in the suburbs where 87 percent of teens wear seat belts. Lowest use is found in large cities where just 74 percent of teens buckled up, despite the reputation of cities for having the highest incidence of accidents, especially among teen drivers.

12.4 Trend in Seat Belt Use

	Teens	Adults
1992	79%	na
1988	63	65
1985	49	40
1982	20	17
1977	23	22

12.5 Seat Belt Use

Thinking about the last time you got into a car, did you use a seat belt, or not?

	September – October 1992	
	Yes	No
National	**79%**	**21%**
Male	77	23
Female	81	19
Ages 13 – 15	80	20
Ages 16 – 17	79	21
White	80	20
Non-white	75	25
White-collar background	84	16
Blue-collar background	72	28
Both parents attended college	90	10
One parent attended college	87	13
Neither parent attended college	69	31
Above-average students	86	14
Average and below	70	30
East	74	26
Midwest	79	21
South	83	17
West	77	23
Large city	74	26
Suburb	87	13
Small town	78	22
Rural	81	19
Republican	82	18
Democrat	82	18
Independent	77	23
Protestant	77	23
Catholic	83	17
Church attender	85	15
Non-attender	74	26

GO 12869; Q. 52

SPORTS, RECREATION, ENTERTAINMENT

Favorite Evening Pastimes

Teens increasingly say their favorite way to spend an evening is to visit with one another. Other favorite evening pastimes include playing sports and exercising, while more sedentary activities such as watching television or going to the movies are declining in popularity.

Young women are more likely than young men to seek an evening with friends, by a margin of 40 percent to 28 percent. Interest in visiting with friends increases as teens grow older, and so does the desire to go out dating, partying, or dancing.

The number of teens who are content to stay at home to watch television hit an all-time high in 1988, when 22 percent of teens named it as their favorite. Today, just 14 percent still watch TV in favor of other activities. Most likely to be found in front of the TV set are teens ages 13 to 15 (18 percent) and young men (16 percent). An additional 2 percent, mostly young males, like to play video games in the evening.

Movie going apparently runs in cycles as a favorite evening pastime. Currently, 9 percent of teens name it as their first choice—the same proportion as in 1980. In 1985, however, trips to the movie theater peaked with 16 percent of teens naming it as their top form of evening entertainment.

One teen in eight (12 percent) now says playing sports or exercising is the favorite way to spend an evening. Athletic activities are particularly favored by young men (20 percent). By comparison only 3 percent of young women say that athletics or exercising is their favorite after hours pastime.

Listening to music is a favorite activity of 3 percent of teens, and another 3 percent say they prefer a quiet evening of reading or studying. Reading pursuits by teens as a favorite pastime are less than half of what they had been in previous years (7 percent).

In a few teen households if parents are wondering why they never seem to get telephone calls at night, it is because 2 percent of teens list talking on the telephone as their favorite way to while away the night. Almost all the talking apparently is done by young women (5 percent). Young women are also the most likely to say that a shopping trip (3 percent) is a good way to spend an evening.

Two percent of the teens, mostly those who are younger, say they are content to stay at home with their families in the evening. The number of teens making this choice has been declining over the years.

Additional favorite evening pastimes each named by 1 percent of teens or fewer include going to the mall, renting videotaped movies, playing a musical instrument, going to the park, and going to concerts.

13.1 Trends in Evening Entertainment

	1992	1988	1985	1980
Visiting with friends	34%	28%	26%	24%
Watching TV	14	22	20	15
Playing sports or exercising	12	3	5	8
Going to movies	9	12	16	9
Dating, partying, dancing	5	10	17	19
Reading, studying	3	7	7	7
Listening to music	3	2	4	5
At home with family	2	6	5	7
Playing games	2	2	4	4
Talking on the phone	2	*	*	*
Shopping	2	*	*	*

*Less than one half of 1 percent

13.2 Favorite Evening Pastimes

What is your favorite way of spending an evening?

	September – October 1992				
	Visiting friends	Watch TV	Sports exercise	Movie going	Dating, partying
National	**34%**	**14%**	**12%**	**9%**	**5%**
Male	28	16	20	8	6
Female	40	12	3	10	4
Ages 13 – 15	31	18	12	9	2
Ages 16 – 17	39	8	12	9	9
White	36	14	11	9	5
Non-white	27	14	16	9	6
White-collar background	42	11	11	11	5
Blue-collar background	26	20	13	7	4
Above-average students	36	11	12	10	6
Average and below	31	18	12	7	4
East	38	8	8	9	10
Midwest	32	18	12	12	4
South	28	14	16	8	4
West	44	14	9	7	4
Large city	32	17	7	10	8
Suburb	36	9	14	9	8
Small town	35	17	14	9	2
Rural	34	12	12	8	5
Republican	40	11	12	7	6
Democrat	30	15	11	13	6
Independent	32	14	13	9	4
Protestant	37	15	13	7	4
Catholic	32	14	13	11	6
Church attender	33	12	14	11	5
Non-attender	36	15	10	7	5

GO 12869; Q. 1

Where Teens Meet

Young women are more likely than young men to be frequent users of the telephone as a means of "meeting" friends or making plans to see them outside the home. The margin for young women is 83 percent compared with young men (60 percent).

On a combined basis, seven teens in 10 (71 percent) "meet" with their friends on the telephone very often and an additional 18 percent use the phone as a meeting device occasionally.

Schools also function as important teen gathering places, with half of the teens (49 percent) saying they meet their friends often there after school hours and 28 percent reporting they are an occasional place for getting together with friends.

Visiting friends at their homes is even more popular, with six teens in 10 (59 percent) citing them as frequent gathering places, and 27 percent disclosing they go there occasionally. Young women (63 percent) are more likely than young men (55 percent) to name friends' homes as gathering places.

Parties, at home or in school, are next in popularity, with 42 percent of the teens reporting they see their friends at social functions.

Parks and playing fields are used by one teen in four (27 percent) who gather with friends there very often. Young men (31 percent) are slightly more likely than young women (23 percent) to make use of these recreational facilities.

Only one teen in 10 (10 percent) uses a community center, youth center or a "Y" to encounter friends very often. An additional 15 percent say they gather in those places occasionally. However, findings that most teens seldom (19 percent) or never (54 percent) use these centers as meeting places may indicate that they are not available in many communities.

Shopping malls and fast food restaurants also function as meeting places. One teenager in four (24 percent) frequently meets friends at a mall, and 36 percent use them as meeting places occasionally. Young women (28 percent) meet friends at a mall very often compared with young men (20 percent). Fast food places have become popular gathering places for 17 percent of the teens.

13.3 Ways To Meet

For each of the following places [listed below] please tell me how often you meet your friends there — very often, occasionally, seldom or never.

| | March – April 1990 | | |
	National	Male	Female
Meet very often by or at . . .			
Telephone	71%	60%	83%
At friends' homes	59	55	63
School after hours	49	51	47
Parties	42	43	41
While cruising or driving around	30	28	31
Park or playing field	27	31	23
Shopping Malls	24	20	28
On the street or on the corner	17	19	15
Fast food place	17	16	19
Community center, youth center, or "Y"	10	10	11

Cars and Public Transportation

Driving an automobile or "cruising" has seen a revival in popularity, and some municipalities have even found it necessary to pass "anti-cruising" laws in order to diminish the number of teen-age traffic jams on Main Street on Saturday night.

Three teens in 10 (30 percent) report they often encounter their friends while cruising. The proportion who get together this way frequently increases to four in 10 (41 percent) among those who are 16 years of age or older.

Eight teens in 10 who are 16 or 17 years of age have a driver's license or learner's permit. Teen drivers are more likely to be encountered in the suburbs or rural areas than in cities or towns.

Over three teens in four say it is important for students at their school to have their own cars, with 39 percent saying it is very important and 38 percent reporting it is somewhat important.

Teen use of all forms of public transportation has risen over the past several years.

Three teens in four (73 percent) say they took a bus during the preceding year. Teen bus use is uniformly high throughout the country, suggesting that many of these trips probably have been on school buses.

Airplane travel is now the second most frequently used form of public transportation for teens. Three teens in 10 (31 percent) took at least one flight during the previous year. Many of these trips may have been out of the country since 15 percent of teens also report having a passport.

Subway or metros are now used by about one teen in five (22 percent). Perhaps because of their reputation for being unsafe in some areas, young women (16 percent) are far less likely than young men (28 percent) to use the underground rapid transit systems. By comparison, about only one teen in eight (12 percent) took a longer trip on the rails on a train ride.

Boat transportation in the form of passenger ships or ferry boats is used by one teen in five (19 percent).

Travel patterns change somewhat as teens grow older. Younger teens, ages 13 to 15, are more likely than those 16 and older to have taken a bus in the past year, by a margin of 78 percent to 67 percent. The younger teens also make greater use of subways (24 percent to 19 percent) and boat transportation (21 percent to 16 percent). As teens grow older they of course have greater access to cars for transportation and become less dependent upon public transportation. Their taste for car travel also means, however, that older teens (24 percent) are nearly twice as likely as those who are younger (14 percent) to have taken a taxi during the past year.

In general, teens living in large cities and the surrounding suburbs are more likely than their cousins from small towns and rural areas to use all forms of public transportation. Indeed, the urban-oriented teens are about twice as likely to use planes, subways, taxis, and trains.

13.4 Transportation Trends

	1992	1986
Bus	73%	65%
Plane	31	23
Subway or metro	22	17
Taxi	19	16
Boat	19	11
Train	12	9

13.5 Importance of Having a Car at School

How important is it for students at your school to have their own cars?

	September – October 1992			
	Very Important	Somewhat important	Of little importance	Of no importance
National	**39%**	**38%**	**13%**	**9%**
Male	41	38	11	8
Female	37	39	15	9
Ages 13 – 15	32	38	16	14
Ages 16 – 17	49	38	9	2
White	41	39	12	8
Non-white	32	36	20	13
White-collar background	42	39	10	8
Blue-collar background	37	38	15	10
Above-average students	37	37	17	9
Average and below	41	41	8	9
East	39	38	11	9
Midwest	43	37	16	4
South	38	38	10	14
West	37	40	17	6
Large city	38	42	12	8
Suburb	40	34	10	16
Small town	38	41	13	8
Rural	42	36	16	6
Republican	44	35	11	9
Democrat	44	34	13	8
Independent	38	43	13	6
Protestant	34	42	14	10
Catholic	46	32	14	8
Church attender	39	38	13	10
Non-attender	38	40	14	8

Note: Table does not include 1 percent of teens who are no longer attending school.

GO 12869; Q. 51

13.6 Public Transportation

Which, if any, of these forms of transportation have you used in the past 12 months — bus, airplane, subway or metro, taxi, passenger ship or ferry boat, train?

	September — October 1992					
	Bus	**Plane**	**Metro**	**Taxi**	**Boat**	**Train**
National	**73%**	**31%**	**22%**	**19%**	**19%**	**12%**
Male	75	29	28	20	17	13
Female	72	33	16	17	22	12
Ages 13 – 15	78	31	24	14	21	13
Ages 16 – 17	67	32	19	24	16	12
White	72	34	20	18	21	11
Non-white	81	23	32	22	13	16
White-collar background	73	44	27	20	26	13
Blue-collar background	72	16	15	16	11	11
Above-average students	72	35	24	18	23	14
Average and below	76	25	20	18	13	10
East	82	34	31	26	19	28
Midwest	74	26	17	17	16	12
South	70	28	19	16	22	6
West	70	43	26	18	19	9
Large city	79	42	28	32	17	15
Suburb	71	46	34	30	31	18
Small town	72	27	17	12	16	8
Rural	72	21	14	13	16	10
Republican	64	33	15	17	16	12
Democrat	71	30	25	26	22	17
Independent	82	35	26	18	23	9
Protestant	72	26	19	18	18	11
Catholic	73	38	26	21	18	16
Church attender	70	38	22	18	22	12
Non-attender	77	24	22	19	16	12

GO 12869; Q. 50

13.7 Documents

Which, if any, of the following do you, yourself, now have — Library card? Driver's license or learner's permit? Passport?

	September – October 1992		
	Library card	Driver's license	Passport
National	**78%**	**41%**	**15%**
Male	76	40	14
Female	82	42	15
Ages 13 – 15	76	14	14
Ages 16 – 17	82	80	16
White	79	44	13
Non-white	76	30	21
Black	77	31	15
Hispanic	72	21	29
White-collar background	83	39	19
Blue-collar background	75	38	9
Above-average students	84	42	16
Average and below	72	39	12
East	81	39	24
Midwest	81	45	8
South	74	44	12
West	80	34	9
Large city	88	32	16
Suburb	86	48	22
Small town	74	39	14
Rural	76	48	9
Republican	78	43	18
Democrat	81	44	14
Independent	84	44	13
Protestant	78	40	9
Catholic	83	42	20
Church attender	79	42	17
Non-attender	79	40	12

GO 12869; Q. 8

Attendance

Professional sports headed the list of events attended by teens in 1992, with nearly half (44 percent) reporting they had gone to at least one game during the previous year. Young men are more likely than young women to attend pro sports events, by a margin of 51 percent to 36 percent. Pro sports reached a record level in 1986 when 49 percent attended a game.

Art museums or art centers were visited by three teens in 10 (31 percent) in 1992. In 1978, a record 37 percent of teens went through an art museum. Other types of museums (such as history and natural science) experienced their lowest teen turnout ever in 1992, with just one in four (26 percent) saying he had gone to one during the year. By comparison, 33 percent had visited a non-art museum in 1978.

Rock concerts drew 28 percent of teens in 1992. The teen draw has been diminishing steadily since 1978, when 42 percent of all teens went to at least one rock concert a year.

Cultural events over the years have drawn comparatively smaller but steady teen audiences. In 1992, attendance at a symphony orchestra concert was reported by 11 percent of teens, a ballet performance was seen by 7 percent, and 4 percent went to an opera.

Family background can have considerable impact upon attendance figures. Teens from white-collar households are more likely to have attended all the types of events tested on the survey than are those from blue-collar families.

Similarly, teens from families where the parents went to college, particularly those where both went, are far more likely than young people whose parents did not have a college education to attend events. Students who themselves report doing above-average work at school are far more likely than academic underachievers to attend all kinds of events more frequently.

Suburban teens, who more often come from white-collar families where parents attended college, usually then are also those most likely to be attending the various events. Residents of large cities may often not have as much affluence or as many advantages as their suburban cousins, but they do usually have much closer access to all kinds of events. As a consequence, metropolitan teens more often report attendance than do those living in small town and rural areas.

As teens grow older their attendance tastes change slightly. Teens who are 16 and older are more likely than their younger brothers and sisters to go to professional sports events (46 percent) and rock concerts (35 percent). Those who are ages 13 to 15, more often than average are found at non-art museums (28 percent), symphony orchestra concerts (13 percent), and even the opera (5 percent). Note, however, that the events and places that younger teens visit in greater numbers often are those included in class trips as part of their studies and cultural enrichment. Their attendance at the events should not be necessarily interpreted as a signal of a cultural reawakening among the younger generation. Older teens, who presumably have greater freedom of choice of where to go, more often are heading for the pro sports arena or the rock venue instead of the concert hall or the museum.

13.8 Attendance Trends

	1992	1988	1986	1984	1978
Pro sports event	44%	44%	49%	43%	43%
Art museum	31	34	30	30	37
Other museums	26	29	30	21	33
Rock concert	28	34	30	32	42
Symphony orchestra concert	11	15	16	12	16
Ballet	7	8	8	7	9
Opera	4	4	3	3	5

13.9 Event Attendance

Which of the following have you, yourself, gone to or attended in the past 12 months — a professional sports event, an art museum or art center, any other museum, a rock concert, a symphony orchestra concert, a ballet performance, an opera?

| | September – October 1992 | | | | | | |
	Pro sports	Art museum	Other museum	Rock concert	Symph. concert	Ballet	Opera
National	**44%**	**31%**	**26%**	**28%**	**11%**	**7%**	**4%**
Male	51	34	28	20	11	6	5
Female	36	28	23	26	11	8	4
Ages 13 – 15	42	32	24	27	16	9	5
Ages 16 – 17	46	30	23	35	7	6	3
White	46	31	27	29	12	6	4
Non-white	37	32	22	22	6	9	6
White-collar background	50	32	30	31	13	8	4
Blue-collar background	36	30	20	26	9	6	3
Both parents attended college	54	46	31	31	15	7	2
Only one attended college	48	38	28	30	12	7	2
Neither attended college	43	23	25	26	10	7	7
Above-average students	49	35	29	31	13	7	5
Average and below	26	23	21	23	9	6	3
East	47	30	32	38	10	8	4
Midwest	50	33	26	28	14	3	6
South	40	29	23	22	5	6	3
West	39	33	24	29	16	10	4
Large city	50	36	26	32	11	9	4
Suburb	60	39	32	26	16	8	6
Small town	41	25	21	28	9	5	3
Rural	35	33	26	30	8	8	4
Republican	43	30	20	30	13	6	6
Democrat	54	33	32	30	11	5	4
Independent	47	34	28	27	10	8	4
Protestant	38	31	27	23	9	6	2
Catholic	53	28	21	30	9	7	7
Church attender	50	35	24	28	11	8	4
Non-attender	36	28	28	27	11	6	5

GO 12869; Q. 2

Sports Participation

There was a sharp drop in team sports participation by teen-agers in 1991. Teens instead now appear to be placing greater emphasis on individual sports and exercise activities to keep themselves physically fit.

Overall, nearly all teens report sports or physical fitness participation during the 12-month period preceding the time of interview, but these activities can take many forms. Team sports such as basketball, touch or tackle football, and softball have skidded to all-time lows in teen participation.

Taking the place of team sports for many teens are individual sports and exercise programs and activities. While some may lament the decrease in team sports, health and physical education experts generally maintain it is far better for young people to develop skills and interest in individual sports and exercise activities that can be readily continued throughout their adult years.

13.10 Sports Participation

	Total	Male	Female
Basketball	56%	65%	47%
Swimming	50	46	54
Bicycling	47	47	47
Jogging	46	48	44
Touch football	45	61	29
Tackle football	43	68	17
Weight training	43	56	30
Regular fitness program	42	43	41
Bowling	41	42	40
Fishing	36	46	26
Tennis	34	34	34
Roller/rollerblade skating	31	27	36
Soccer	30	33	28
Softball	28	20	36
Aerobic dancing/jazzercise	26	6	46
Hunting	19	32	6
Water skiing	17	14	20
Snow skiing	16	17	15
Golf	16	24	9
Hockey	13	15	11
Skateboarding	12	20	4

GO 2150220; Q. 9

13.11 Sports Participation Trend

Which of these sports or activities have you, yourself participated in or played within the past 12 months?

	1991	1987	1985	1983	1979	1978
Bicycling	47%	78%	82%	78%	na	na
Basketball	56	76	78	75	68	68
Softball	28	71	69	77	74	64
Football (touch)	45	60	67	64	na	na
Jogging	46	55	62	55	na	na
Weight training	43	49	62	na	na	na
Rollerskating	31	55	59	68	57	52
Swimming	50	65	57	67	75	62
Bowling	41	48	55	50	59	59
Fishing	36	44	51	48	54	51
Tennis	34	46	36	52	54	47
Soccer	30	na	na	na	na	na
Aerobic dancing	26	28	34	na	na	na
Snow skiing	16	23	28	24	21	22
Hunting	19	21	26	22	23	27
Ice skating	na	21	25	26	29	34
Racquetball	na	14	20	na	20	14
Horseback riding	19	20	na	32	31	16
Golf	16	18	20	19	18	16
Sailing	na	8	12	na	na	na
Regular fitness program	42	na	na	na	na	na
Skateboarding	12	na	na	na	na	na

Spectator Sports

Teens name football as their favorite sport to watch. Basketball is second in popularity among teens and baseball is third. Baseball is equally popular with both sexes, but basketball is more often named by young women than young men as their favorite, by a margin of 25 percent to 18 percent. Non-white teens (47 percent) are nearly three times as likely as white teens (17 percent) to say they favor basketball viewing over all other sports.

When compared to the vote for previous years, basketball emerges as the fastest growing spectator sport.

13.12 Teens' Favorite Spectator Sports

	Total	Male	Female
Football	41%	49%	33%
Basketball	22	18	25
Baseball	13	12	13
Hockey	4	5	3
Tennis	3	1	5
Soccer	2	–	4
Volleyball	2	–	4
Wrestling	2	2	1
Swimming, diving	2	1	2
Miscellaneous	7	10	5
None	1	1	2

Note: Total adds to more than 100 percent, because some teens named more than one favorite sport.

13.13 Favorite Sport Trend

	1991	1987	1985	1977
Football	41%	40%	35%	40%
Baseball	13	14	13	17
Basketball	22	13	23	14

MEDIA

Media Used Yesterday

Nine in 10 teens (88 percent) in 1991 reported listening to radio on the day preceding the interview. The same proportion watched television. Young women were more likely than young men to listen to the radio, by a margin of 95 percent to 88 percent.

Two teens in three (88 percent) read a newspaper yesterday. This represented a significant increase over the level of readership in previous years.

Magazines were read or looked at by 58 percent of the teens.

Readership of both newspapers and magazines was higher among students who said they were doing above average work at school. Newspapers were read, by 72 percent of the above-average students, compared to just 64 percent of those who said their academic work was average or below average. Magazines were read by 59 percent of the above-average students, and by 54 percent of the academic underachievers.

Overall, only 11 percent of the teens said they looked at a comic book yesterday

14.1 Trend in Media Used Yesterday

	1991	1990	1989	1986	1984	1983
Radio	88%	90%	93%	91%	95%	93%
TV	88	76%	93	89	89	91
Cable TV	na	63	na	na	na	na
VCR	na	39	na	na	na	na
Newspaper	88	63	61	68	71	73
Magazine	58	71	57	54	58	54
Comic book	11	10	18	17	14	15

14.2 Electronic Media

Did you, yourself, do any of the following things yesterday — listen to the radio, watch television?

	Radio	TV
National	**88%**	**88%**
Male	87	90
Female	90	86
Ages 13 – 15	87	90
Ages 16 – 17	90	86
White	90	87
Non-white	81	94
White-collar background	88	86
Blue-collar background	90	91
Above-average students	90	88
Average and below	86	89
East	93	90
Midwest	90	87
South	86	91
West	83	85
Large city	86	94
Suburb	81	94
Small town, rural	89	87
Protestant	88	89
Catholic	89	90
Church attender	88	89
Non-attender	89	89

14.3 Watching TV

About how much time, if any, did you spend yesterday on each of these activities — watching TV?

| | September – October 1992 | | | |
	None	Less than 1 hour	1 – 2 hours	3 or more hours
National	**12%**	**22%**	**47%**	**17%**
Male	9	21	50	16
Female	15	23	44	15
Ages 13 – 15	11	19	50	18
Ages 16 – 17	14	26	44	17
White	12	24	47	17
Non-white	12	15	50	21
White-collar background	13	24	51	12
Blue-collar background	13	20	42	23
Both parents attended college	10	23	52	14
Only one attended college	11	21	51	16
Neither attended college	14	24	43	17
Above-average students	15	22	50	11
Average and below	8	21	45	18
East	10	26	45	17
Midwest	14	20	52	12
South	10	20	50	19
West	14	25	39	21
Large city	12	24	39	24
Suburb	11	22	48	19
Small town	10	20	48	20
Rural	19	24	49	7
Republican	11	19	47	21
Democrat	11	22	45	20
Independent	14	25	45	14
Protestant	11	17	52	19
Catholic	13	27	46	13
Church attender	13	23	44	18
Non-attender	11	22	51	15

GO 12869; Q. 7b

Favorite TV Programming

Almost two teens in three (63 percent) in 1990 named comedy as the type of television fare they like to watch most. Comedy is favored in particular by young women (66 percent) and by teens living in the South (68 percent) and West (69 percent).

Next in popularity among teen audiences are regular dramatic series, which were named by 1 teen in 10 (11 percent). Televised dramatic presentations achieved their highest audience ratings in the East where they were chosen by 16 percent of the teen-agers. TV miniseries or special dramatic presentations, however, were the programming choice of only 2 percent.

Motion pictures are the favorite TV fare of 5 percent of the teens. Films achieve their highest rating in the West where they were the choice of 8 percent of the teens.

Sports were chosen by 4 percent of the teens overall, but most often were named by young men rather than young women, by a margin of 7 percent to 1 percent. Midwestern teens (9 percent) are most likely to watch a sports event on television.

Music or rock videos were named by only 4 percent of the teens. Music or rock videos enjoy their greatest popularity in the West (7 percent), and least often are the programming choice of teens living in the East and Midwest (2 percent).

Soap operas were voted the top choice of only 2 percent.

News programs were chosen as their favorite by a mere 2 percent of the teenagers overall, but preference for this type of presentation increased to 7 percent among teens 16 years of age or older.

14.4 Favorite TV Programs

What is your favorite type of TV program?

	March – April 1990		
	National	**Male**	**Female**
Comedy	63%	60%	66%
Drama	11	11	12
Movies	5	6	4
Sports	4	7	1
Music or rock videos	4	3	5
Cartoons	3	4	2
Miniseries, specials	2	2	3
Soap operas	2	–	4
News	2	2	1
Other	4	3	5
No opinion	4	5	4

Note: Columns add to more than 100% because some teens named more than one type of program.

Books

Book reading is reported by 85 percent of teens. This may have include required reading, with 76 percent saying they had read or looked at a school text book the previous day. But a majority of the teenagers (56 percent) also said that they read a book other than those required in school on the day preceding the interview.

Above-average students (79 percent) are only slightly more likely than those doing average or below-average work in school (73 percent) to say they recently used their school books for study. Reading for pleasure, however, is more likely to be found among the academically proficient (62 percent) than among underachievers (49 percent).

When asked to name their favorite types of books, teenagers generally cite fictional categories far more often than non-fiction.

Mystery, spy or suspense novels are the favorites of one teen in four (25 percent).

Second in popularity are action, adventure, and war stories. Mystery books more often are chosen as favorites by young women (31 percent) than by young men (20 percent). Young men, by a margin of 25 percent to 12 percent, more often name fiction with action, adventure or war themes as their favorites.

Mysteries and spy novels appeal somewhat more to above-average students (29 percent) than to average or below-average students (23 percent). Books with action and adventure themes exert a greater pull among the average and below-average students (24 percent) than among those getting higher grades (15 percent).

Romance novels are far more often selected by young women (20 percent) than by young men (3 percent). Science fiction once was almost exclusively the domain of male readers, and although young men still are leading (15 percent), the ranks of female readers (7 percent) interested in alternative futures is growing.

A broad range of current popular fiction or best sellers are named as favorites by 7 percent of the teens but only 2 percent say they prefer the classics.

Books featuring horror, the occult or the supernatural are the choice of 4 percent of the teens. Rounding out the fictional favorites are drama (1 percent) and novels about teen-agers (1 percent).

Biographies and autobiographies head the list of non-fiction themes named as favorites, but garner the votes of only one teen in 20 (5 percent).

Books about sports are favored by 8 percent of the young men, but fail to find any female interest. Humor finds a wider audience and is named by 5 percent of the young men 3 percent of the young women. History books are favored by a mere 1 percent of the teens.

14.5 Favorite Kinds of Books

	National	Male	Female
Mystery, spy, suspense	25%	20%	31%
Action, adventure, war	19	25	12
Romance	11	3	20
Science fiction	11	15	7
Popular fiction, best sellers	7	6	9
Horror, occult, supernatural	4	5	4
Classics	2	2	3
Drama	1	1	1
Teen fiction	1	–	2
Biography	5	3	6
Sports	4	8	–
Comics, humor	4	5	3
History	1	1	2
Other non-fiction	4	5	3

14.6 Time Spent Reading Books Yesterday

About how much time, if any, did you spend yesterday at each of these activities — reading for fun or pleasure?

	September – October 1992			
	None	Less than 1 hour	1 – 2 hours	3 or more hours
National	**43%**	**35%**	**20%**	**2%**
Male	42	37	19	2
Female	43	34	22	2
Ages 13 – 15	40	39	19	2
Ages 16 – 17	45	31	22	2
White	45	35	18	2
Non-white	31	38	28	3
White-collar background	39	40	18	2
Blue-collar background	49	31	19	1
Both parents attended college	35	42	21	2
Only one attended college	38	39	21	2
Neither attended college	46	32	19	2
Above-average students	36	40	22	2
Average and below	51	29	17	2
East	30	37	30	2
Midwest	43	39	18	–
South	48	30	19	2
West	43	38	17	2
Large city	27	48	22	3
Suburb	41	40	16	3
Small town	51	30	18	1
Rural	38	32	27	2
Republican	44	33	21	2
Democrat	39	38	21	2
Independent	40	36	21	3
Protestant	43	36	18	3
Catholic	42	36	21	1
Church attender	38	35	24	2
Non-attender	47	36	16	1

GO 12869; Q. 7a

14.7 Print Media Readership

Did you, yourself, do any of the following this yesterday — read or look at a newspaper, read or look at a magazine, read or look at a comic book?

	June – July 1991		
	Newspapers	**Magazines**	**Comic books**
National	**68%**	**58%**	**11%**
Male	68	58	12
Female	69	57	9
Ages 13 – 15	64	62	14
Ages 16 – 17	75	52	6
Above-average students	72	59	9
Average or below	64	55	13
White-collar family background	71	60	11
Blue-collar family background	70	58	10
East	74	56	11
Midwest	74	73	11
South	66	52	11
West	60	48	9
Large city	72	52	20
Suburb	68	56	10
Small town, rural	68	59	9
Protestant	70	54	8
Catholic	67	60	14
Church attender	66	61	13
Non-attender	71	54	9

14.8 Daily Newspaper Readership

About how often would you say you read or look at anything in a daily newspaper — daily or almost daily, one or two times a week, one or two times a month, a few times a year, almost never or never?

	June – July 1991			
	About daily	**1 – 2 weekly**	**1 – 2 monthly**	**Seldom or never**
National	**52%**	**36%**	**6%**	**5%**
Male	55	34	6	5
Female	48	39	6	6
Ages 13 – 15	48	38	6	6
Ages 16 – 17	56	33	5	5
White	54	35	6	4
Non-white	45	38	4	10
White-collar background	56	33	3	6
Blue-collar background	49	40	9	2
Above-average students	54	34	5	5
Average and below	48	39	7	6
East	52	39	4	4
Midwest	60	32	3	5
South	47	38	8	6
West	48	36	7	7
Large city	54	30	6	9
Suburb	50	43	2	5
Small town, rural	51	37	6	5
Protestant	50	41	5	4
Catholic	56	30	5	7
Church attender	57	31	5	5
Non-attender	47	41	7	5

Note: 1 percent of teens did not report on their frequency of reading.

GO 224007; Q. 2

Which of these, if any, have your read or looked at in a daily newspaper in the past seven days — front page headlines, movie reviews, comics, sports, TV listings, help wanted ads?

	June – July 1991					
	Head-lines	Movie reviews	Comics	Sports	TV listings	Want ads
National	**71%**	**60%**	**55%**	**54%**	**53%**	**43%**
Male	68	60	55	71	53	41
Female	73	61	56	37	53	44
Ages 13 – 15	58	61	61	53	56	39
Ages 16 – 17	75	59	47	56	50	48
White	73	60	58	56	53	43
Non-white	63	59	47	50	56	42
White-collar background	74	64	59	58	57	38
Blue-collar background	72	58	54	54	52	49
Above-average students	73	60	60	56	55	38
Average and below	69	61	49	52	51	48
East	70	56	62	55	56	46
Midwest	83	63	57	50	54	51
South	66	62	54	55	50	36
West	65	59	48	57	54	37
Large city	72	71	48	49	52	26
Suburb	74	70	49	55	51	46
Small town, rural	70	58	57	55	53	45
Protestant	73	60	54	55	57	43
Catholic	70	62	59	61	52	45
Church attender	74	66	57	55	58	38
Non-attender	69	55	61	54	49	47

Q. 224007; Q. 3

14.9b Daily Newspaper Sections Read Last Week

. . . Horoscopes, ads from stores, national or international news, columnists such as "Dear Abby," Editorials?

	June – July 1991				
	Horo-scopes	Store ads	News	Column-ists	Editorials
National	**42%**	**40%**	**40%**	**24%**	**22%**
Male	26	33	38	12	20
Female	58	48	42	36	24
Ages 13 – 15	56	46	36	35	21
Ages 16 – 17	44	45	47	25	25
White	42	41	40	25	23
Non-white	41	38	37	18	19
White-collar background	42	41	40	25	23
Blue-collar background	46	44	41	23	27
Above-average students	42	39	44	26	26
Average and below	43	43	34	20	17
East	51	41	37	29	27
Midwest	45	48	44	27	22
South	41	43	37	22	22
West	31	29	41	17	19
Large city	46	43	29	25	17
Suburb	29	58	48	21	21
Small town, rural	43	39	41	24	23
Rural					
Protestant	42	40	42	22	24
Catholic	45	42	37	28	19
Church attender	36	40	41	24	25
Non-attender	48	42	39	24	20

GO 224007; Q. 3

Cats and Dogs Reign in the Comics!
Comics Going to the Dogs (and Cats)!

If a Sunday comic strip doesn't feature a cat or dog, it probably had better at least show one in a supporting role to win teen readers.

The current line-up of teen favorites is headed by "Garfield," a bombastic, overweight cat whose chief pleasure in life is driving his companion, a droopy-eared hound, Odie, to distraction.

While Garfield is a garrulous tabby cat, Hobbes from "Calvin and Hobbes" is a gentle philosophical stuffed tiger who comes alive when he is alone with Calvin. The strip which has become a favorite on the nation's college campuses is now second in popularity among teens.

"Peanuts" is in third place and undoubtedly owes much of its popularity to Snoopy, a beagle of many talents, who often steals the show from Charlie Brown, Lucy, Linus and friends. Snoopy even has his own supporting cast, consisting of Woodstock and a flock of birds of undetermined species.

Gary Larson's "The Far Side" is in fourth place and often features a variety of animals engaged in off-beat and outrageous behavior.

"Blondie," in fifth place, made headlines in the news sections of the nation's newspapers when she declared her independence by starting her own catering business. Undoubtedly, it is comforting for her to know that while she is away on business, her home is being guarded by the family dog, Daisy. Now, if she could just teach Daisy to guard the refrigerator against raids by Dogwood.

The "Family Circus" won sixth place in the hearts of teens. Of course, no comic family would be complete without a dog who regularly gets into mischief but in the end wins the affection of parent and child alike.

The War in the Gulf may be over, and the "Evil Empire" no longer a threat, but Beetle Bailey and the soldiers at Camp Swampy still carry on the military life. "Bailey" in seventh place often features Otto, Sarge's beer-guzzling bulldog who appears in military uniform.

Favorite Comics

1. **Garfield**
2. **Calvin and Hobbes**
3. **Peanuts**
4. **Far Side**
5. **Blondie**
6. **Family Circus**
7. **Beetle Bailey**
8. **Cathy**
9. **Marvin**
10. **For Better or For Worse**

GARFIELD: © 1978 United Feature Syndicate, Inc.

When eighth-place "Cathy" comes home exhausted from another hard day at the office, all too often she is greeted by her lovable puppy who: has had an "accident," has torn up the place or somehow manages to scare off a boyfriend.

Rounding out the top-10 list are "Marvin," who of course has a dog, and "For Better or Worse."

Not in the overall top-10 list, but among the 10 favorite comics of young men are "B.C." and "Mother Goose and Grimm." Grimm is yet another comic strip dog.

Young women include on their list "Heathcliff," another fat tabby cat, whose specialty is tossing garbage cans and terrorizing the neighborhood fish store in his never-ending quest for seafood. "Funky Winkerbean" also appears on the list of favorites of young women.

14.10 Favorite Comics

Do you regularly read a Sunday newspaper?
Do you regularly read or look at any of the color comics on Sunday?
What is your favorite comic? What are your other favorite comics?

All Teens

1992	1988	1984	1980
1. Garfield	1. Garfield	1. Garfield	1. Garfield
2. Calvin & Hobbes	2. Peanuts	2. Peanuts	2. Peanuts
3. Peanuts	3. Blondie	3. Blondie	3. Blondie
4. The Far Side	4. Calvin & Hobbes	4. Beetle Bailey	4. Family Circus
5. Blondie	5. Family Circus	5. Family Circus	5. Ziggy
6. Family Circus	6. The Far Side	6. Bloom County	6. Beetle Bailey
7. Beetle Bailey	7. Bloom County	7. Marvin	7. Hagar
8. Cathy	8. Beetle Bailey	8. Doonesbury	8. Nancy
9. Marvin	9. Heathcliff	9. Ziggy	9. Spider-Man
10. For Better or for worse	10. Dennis the Menace	10. Nancy	10. Dennis the Menace

Male

1992	1988	1984	1980
1. Garfield	1. Garfield	1. Garfield	1. Garfield
2. The Far Side	2. Peanuts	2. Peanuts	2. Peanuts
3. Calvin & Hobbes	3. Bloom County	3. Beetle Bailey	3. Blondie
4. Peanuts	4. Calvin & Hobbes	4. Blondie	4. Beetle Bailey
5. Beetle Bailey	5. The Far Side	5. Bloom County	5. Spider-Man
6. Marvin	6. Beetle Bailey	6. Doonesbury	6. Hagar
7. Blondie	7. Family Circus	7. Family Circus	7. Family Circus
8. Family Circus	8. Blondie	8. Marvin	8. B.C.
9. B.C.	9. Heathcliff	9. Spider-Man	9. Ziggy
10. Better or Worse	10. Dennis, Doonesbury	10. Ziggy	10. Heathcliff

Female

1992	1988	1984	1980
1. Garfield	1. Garfield	1. Garfield	1. Garfield
2. Peanuts	2. Peanuts	2. Peanuts	2. Peanuts
3. Calvin & Hobbes	3. Blondie	3. Blondie	3. Blondie
4. Cathy	4. Family Circus	4. Family Circus	4. Family Circus
5. Blondie	5. Calvin & Hobbes	5. Beetle Bailey	5. Ziggy
6. Family Circus	6. The Far Side	6. Nancy	6. Nancy
7. Better or Worse	7. Cathy	7. Bloom County	7. Dennis
8. The Far Side	8. Marvin	8. Marvin	8. Doonesbury
9. Marvin	9. Bloom County	9. Cathy	9. Beetle Bailey
10. Heathcliff, Funky Winkerbean	10. Better or Worse	10. Ziggy	10. Born Loser

14.11 Sunday Newspaper and Comic Readership

Do your regularly read or look at a Sunday newspaper?
Do you regularly read or look at any of the color comics on Sunday or on weekends?

	December 1991	
	Read Sunday newspapers	Read color comics
National	**70%**	**51%**
Male	71	54
Female	68	48
Ages 13 – 15	69	54
Ages 16 – 17	70	46
White	70	52
Non-white	69	70
White-collar background	71	50
Blue-collar background	67	49
Above-average students	71	53
Average and below	67	47
East	73	56
Midwest	75	50
South	67	48
West	70	51
Protestant	71	53
Catholic	72	48
Church attender	68	52
Non-attender	71	49

GO 21504500; Q. 21–22

Newspaper Needs

Teens are certainly interested in reading about the affairs of the adult world, but many would like to see their daily newspaper present more information on what their fellow teens are thinking. They also would like more coverage of the local high school sports scene and to be able to read music and movie reviews by people of their own age.

14.12 What Teens Would Like To See in Newspapers

I am going to read you a list of stories that a daily newspaper might carry. For each, please tell me if you would be very interested in reading that type of store in a daily newspaper, somewhat interested, not too interested, or not at all interested.

	June – July 1991		
	Very interested	Somewhat interested	Little or no interest
Results of local student polls	52%	33%	14%
Local high school sports results	48	29	22
News about local schools	46	38	15
Rock recording and video reviews by teens	43	30	26
Results of national teen opinion polls	42	40	18
Movie reviews by teens	40	40	19
Reviews of local school plays and musical performances	15	33	51

Note: 1 percent of teens did not express their interests.

GO 224007; Q. 4

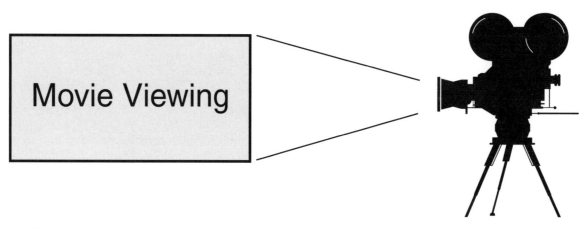

Movie Viewing

Movie moguls in the past used to count the number of teens lined up at the box office to measure the success or failure of their new films. Today, however, they have to peer into living and recreation rooms and count "couch potatoes" to keep pace with teen movie viewing on television. Most teens still go out to the movies, but they watch far more films at home.

The teens now present a mixed picture for the film industry. The striking finding for attendance in 1991 was that nearly all teens (95 percent) went out to the movies at least once during the year. That reverses a long-term downward trend in teen movie attendance that hit its lowest point in 1989, when only 64 percent had gone to the movies during the previous year. Unfortunately for the film industry, while more teens may be going out to the movies, they are going less often. The nation's ticket sellers may be seeing more different teen faces, but they are selling fewer tickets to them.

Today's teens of course do not have to rely upon the local movie house to see the latest films, but can choose instead to rent a film from their local videotape outlet, or switch to one of the movie channels if they have cable television at home, or wait until the movie is finally released on regular broadcast TV.

14.13 Movie Media Trend

Percent of teens using each medium to view movies	VCR	Theater	Broadcast television	Cable TV
1991	97%	95%	93%	82%
1989	94	64	91	76
1988	93	74	94	76
1987	91	84	88	70
1986	87	91	90	67
1985	75	92	88	69
Average annual number seen:				
1991	26	9	26	28
1989	28	10	27	30
1988	34	12	31	32
1987	25	27	27	30
1986	24	11	28	26
1985	20	15	28	38

14.14 How Movies Are Seen

About how many times, if any, did you, yourself, go out to the movies within the last 12 months?
About how many times, if any, in the past 12 months have you seen movies in each of the following ways — On cable television? On regular television? On a videocassette recorder (VCR)?

	December 1991			
	VCR	Theater	Broadcast television	Cable TV
National	**97%**	**95%**	**93%**	**82%**
Male	98	93	91	81
Female	97	96	94	83
Ages 13 – 15	97	95	92	83
Ages 16 – 17	98	94	94	83
White	98	95	92	81
Non-white	96	95	94	93
White-collar background	97	97	93	85
Blue-collar background	99	93	96	78
Above-average students	99	97	94	81
Average or below	94	91	91	84
East	99	91	87	69
Midwest	98	95	97	88
South	96	96	94	82
West	100	90	86	74
Protestant	99	95	96	79
Catholic	98	94	93	80
Church attender	97	96	97	82
Non-attender	97	94	88	83

GO 21504500; Q. 5–6

247

14.15 Videotape Renter Profile

We are trying to find out what teens like yourself are currently doing in several areas. Please tell me if you personally have or have not done each of the following activities in the past 30 days. In the past 30 days, have you rented a video?

	June – July 1992	
	Yes	No
National	**70%**	**30%**
Male	78	22
Female	70	30
Ages 12 – 13	68	32
Ages 14 – 15	73	27
Ages 16 – 17	69	31
White	74	26
Non-white	53	47
Black	46	54
Hispanic	72	28
White-collar background	71	29
Blue-collar background	65	35
Above-average students	74	26
Average and below	65	35
East	64	36
Midwest	71	29
South	72	28
West	71	29
Large city	68	32
Suburb	74	26
Small town	68	32
Rural	73	27
Protestant	66	34
Catholic	76	24
Church attender	71	29
Non-attender	69	31

GO 21505702; Q. S4

248

Computers

Two teens in three in 1992 were taking computer courses at school (30 percent) or had taken them in the past (38 percent). Also that year, four teens in 10 (41 percent) reported there is a computer at home. Almost all who have one at home are given access to it by their parents.

Among teens who plan to attend college, three in four (74 percent) in 1988 said they expect to take one or more computer courses. Interest in studying computers at college peaked at 81 percent in 1984; it declined in ensuing years, and by 1987 had fallen to 68 percent of college-bound teens.

Similarly, 44 percent of teens said there is at least some likelihood they will major in a field such as computer science, computer programming or computer engineering. Of college-bound teens, 15 percent say it is very likely they will major in computer studies, while 29 percent say it is fairly likely. Disagreeing are 55 percent, who say it is not at all likely they will major in computer studies. The highest level of interest in a computer major was recorded in 1984 (45 percent).

A majority (54 percent) of younger teens, 13 to 15, are contemplating a computer-related major in college, but such intentions drop sharply to 31 percent among those 16 or older, who are nearing their entrance into college.

There has recently been much discussion among educators and computer experts about an emerging "gender gap" in computer use, but the survey evidence suggests the gap may be a narrow one for teens. Young men (68 percent) and young women (68 percent) are equally as likely to have studied computers before entering college. They also have equal access to them at home, but young men are more likely to have used it there than are young women.

The intention of young men to study computers in college is only slightly greater than that of young women, by a margin of 76 percent to 72 percent. But a somewhat wider gap appears among those contemplating a computer major in college, with young men (50 percent) showing greater interest than young women (41 percent).

To some teens, a computer career may promise upward mobility, as teens from blue-collar households (49 percent) show more interest than is true of white-collar teens (39 percent) in a computer major.

14.16 Computer Studies Trend

	1992	1988	1987	1986	1985	1984	1983	1981
Studied computers in high school	68%	58	55%	55%	51%	40%	29%	21%
Plan to take computer courses in college	na	64	68	71	78	81	69	55
Likely to major in computer studies	na	44	32	37	43	45	43	37

14.17 Computer Courses at School

Have you ever taken, or are you now taking, a computer course at school?

	September – October 1992		
	Now taking	Taken in past	Never taken
National	**30%**	**38%**	**32%**
Male	29	39	32
Female	30	38	32
Ages 13 – 15	27	36	37
Ages 16 – 17	33	42	25
White	29	40	31
Non-white	34	30	36
White-collar background	30	42	28
Blue-collar background	34	33	33
Above-average students	32	42	26
Average and below	34	34	32
East	37	38	25
Midwest	30	40	30
South	24	35	41
West	32	41	27
Large city	30	34	36
Suburb	31	44	25
Small town	34	33	33
Rural	25	43	32
Republican	28	48	24
Democrat	37	34	29
Independent	31	34	35
Protestant	27	39	34
Catholic	33	38	29
Church attender	28	38	34
Non-attender	32	38	30

GO 12869; Q. 4

14.18 Computer Use at Home

Do you or does anyone else in your household now have a computer at home?
About how much time, if any, did you spend yesterday at each of these activities — using a computer at home?

| | September – October 1992 | | | |
	Computer at home	Used it yesterday	Used less than 1 hr.	Used 1 hr. or more
National	**41%**	**34%**	**18%**	**16%**
Male	40	47	22	25
Female	41	21	14	7
Ages 13 – 15	40	33	20	13
Ages 16 – 17	41	35	16	19
White	44	32	19	13
Non-white	28	43	13	30
White-collar background	49	40	23	17
Blue-collar background	33	20	8	12
Above-average students	49	38	21	17
Average and below	29	26	13	13
East	48	31	13	18
Midwest	35	34	20	14
South	36	33	21	12
West	49	37	18	19
Large city	33	39	26	13
Suburb	52	45	19	26
Small town	35	32	18	14
Rural	48	24	18	6
Republican	47	29	18	11
Democrat	46	35	19	16
Independent	37	28	15	13
Protestant	39	32	17	15
Catholic	38	37	24	13
Church attender	39	35	17	18
Non-attender	42	33	19	14

GO 12869; Q. 5, 7b

Calculators and Videogames

Nearly half of the teens interviewed in a 1990 survey (44 percent) reported using a hand-held calculator on the day preceding the interview. Above-average students are far more likely than average students or academic underachievers to make use of calculators for mathematics, by a margin of 52 percent to 35 percent. Calculators also are more often used in white-collar households (51 percent) than by members of blue-collar families (37 percent).

Young women (48 percent) somewhat more often than young men (41 percent) report use of calculators. The handheld devices also are more likely to be employed by teens who are age 16 or older (50 percent) than by those who are 13 to 15 years old (40 percent).

The reverse is true of home video games, with the highest incidence of daily use being found among younger male teens (51 percent). Overall, young men of all ages are more likely than young women to play video games, by a margin of 43 percent to 27 percent; and young teens (41 percent) more often play them than do older teen-agers (27 percent).

Those who are doing average or below-average schoolwork (39 percent) more than above-average students (32 percent) said that they have been spending time on video games. The games also are more often found in blue-collar households (37 percent) than in white collar families (33 percent).

14.19 Use of Electronic Devices

Which of the following did you, yourself do yesterday — Use a hand-held calculator? Played a Nintendo or other home video game?

	March – April 1990	
	Calculator	**Video game**
National	**44%**	**35%**
Male	41	43
Female	48	27
Ages 13 – 15	40	41
Ages 16 – 17	50	27
Above-average students	52	32
Average and below	35	39
White-collar background	51	33
Blue-collar background	37	37

Favorite form

Sources

Elvis Presley

Favorite Form of Music

Rap is at the top of the charts, radio's "Top 40" is fading, while rock endures, and country & western music is making a comeback in the 1990s.

Rap, which was not even mentioned on past Gallup Youth Survey music audits, ranked first as the favorite form of music named by teens in 1992. The various forms of hard rock that over the years have been characterized as "acid" or "heavy metal" have always been first or second on the teen charts since these votes began in 1981. Rock currently is the first choice of 25 percent of the teens. The hard forms of rock draw far more white teen fans (30 percent) than non-white (9 percent).

Country and western music had been slipping in popularity among teens in recent years, but may now be making a big comeback, with one teen in eight naming it as a favorite.

The big losers in 1992 were radio's Top-40 format and "new wave" sounds. Top 40 had been at the head of the list in recent years, but slid to third place in 1992. New wave, a collective term used to describe a wide range of experimental and emerging forms, over the years had drawn a steady audience of about 15 percent of the teens, but now has dropped almost out of sight.

Rhythm 'n' blues has long been a favorite of many black teens, and now is second among them in popularity, and finds few white teen fans.

"Easy listening" music (often disparagingly called "elevator" or "wallpaper" music), classical music, and Jazz now draw few fans.

One final word of consolation to parents and grandparents who may not like either rap or rock — the only thing certain about teen musical taste is that it probably will change quickly.

15.1 Teen Musical Taste Trend

	1992	1988	1987	1986	1983	1982	1981
Rap	26%	na	na	na	na	na	na
Top 40	16	30	35	34	27	23	25
Rock	25	28	21	22	26	26	30
New Wave	4	16	16	18	12	14	16
Easy Listening	4	9	9	8	8	10	na
Country & Western	12	7	4	7	9	8	13
Rhythm 'n' Blues	4	5	5	4	5	5	6
Classical	3	2	3	3	2	3	3
Jazz	1	1	6	3	2	6	6

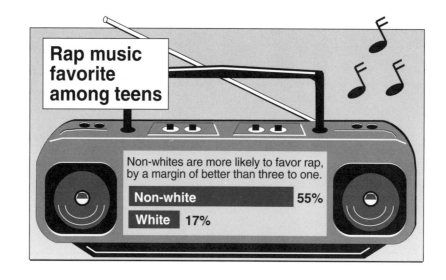

Rap music favorite among teens

Non-whites are more likely to favor rap, by a margin of better than three to one.

Non-white 55%

White 17%

15.2 Favorite Form of Music

What is your favorite form of music?

	April — May 1992				
	Rap	Hard rock	Top 40	Country & western	Rhythm 'n' blues
National	**26%**	**25%**	**16%**	**12%**	**4%**
Male	29	27	10	14	2
Female	23	23	22	11	6
Ages 13 – 15	33	25	17	10	2
Ages 16 – 17	18	24	13	15	7
White	17	30	19	15	2
Non-white	55	9	6	5	12
Black	67	4	4	2	17
White-collar background	22	25	19	9	6
Blue-collar background	31	21	13	16	4
Above-average students	25	24	17	9	6
Average and below	29	27	13	16	2
East	30	28	20	2	6
Midwest	20	31	17	10	5
South	28	13	16	21	2
West	28	31	8	12	5
Republican	19	28	20	11	4
Democrat	27	23	11	17	8
Independent	32	23	14	10	3
Protestant	24	22	20	11	5
Catholic	28	27	16	11	1
Church attender	26	23	18	11	6
Non-attender	27	28	12	14	2

GO 21504500; Q. 1

Music Sources

In 1992, over nine teens in 10 (92 percent) reported they listened to music on FM radio yesterday. FM radio consistently has been the most popular source of music for teens since 1984 when this question was first asked. AM radio is cited as a source by only 17 percent of the teens. Non-white teens (25 percent) are those most likely to listen to AM radio.

Nearly nine teens in 10 (88 percent) said they heard music from a recording yesterday. The number of teens using compact discs, records, tapes, or cassettes for music listening is up sharply since 1986 (68 percent) and 1984 (70 percent) when only seven in 10 opted for recorded music.

The market for music videos among teens is growing fast. Over half of the teens reported watching a music video on cable television yesterday. A sharp increase in the number watching on broadcast TV was recorded in 1992 when 43 percent watched yesterday. The broadcast share of the teen audience had dropped very low in previous years.

Over the years, attendance at live music performances yesterday has of course been relatively uncommon, and in 1992 only 3 percent reported having had this opportunity.

15.3 Listening Trend

	1992	1988	1986	1984
FM radio	92%	88%	88%	91%
AM radio	17	11	13	23
Recordings	88	82	68	70
Music video (cable TV)	55	38	36	44
Music video (broadcast TV)	43	14	15	37
Live concert	4	3	3	2

15.4 Music Sources

Did you, yourself, listen to music yesterday in any of the following ways — Listening to a recording such a CD, record, tape, or cassette? FM radio? AM radio? Music video on cable TV? Music video on regular TV? Attended a live concert?

	September – October 1992					
	FM radio	AM radio	Recording	Cable video	TV video	Live concert
National	**92%**	**17%**	**88%**	**55%**	**43%**	**4%**
Male	90	19	87	57	43	4
Female	95	16	89	54	43	3
Ages 13 – 15	91	19	85	53	43	4
Ages 16 – 17	95	16	92	58	44	4
White	92	15	85	53	43	4
Non-white	95	25	92	69	51	6
White-collar background	94	17	91	55	45	3
Blue-collar background	91	17	84	56	44	3
Above-average students	93	15	87	55	42	4
Average and below	91	20	89	55	44	4
East	96	19	87	63	45	8
Midwest	93	15	93	55	42	3
South	92	15	83	52	41	2
West	89	22	91	54	46	5
Large city	95	19	89	51	41	5
Suburb	92	23	92	68	50	3
Small town	89	13	84	58	43	4
Rural	97	19	91	43	41	1
Republican	94	16	92	54	42	5
Democrat	92	19	87	64	43	4
Independent	92	17	89	54	43	2
Protestant	94	17	86	51	43	3
Catholic	94	18	89	62	50	4
Church attender	94	19	87	59	45	5
Non-attender	94	18	92	62	50	4

Note: 1 percent of teens said they did not hear music from any of these sources on the previous day.

GO 12869: Q. 3

Teens Prefer Younger Elvis

In the Spring of 1992 the U.S. Postal Service asked people to vote on whether they would prefer to see a younger or older Elvis Presley depicted on the nation's postage stamps. They received over 1.1 million ballots and reported that the younger Elvis design was preferred over the older version by a three-to-one margin. At least 25 private polls were conducted by local newspapers and rock format radio stations, with about the same results.

Despite these seemingly impressive numbers, the results are not considered scientific, but are called "straw polls." They are unscientific because instead of being based on randomly selected representative samples, the respondents to the polls are volunteers who are interested in the subject. Indeed, some were so interested that according to newspaper accounts of the period they stuffed the ballot box by voting as many as 25 times for their favorite version of the stamp.

A Gallup Youth Survey conducted during the same period as the Postal Service "poll" may very well be the only scientific poll of opinion on the topic. At that time seven teens in 10 (73 percent) said they had heard of the plans to issue the stamp. In follow-up questions those who had not heard about the stamp were informed about it, and then all teens were asked for their preferences.

Overall, better than three teens in four (78 percent) said they thought it is a good idea that the Postal Service is issuing the Elvis Presley commemorative stamp. Only 13 percent thought it is a bad idea, and 9 percent had no opinion.

When asked to choose between the two versions, by a four-to-one margin, teens expressed preference for a stamp showing him as a younger singer (74 percent) than as an older singer (18 percent). An additional 5 percent said either version would be fine by them, while 1 percent said they disliked both, and 2 percent had no opinion.

Young women were more likely than young men to express preference for the younger Elvis version of the stamp, by a margin of 78 percent to 68 percent.

Although 28 percent of the teens said they planned to get office Postal Service ballots to cast their votes on the stamp, only 2 percent said they actually had done so.

15.5 The Elvis Presley Stamp

Have you heard about the Elvis Presley stamps that the Postal Service is going to issue this year? The Postal Service ask people to choose between two pictures for the Elvis Presley stamp — one that shows him when he was a younger singer and one that shows him as an older singer — which one would you, yourself prefer? Do you think it is a good idea or poor idea that the Postal Service is honoring Elvis Presley with a postage stamp?

	April – May 1992			
	Heard of stamp	Approve of stamp	Prefer younger Elvis	Prefer older Elvis
National	**73%**	**78%**	**74%**	**18%**
Male	73	75	70	21
Female	72	81	78	15
Ages 13 – 15	70	79	74	19
Ages 16 – 17	78	75	73	18
White	79	80	76	17
Non-white	56	72	69	22
White-collar background	75	74	76	16
Blue-collar background	74	85	71	22
Above-average students	76	77	77	14
Average and below	70	79	70	24
East	78	77	68	23
Midwest	72	77	75	15
South	75	78	76	17
West	67	81	73	19
Republican	78	80	77	18
Democrat	74	73	71	19
Independent	71	80	74	18
Protestant	77	76	72	20
Catholic	75	80	80	15
Church attender	73	76	73	20
Non-attender	73	80	74	16

GO 21504500; Q. 2, 3, 5

Economic Outlook

Banking

Value of Space Program

ECONOMICS

Economic Outlook

Teen-agers usually are optimistic about the future of their family's financial situation, but there were signs in 1992 that all may not have been well in many of the nation's teen households. A substantial number of teens said their family's financial situation was worse than the previous year, and many felt it was not a good time to buy the things they wanted. Further evidence of the financial pressures was a surprisingly high number who reported their families depended upon them to work and earn money to help make ends meet.

An improvement in the family financial situation over the past year is reported by 42 percent of teens, but one teen in three (33 percent) says it has grown worse. Among the remaining teens, 20 percent say there has been no change and 5 percent have no opinion.

Maybe it is just another case of youthful optimism, but three teens in four (73 percent) expect their family's financial picture to improve next year. Just 13 percent expect their situation to grow worse, while 7 percent believe it will stay about the same as now.

Despite this glowing forecast, many teens still seem to lack confidence, as measured by their buying intentions, in the future of the economy. While 47 percent say this might now be a good time to buy the things they want, half (50 percent) of the nation's young people feel it is a poor time.

Many teens appear to have direct knowledge of their family's true financial picture, because they feel others in the household are now counting upon them to help make ends meet. In total, over half of the teens interviewed say their families depend upon them to at least some extent to help out. For 7 percent of the teens, there is a feeling that the family depends upon them a great deal, and 21 percent say there is a fair amount of dependency upon their earnings. For one teen in four (25 percent) the feeling of financial dependency may not be as urgent, but they are still expected to pitch in at least "a little." The remaining 47 percent of teens say their families are not at all dependent upon them to help out financially.

Most frequently reporting that their families depend upon them a great or a fair amount are non-white teens (35 percent) and those from blue-collar households (31 percent). While undoubtedly the early work experience may be valuable in later life, there is some evidence to suggest it may now be taking its toll upon educational performance. Students who say they are getting above-average grades in school (22 percent) are less likely than those getting average or below-average grades (35 percent) to feel they should be working to help out their families.

In the 1992 election year it was significant to note that teen Republicans had the rosiest economic reports, with 48 percent reporting their families made financial gains the past year, and only 18 percent feeling their households depended upon them at least a fair amount to help out. Teen Democrats (40 percent) and independents (36 percent) were more likely to believe their families lost financial ground over the past year. As a consequence, both teen Democrats (34 percent) and independents (29 percent) felt at least a fair amount of obligation to help out with the family finances.

16.1 Changes in Financial Situation

We are interested in how peoples' financial situation may have changed. Would you say that your family is financially better off now than you were a year ago, or are financially worse off now?

| | April – May 1992 | | |
	Better	Same	Worse
National	**42%**	**20%**	**33%**
Male	45	23	27
Female	38	18	39
Ages 13 – 15	43	20	30
Ages 16 – 17	41	20	37
White	40	24	31
Non-white	46	10	41
White-collar background	41	22	34
Blue-collar background	40	16	38
Above-average students	43	21	31
Average and below	39	20	36
East	28	18	44
Midwest	42	21	34
South	49	24	22
West	45	17	35
Republican	48	24	24
Democrat	38	17	40
Independent	40	18	36
Protestant	46	21	28
Catholic	43	21	29
Church attender	45	21	29
Non-attender	38	20	37

Note: 5 percent of teens were unable to give an estimate.

GO 21504500; Q. 7

16.2 Current Financial Situation

Thinking of your own financial situation just now, do you feel you are in a good position to buy some of the things you would like to have, or is now a rather bad time for you to spend money?

	April — May 1992	
	Good time	Bad time
National	**47%**	**50%**
Male	49	48
Female	45	52
Ages 13 – 15	51	47
Ages 16 – 17	42	55
White	47	51
Non-white	42	55
White-collar background	46	53
Blue-collar background	46	52
Above-average students	50	47
Average and below	42	57
East	53	44
Midwest	48	50
South	45	52
West	43	55
Republican	47	50
Democrat	47	50
Independent	49	50
Protestant	55	43
Catholic	43	54
Church attender	48	50
Non-attender	46	52

Note: 3 percent of teens had no opinion.

GO 21504500; Q. 9

264

16.3 Financial Outlook

Now looking ahead, do you expect that at this time next year you will be financially better off than now, or worse off than now?

	April – May 1992		
	Better	Same	Worse
National	**73%**	**7%**	**13%**
Male	71	7	15
Female	76	7	11
Ages 13 – 15	74	9	10
Ages 16 – 17	73	5	18
White	71	8	14
Non-white	81	5	11
White-collar background	77	6	12
Blue-collar background	71	6	18
Above-average students	74	7	13
Average and below	74	8	12
East	64	7	19
Midwest	75	10	12
South	78	7	9
West	75	5	15
Republican	75	8	9
Democrat	75	6	16
Independent	77	5	13
Protestant	76	5	12
Catholic	71	7	14
Church attender	75	8	11
Non-attender	72	6	16

Note: 7 percent of teens were unable to give an estimate.

GO 21504500; Q. 8

16.4 Contribution to Family Finances

How much does your family depend upon you to work and earn money — a great deal, a fair amount, a little, or not at all?

	April – May 1992			
	Great deal	Fair amount	Little	Not at all
National	**7%**	**21%**	**25%**	**46%**
Male	7	23	26	44
Female	6	19	24	50
Ages 13 – 15	6	22	25	46
Ages 16 – 17	8	18	26	48
White	5	19	27	47
Non-white	11	24	18	47
White-collar background	5	19	26	50
Blue-collar background	9	23	25	43
Above-average students	5	17	25	53
Average and below	10	26	25	38
East	11	17	23	50
Midwest	6	20	25	48
South	6	24	23	48
West	4	21	31	41
Republican	4	14	27	54
Democrat	2	32	22	42
Independent	10	19	26	44
Protestant	7	14	25	53
Catholic	8	17	30	45
Church attender	5	20	25	50
Non-attender	9	21	25	43

Note: 1 percent of teens had no opinion.

GO 21504500; Q. 10

Teen Banking

Social Security numbers become necessary as young people begin to get jobs, open savings accounts, or engage in any kind of banking or investment activity. As such, measurements of the number of teens who have Social Security numbers or cards become significant measurements of their participation in the economic affairs of the country. The number of teens who are registered for Social Security has been growing, so that by 1992, 86 percent of teens had a Social Security card. By age 16, nearly all teens (97 percent) had one. More and more, the numbers are being required by the U.S. Internal Revenue Service and other agencies even for those who have had no taxable income.

A savings account passbook is the financial document most likely to be owned by teens, with 62 percent of all teens reporting they have one. The level of savings has been about the same since 1984.

The number of teens with their own checking accounts just about doubled between 1988 (10 percent) and 1992 (19 percent). By age 16, three teens in 10 (29 percent) are able to write their own checks.

Only one teen in 25 (4 percent) has his or her own credit card Even by age 16, teen credit card use is found only among 6 percent of the older teens.

16.5 Financial Account Trends

	1992	1988	1984
Social Security card	86%	78%	80%
Savings account	62	62	64
Checking account	19	10	na
Credit card	4	4	5

16.6 Economic Documents

Which, if any, of the following do you, yourself, now have — Social security card? Savings account? Checking account? Credit card?

	September – October 1992			
	Social security card	Savings account	Checking account	Credit card
National	**86%**	**62%**	**19%**	**4%**
Male	84	63	18	2
Female	87	62	21	6
Ages 13 – 15	78	57	12	3
Ages 16 – 17	97	70	29	6
White	85	68	21	4
Non-white	88	39	12	4
White-collar background	84	73	22	5
Blue-collar background	88	54	19	4
Above-average students	84	67	21	5
Average and below	88	55	17	3
East	86	52	19	5
Midwest	91	71	26	6
South	86	52	16	1
West	79	62	17	6
Large city	81	58	16	5
Suburb	84	76	28	6
Small town	88	59	17	2
Rural	88	65	20	6
Republican	86	66	20	7
Democrat	90	58	20	6
Independent	84	66	22	2
Protestant	85	56	20	4
Catholic	88	66	20	5
Church attender	87	65	20	4
Non-attender	84	59	18	5

GO 12869: Q. 8

Space Program Expenditures

"Star Trek" has started its third series and preliminary indications are that the venerable exploration of "the final frontier" continues to draw great interest from teen-agers, but the same no longer holds true for today's space program. For the first time, the Gallup Youth Survey has found that teens believe the money the U.S. government has spent on the space program has not been a worthwhile investment, and might have been better spent on other national problems.

Only one teen in three (35 percent) in 1992 endorsed the space program. Calling for re-allocation of federal funds on the program to other pressing needs are 62 percent of the teens.

Just seven years ago in 1985, almost the opposite opinion was put forth by teens, with 62 percent at that time endorsing the space program and only 36 percent opposing it. Until then support had grown from 52 percent approval in 1980 to 58 percent in 1983.

Even at the height of enthusiasm for the space program in 1985, the majority of teens (56 percent) believed there was little or no chance that they, themselves, would some day have the opportunity to travel in outer space. One teen in three (32 percent) at that time felt "some" likelihood of being a future space traveler, while 11 percent said they felt very confident this possibility would exist in their lifetime. At best most teens felt they would just watch the space shuttle take-offs and landings on television, which 88 percent had viewed.

Later negative attitudes towards the space program may be a consequence of the economic recession affecting the country and people's outlooks on life at the time of the survey. When teens were asked on the same survey to identify the nation's leading problem, two in three (65 percent) cited a wide range of social ills they felt required priority attention, and an additional 21 percent singled out economic woes and their consequences. That level of opinion leaves little room for investment in space technology.

Non-white teens, who are usually more likely than whites to bear the brunt of recessionary pressures, show less enthusiasm for the space program, by a margin of 38 percent to 29 percent. Similar low levels of support are found in the economically hard-hit large inner cities (29 percent) and rural areas (also, 29 percent), compared to support of 44 percent of teens from the suburbs and 36 percent from those living in small towns. There is no difference found, however, in support for the space program between teens from white-collar and blue-collar backgrounds (35 percent, each).

16.7 Opinion of U.S. Space Program Value

	Worthwhile investment	Other problems more worthy
1992	35%	62%
1985	62	36
1983	58	32
1980	52	43

16.8 Opinion of U.S. Space Program Expenditures

All things considered, do you think the money spent by the U.S. government on the space program has been a worthwhile investment, or do you feel that this money might have been better spent on other national problems?

	September – October 1992	
	Worthwhile investment	Other problems more worthy
National	**35%**	**62%**
Male	38	58
Female	32	65
Ages 13 – 15	39	58
Ages 16 – 17	29	66
White	38	58
Non-white	29	66
White-collar background	35	63
Blue-collar background	35	61
Above-average students	36	61
Average and below	33	63
East	35	56
Midwest	39	60
South	34	62
West	32	66
Large city	29	68
Suburb	44	54
Small town	36	60
Rural	29	67
Republican	41	56
Democrat	31	67
Independent	34	64
Protestant	33	63
Catholic	32	65
Church attender	34	63
Non-attender	36	60

Note: Table does not include 3 percent of teens who did not have an opinion.

GO 12869; Q. 38

THE ENVIRONMENT

World environmental quality

National environmental problems

Community environmental quality

Solutions

Actions

Protecting nature

Animal rights

World Environmental Quality

America's teen-agers not only show high awareness of the world's environmental condition, they are very seriously concerned about a host of its problems. While adults expressed their concerns in debates on environmental issues during the world conference in Rio de Janeiro in 1992, teens in comparison often showed levels of concern that were even higher.

Overall, only four teens in 10 consider worldwide environmental conditions to be very good or fairly good. A more negative view is taken by 40 percent who rate worldwide environmental quality as fairly bad and 19 percent who say it is very bad. Just 2 percent of teens have no opinion about the world's environmental health. By comparison, 26 percent of American adults say worldwide environmental conditions are good, and 66 percent rate them as bad. These findings were echoed throughout the world in surveys taken in 1992 that showed majorities in nearly every country had great concern about the planet's environmental condition.

The power of communications in the "global village" of our world today is demonstrated by the high levels of awareness in every land surveyed of the potential damaging effects of the ozone hole in the earth's atmosphere. It is likely that only a few years ago most people throughout the world probably were not even aware of an ozone layer in the atmosphere. Now, in this country, three teen-agers in four join two adults in three in rating the ozone depletion problem as very serious.

The polluted condition of the world's rivers, lakes and oceans is of very serious concern to 74 percent of teens and 71 percent of adults.

The importance of the loss of valuable rain forests is another example of a problem that has captured worldwide interest and concern. In the U.S., 72 percent of teens, compared to 63 percent of adults, rate the loss of rain forests as very serious.

Air pollution and smog have long ceased to be the butt of comedians' jokes about Los Angeles or New Jersey and are now of serious concern to 70 percent of teens and to six adults in 10.

Some people may shake their heads about Spotted Owls or small fish called Snail Darters, but 63 percent of teens rate the loss of plant and animal species throughout the world as a very serious problem. Half of the adults surveyed share the belief that this a matter of very serious concern.

Teens and adults (54 percent each) are equally very concerned about worldwide effects of soil erosion.

The threat of global warming or the "greenhouse effect" is not taken lightly by teens, with slightly over half (52 percent) saying it is a very serious concern. Among adults, 47 percent feel the same way.

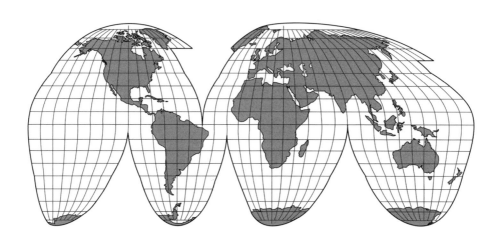

17.1 Concern About the Environment

How concerned are you personally about environmental problems — Would you say a great deal, a fair amount, not very much, or not at all?

Q. 18	April 1992			
	Great deal	Fair amount	Not very much	Not at all
National	**40%**	**51%**	**7%**	**2%**
Male	35	53	9	3
Female	45	48	5	2
Ages 13 – 15	41	49	8	2
Ages 16 – 17	38	54	6	2
White	38	55	7	*
Non-white	46	39	9	6
White-collar background	39	53	6	2
Blue-collar background	42	49	7	2
Above-average students	42	52	5	1
Average and below	38	48	11	3
East	44	49	5	2
Midwest	34	57	7	2
South	40	48	10	2
West	43	49	7	1
Republican	35	57	7	1
Democrat	38	52	8	2
Independent	48	43	7	2
Protestant	33	55	10	2
Catholic	48	47	4	1
Church attender	37	51	10	2
Non-attender	42	49	8	1
Adults	*38*	*47*	*12*	*2*

*Less than one-half of 1 percent

Note: 1 percent of adults had no opinion.

GO 21504500; Q. 18

17.2 Rating of the World Environment

Overall, how would you rate the quality of the environment of the world as a whole — very good, fairly good, fairly bad, or very bad?

	April 1992			
	Very good	Fairly good	Fairly bad	Very bad
National	3%	36%	40%	19%
Male	3	38	39	18
Female	3	34	41	20
Ages 13 – 15	1	41	37	19
Ages 16 – 17	5	30	44	19
White	3	36	44	16
Non-white	3	37	29	28
White-collar background	2	34	47	16
Blue-collar background	2	39	32	25
Above-average students	2	34	43	19
Average and below	4	38	35	19
East	4	35	39	21
Midwest	2	38	43	14
South	3	42	38	16
West	3	27	40	28
Republican	4	43	38	14
Democrat	3	32	44	19
Independent	2	34	39	22
Protestant	3	40	38	15
Catholic	6	36	38	18
Church attender	3	42	37	17
Non-attender	3	31	42	21
Adults	*2*	*24*	*44*	*22*

Note: 2 percent of teens and 8 percent of adults had no opinion.

GO 21504500; Q. 17c

17.3 Worldwide Environmental Problems

Here is a list of environmental issues that may be affecting the world as a whole. As I read each one, please tell me how serious a problem you personally believe it to be in the world — very serious, somewhat serious, not very serious, or not serious at all — or you don't know enough about it to judge?

	April 1992				
	Very serious	Somewhat serious	Not very serious	Not at all serious	Cannot judge
Loss of ozone in the earth's atmosphere	77%	14%	3%	1%	5%
Pollution of rivers, lakes, and oceans	74	19	3	1	3
Loss of the rain forests and jungles	72	14	5	2	7
Air pollution and smog	70	23	5	1	1
Global warming or the "greenhouse effect"	52	24	9	3	12
Loss of animal and plant species	63	22	6	3	6
Soil erosion, polluted land, and loss of farmland	54	26	9	1	10

GO 21504500; Q. 20

17.4a Very Serious Worldwide Environmental Problems

. . . Loss of ozone in the earth's atmosphere?
. . . Pollution of rivers, lakes, and oceans?
. . . Loss of the rain forests and jungles?
. . . Air pollution and smog?

	April 1992			
	Ozone loss	Water pollution	Rain forests	Air pollution
National	**77%**	**74%**	**72%**	**70%**
Male	72	72	70	67
Female	81	77	74	72
Ages 13 – 15	79	71	71	72
Ages 16 – 17	74	79	73	67
White	77	73	64	68
Non-white	76	77	56	76
White-collar background	78	74	74	67
Blue-collar background	78	74	69	72
Above-average students	77	74	76	71
Average and below	76	74	65	69
East	81	74	69	65
Midwest	74	70	67	72
South	71	74	72	61
West	84	80	79	84
Republican	77	72	73	68
Democrat	74	62	65	69
Independent	78	84	76	71
Protestant	71	67	71	62
Catholic	78	80	74	73
Church attender	72	69	69	66
Non-attender	82	79	74	74
Adults	*56*	*71*	*63*	*60*

GO 21504500; Q. 20

17.4b Very Serious Worldwide Environmental Problems

. . . Loss of animal and plant species?
. . . Soil erosion, polluted land, and loss of farmland?
. . . Global warming?

	April 1992		
	Species loss	**Soil loss**	**Global warming**
National	**63%**	**54%**	**52%**
Male	62	52	55
Female	64	56	50
Ages 13 – 15	61	54	54
Ages 16 – 17	65	54	50
White	62	52	53
Non-white	64	59	52
White-collar background	62	51	56
Blue-collar background	65	52	48
Above-average students	63	52	54
Average and below	63	57	51
East	62	55	61
Midwest	57	52	45
South	60	50	47
West	75	60	61
Republican	56	57	46
Democrat	61	43	48
Independent	68	60	59
Protestant	54	47	45
Catholic	70	56	55
Church attender	56	50	49
Non-attender	70	58	56
Adults	*50*	*54*	*47*

GO 21504500; Q. 20

National Environmental Problems

At best, America's teen-agers rate the country's environmental quality as only fairly good, and a majority think it is poor. While they view a wide range of institutions and conditions as being responsible for the current sorry state of affairs, they feel that the greatest blame should placed on the wasteful habits of individuals like themselves. Or as Walt Kelly's "Pogo" said to their parents' generation: "We have met the enemy, and he is us."

Teens put the blame for the nation's environmental ills squarely upon themselves and other individuals. Seven teens in 10 feel that individuals who consume more than they need and throw away too much contribute a great deal to the problem. Somewhat fewer adults (58 percent) hold a similar view.

A majority of teens feel that business and industry are major contributors to the problems because they are thought to favor growth over protecting the environment. Adults (70 percent) view business and industrial interests as the *leading* cause of the nation's environmental woes.

About half of the teens think that a lack of education is contributing a great deal to national environmental problems because people just do not know what to do to improve conditions. Adults (61 percent) are even more inclined to want more educational efforts to raise environmental consciousness.

Teens (48 percent) are less likely than their parents and other adults (60 percent) to view technology as part of the problem rather than the solution because production in this country is thought to waste too many resources and to create too much pollution.

Nearly half of the nation's teens and adults feel that a great deal of the blame should be placed on government because it is believed to put too little emphasis on protecting the environment.

The attitudes of teen-agers towards family planning take on great importance because they can greatly influence future population growth patterns. Teens are more likely than adults, by a margin of 43 percent to 30 percent, to believe that overpopulation or the use of resources by too many people contributes a great deal to the nation's environmental problems.

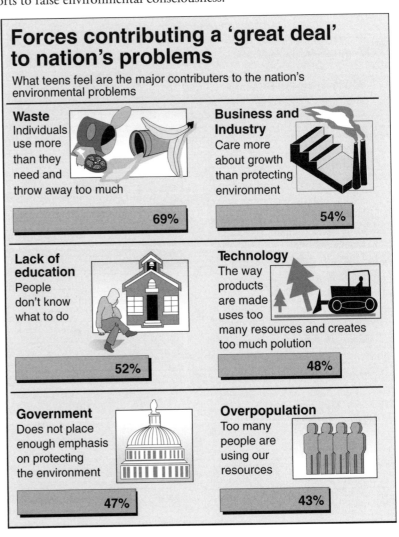

Forces contributing a 'great deal' to nation's problems

What teens feel are the major contributers to the nation's environmental problems

Waste
Individuals use more than they need and throw away too much
69%

Business and Industry
Care more about growth than protecting environment
54%

Lack of education
People don't know what to do
52%

Technology
The way products are made uses too many resources and creates too much polution
48%

Government
Does not place enough emphasis on protecting the environment
47%

Overpopulation
Too many people are using our resources
43%

17.5 Rating of the National Environment

Overall, how would you rate the quality of the environment in our nation — very good, fairly good, fairly bad, or very bad?

	April 1992			
	Very good	Fairly good	Fairly bad	Very bad
National	**4%**	**42%**	**39%**	**15%**
Male	4	47	36	13
Female	4	36	42	17
Ages 13 – 15	2	42	40	14
Ages 16 – 17	6	41	38	16
White	4	44	41	11
Non-white	4	37	32	25
White-collar background	2	40	44	13
Blue-collar background	2	44	37	16
Above-average students	3	42	42	13
Average and below	5	42	34	18
East	4	36	41	18
Midwest	5	50	35	10
South	4	47	36	12
West	1	29	47	22
Republican	6	49	36	10
Democrat	2	40	41	15
Independent	4	36	42	18
Protestant	2	51	34	11
Catholic	6	39	38	17
Church attender	4	44	38	13
Non-attender	3	39	40	16
Adults	*3*	*49*	*35*	*10*

Note: 3 percent of adults had no opinion.

GO 21504500; Q. 17a

17.6a Factors Contributing a Great Deal to Environmental Problems

Now I'm going to read you a list of possible causes of our nation's environmental problems. As I read each item, please tell me how much you think it contributes to the environmental problems here in our nation — a great deal, a fair amount, not very much, or not at all?

| | April 1992 | | |
	Waste	Business & industry	Lack of education
National	**69%**	**54%**	**52%**
Male	66	55	46
Female	72	52	58
Ages 13 – 15	67	53	50
Ages 16 – 17	73	54	56
White	70	52	50
Non-white	67	58	58
White-collar background	71	56	52
Blue-collar background	64	48	46
Above-average students	73	53	52
Average and below	63	53	51
East	67	56	53
Midwest	67	45	48
South	67	55	55
West	75	60	54
Republican	63	42	52
Democrat	77	57	54
Independent	69t	58	53
Protestant	62	42	53
Catholic	74	54	54
Church attender	67	52	54
Non-attender	72	56	51
Adults	*73*	*69*	*53*

GO 21504500; Q. 21

17.6b Factors Contributing a Great Deal to Environmental Problems

. . . Technology — the way products are made uses too many resources and creates too much pollution?
. . . The government — it does not place enough emphasis on protecting the environment?
. . . Overpopulation — there are too many people using up our resources?

	April 1992		
	Technology	Government	Over-population
National	**48%**	**47%**	**43%**
Male	45	45	43
Female	51	49	44
Ages 13 – 15	48	44	43
Ages 16 – 17	48	52	43
White	46	45	42
Non-white	53	54	46
White-collar background	47	48	40
Blue-collar background	47	40	47
Above-average students	47	46	41
Average and below	49	49	46
East	54	52	42
Midwest	42	40	39
South	49	44	47
West	47	53	45
Republican	46	30	44
Democrat	44	51	44
Independent	53	58	43
Protestant	39	39	43
Catholic	54	43	41
Church attender	48	42	41
Non-attender	48	52	46
Adults	*50*	*45*	*36*

GO 21504500; Q. 21

Community Environmental Quality

As many parents have discovered, their children are no longer just studying the "the 3 Rs" at school, but are also busy acquiring many new skills necessary to live in the modern world. This is most evident in how teen-agers now view the environment. Teens have learned to regard environmental protection not just as a worldwide or a national problem but as something they can deal with locally, starting in their own homes and communities.

Their potential commitment to local action is significant, because few teens rate the quality of the environment in their local communities as being very good. Near majorities, according to the findings of a 1992 study, say poor water quality, poor air quality, and inadequate sewage and garbage disposal facilities are very serious community problems.

Quality of local community environment

How teens rate the environment in their own communities

Very good	18%
Fairly good	64
Fairly bad	10
Very bad	8
Not sure	*

* Less than one-half of 1 percent

About two teens in three say the overall environmental quality of their community is only fairly good and just 18 percent consider local conditions to be very good. American adults hold somewhat more negative views than their children towards the environment.

When it comes to specific aspects of the local environment, America's teen-agers are far more critical of it than are their elders.

Even though unsafe drinking water seldom is a problem in the United States, teens are twice as likely as adults (22 percent) to say poor water quality is a very serious local problem.

Many teens also take a dim view of local sanitation, garbage and sewage disposal facilities, with 44 percent considering it a very serious problem, compared to only 18 percent of adults who have a similar view. Three times as many teens as adults feel local contaminated soil is a very serious problem.

Poor local air quality is reported as a very serious problem by 43 percent of the teens. Three adults in 10 share the concern of teens that the problem of local air quality is very serious. Teens are twice as likely as adults to believe overpopulation in the local community has become a very serious problem.

Although some adults may consider the "boom boxes" and loud mufflers that some teens seem to regard as necessary to their happiness to be the major sources of noise pollution, among teens themselves, 11 percent rate local noise conditions as very serious and 24 percent say the din is a somewhat serious problem. They are joined by 29 percent of adults who would like to see the local noise volume turned down.

17.7 Community Environmental Quality — Overall Rating

Overall, how would you rate the quality of the environment here in your local community — very good, fairly good, fairly bad, or very bad?

	April 1992			
	Very good	Fairly good	Fairly bad	Very bad
National	**18%**	**64%**	**10%**	**8%**
Male	25	59	8	8
Female	11	69	13	7
Ages 13 – 15	17	67	7	9
Ages 16 – 17	20	58	16	6
White	20	67	8	5
Non-white	12	54	18	16
White-collar background	19	65	11	5
Blue-collar background	13	64	10	13
Above-average students	19	62	11	8
Average and below	18	66	9	7
East	18	61	13	8
Midwest	22	64	9	5
South	16	69	8	7
West	17	58	14	11
Republican	21	66	10	3
Democrat	16	61	16	7
Independent	18	63	7	12
Protestant	18	65	10	7
Catholic	23	60	11	5
Church attender	20	63	12	5
Non-attender	16	65	9	10
Adults	*17*	*54*	*22*	*5*

Note: 2 percent of adults gave no opinion.

GO 21504500; Q. 17b

17.8 Aspects of Community Environmental Quality

Here is a list of environmental problems facing many communities. Please tell me how serious you consider each one to be here in your community — very serious, somewhat serious, not very serious, or not serious at all.

	April 1992			
	Very serious	Somewhat serious	Not very serious	Not at all serious
Poor water quality	45%	19%	22%	14%
Inadequate sewage, sanitation, and garbage disposal	44	19	24	13
Poor air quality	43	20	25	12
Contaminated soil	35	18	29	16
Too many people, overcrowded	22	26	34	18
Too much noise	11	24	43	22

GO 21504500; Q. 19

17.9a Very Serious Community Environmental Problems

. . . Poor water quality?
. . . Inadequate sewage, sanitation and garbage disposal?
. . . Poor air quality?

	April 1992		
	Poor water quality	Poor sewage	Poor air quality
National	**45%**	**44%**	**43%**
Male	46	43	41
Female	44	46	45
Ages 13 – 15	42	41	44
Ages 16 – 17	49	48	41
White	40	40	38
Non-white	59	60	55
White-collar background	43	43	42
Blue-collar background	44	44	46
Above-average students	43	41	43
Average and below	46	50	42
East	46	48	45
Midwest	42	39	40
South	43	44	40
West	49	47	47
Republican	40	40	36
Democrat	42	47	43
Independent	51	48	50
Protestant	46	42	42
Catholic	43	48	41
Church attender	46	43	42
Non-attender	44	46	43
Adults	*22*	*18*	*18*

GO 21504500; Q. 19

17.9b Very Serious Community Environmental Problems

. . . Contaminated soil?
. . . Too many people, overcrowding?
. . . Too much noise?

	April 1992		
	Bad soil	Too many people	Too much noise
National	**35%**	**22%**	**11%**
Male	38	20	11
Female	33	24	12
Ages 13 – 15	36	22	10
Ages 16 – 17	34	22	14
White	29	17	8
Non-white	54	36	20
White-collar background	34	22	11
Blue-collar background	34	20	14
Above-average students	34	24	10
Average and below	38	19	12
East	39	26	13
Midwest	35	20	8
South	37	20	15
West	29	21	9
Republican	31	15	11
Democrat	33	24	15
Independent	42	26	10
Protestant	31	24	6
Catholic	31	19	10
Church attender	37	21	12
Non-attender	34	24	11
Adults	*12*	*11*	*7*

GO 21504500; Q. 19

Environmental Solutions

America's teen-agers support a wide range of proposed solutions to help solve the nation's environmental problems and are willing to pay the cost. Teens particularly want to see increased governmental activity to support scientific research and to control business, industry, and product marketing activities.

Adults often show stronger support for increased governmental action, but as teens grow older, they usually begin to mirror the high environmental commitment of adult Americans.

17.10 Support for Environmental Solutions
(Percent strongly or somewhat favoring each proposal)

	April 1992	
	Teens	Adults
Support scientific research to help find new ways to control pollution	91%	92%
Make stronger environmental protection laws for business and industry	86	90
Ban the sale of products that are unsafe for the environment	80	89
Provide family planning information and free birth control to all citizens who want it to help reduce birth rates	80	81
Make laws requiring that all citizens conserve resources and reduce pollution	85	82
Limit exports of our natural resources to other nations	61	73

GO 21504500; Q. 22

17.11a Strongly Favored Environmental Solutions

. . . Support scientific research to help find new ways to control pollution?
. . . Make stronger environmental protection laws for business and industry?
. . . Ban the sale of products that are unsafe for the environment?

	April 1992		
	Support scientific research	Stronger protection laws	Ban unsafe products
National	**64%**	**62%**	**56%**
Male	64	64	54
Female	65	61	59
Ages 13 – 15	62	60	53
Ages 16 – 17	68	66	61
White	63	62	56
Non-white	69	63	57
White-collar background	66	66	58
Blue-collar background	61	58	58
Above-average students	67	65	58
Average and below	60	59	54
East	59	61	64
Midwest	63	56	48
South	61	62	52
West	76	72	64
Republican	65	57	53
Democrat	66	59	56
Independent	63	72	60
Protestant	66	58	56
Catholic	65	65	56
Church attender	66	57	59
Non-attender	63	68	54
Adults	*59*	*56*	*62*

GO 21504500; Q. 22

288

17.11b Strongly Favored Environmental Solutions

. . . Provide family planning information and free birth control, to all citizens who want it, to help reduce birth rates?

. . . Make laws that all citizens conserve resources and reduce pollution?

. . . Limit exports of our natural resources to other nations?

	April 1992		
	Family planning	Conserve resources	Limit exports
National	**52%**	**51%**	**26%**
Male	47	47	28
Female	57	55	24
Ages 13 – 15	49	48	27
Ages 16 – 17	56	54	24
White	51	47	25
Non-white	55	59	29
White-collar background	51	51	26
Blue-collar background	54	56	26
Above-average students	49	52	27
Average and below	57	49	24
East	49	58	27
Midwest	50	48	25
South	53	44	28
West	56	56	24
Republican	44	39	27
Democrat	58	51	23
Independent	56	60	30
Protestant	50	47	22
Catholic	56	54	32
Church attender	45	49	26
Non-attender	60	52	26
Adults	*81*	*82*	*73*

GO 21504500; Q. 22

Environmental Action

When it comes to moving beyond words and taking action to save the environment, America's teens often have shown a deeper commitment than their elders. Teens report they have been particularly active in recycling programs, and in comparison to adults, they far more often join organizations that are actively working towards a better and safer environment. Manufacturers would do well to heed the environmental concerns of the new generation because teens also say they are likely to purchase or avoid products according to their ecological sensitivity.

Nearly nine teens in 10 say they have voluntarily recycled materials during the past year.

Eight teens in 10 report that in the past year they avoided using some products they believe can harm the environment. Seven in 10 say that during the same period they actually went out of their way to purchase certain products because they were thought to be better for the environment than competing products.

By comparison, adults are far less likely to report having avoided use of environmentally harmful products or having increased use of competing products believed to be more beneficial to the environment.

On the home front, about two teens in three say they have been trying to use less water.

During the past year one teen in four reports having been active in a group or organization that works to protect the environment.

AP/S. Kohler

17.12 Environmental Actions Last Year

Have you, yourself, done any of the following things in the past year —
... Voluntarily recycled newspapers, glass, aluminum, motor oil, or other items?
... Avoided using certain products that harm the environment?
... Bought some product specifically because you thought it was better for the environment than competing products?
... Tried to use less water in your household?
... Been active in a group or organization that works to protect the environment?

	April 1992				
	Recy-cled	Avoided products	Sought products	Less water	Activist
National	**88%**	**80%**	**70%**	**64%**	**27%**
Male	88	75	68	58	23
Female	88	84	72	70	31
Ages 13 – 15	86	79	67	64	27
Ages 16 – 17	91	80	73	65	27
White	91	81	73	65	26
Non-white	79	77	61	63	30
White-collar background	91	81	71	64	23
Blue-collar background	84	78	72	66	35
Above-average students	92	85	75	66	28
Average and below	83	73	63	61	24
East	89	82	68	67	24
Midwest	85	81	65	59	28
South	84	74	70	60	33
West	96	84	77	74	20
Republican	90	77	70	62	22
Democrat	87	78	72	63	33
Independent	87	80	67	66	27
Protestant	88	76	63	61	24
Catholic	94	88	74	69	29
Church attender	86	83	66	65	27
Non-attender	90	76	74	64	27
Adults	*75*	*57*	*49*	*66*	*10*

GO 21504500; Q. 24

Protecting Nature

There is a popular myth that many people in this country have a high disregard of nature because they believe the Bible gives them the right to dominate the world and all of its living creatures. Few teen-agers, and for that matter, few of their parents or other elders, accept this view, according to the findings of a special Gallup Youth Survey taken shortly before the environmental conference in Rio de Janeiro in 1992.

Rather than believing that they have license to treat the environment any way they want, better than nine teens in 10 agree with the statement that "Nature is God's creation and therefore it is the duty of humans to take care of the environment." Adults, also 93 percent, are in exact agreement with teens on the matter

.

Almost as many teens (88 percent) also accept the concept that "all living things have the same right to exist as do humans."

Furthermore, just about as many teens (86 percent) go on to agree that not only do they have the right to exist but that "humans have a moral obligation to protect all living things."

Teens were also asked specifically if they agree that "God intended nature to be used by humans, and therefore we should not worry too much about harming the environment." This negative position was accepted by only 13 percent of the teens and adults.

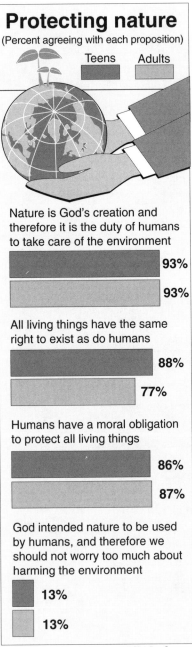

Protecting nature
(Percent agreeing with each proposition)
Teens   Adults

Nature is God's creation and therefore it is the duty of humans to take care of the environment
93%
93%

All living things have the same right to exist as do humans
88%
77%

Humans have a moral obligation to protect all living things
86%
87%

God intended nature to be used by humans, and therefore we should not worry too much about harming the environment
13%
13%

AP/Ed De Gasero

Please tell me whether you agree or not with each of the following —
. . . Nature is God's creation and therefore it is the duty of humans to take care of the environment?
. . . All living things have the same right to exist as do humans?
. . . Humans have a moral obligation to protect all living things?
. . . God intended nature to be used by humans, and therefore we should not worry too much about harming the environment?

	April 1992			
	Duty to protect environment	All creatures have rights	Moral obligation to protect	Do not have to worry
National	**93%**	**88%**	**86%**	**13%**
Male	93	84	84	11
Female	94	92	87	15
Ages 13 – 15	94	91	86	12
Ages 16 – 17	92	83	86	15
White	92	86	84	11
Non-white	99	90	89	19
White-collar background	92	84	85	12
Blue-collar background	97	94	86	15
Above-average students	95	86	87	10
Average and below	93	89	84	17
East	94	89	86	10
Midwest	95	91	83	15
South	95	83	89	15
West	87	89	84	11
Republican	95	84	84	16
Democrat	93	86	82	10
Independent	93	92	89	13
Protestant	98	86	81	16
Catholic	93	90	91	11
Church attender	97	86	84	16
Non-attender	89	90	87	10
Adults	*93*	*77*	*87*	*13*

GO 21504500; Q. 23

Animal Protection and "Rights"

We are an animal loving nation, and so it should come as no surprise that as children who have been devoted to their dogs, cats, and hamsters grow older, they become highly supportive of efforts to protect animal species that are endangered. The scientific and medical communities probably will be alarmed, however, to discover that a majority of the nation's teen-agers also said in a 1991 survey that they support the "animal rights movement," even if would mean the end to laboratory and medical tests that use animals.

Nearly nine teens in 10 say they support protecting endangered species of animals even if it would cost a lot of money.

The animal rights movement, with its frequent emphasis upon militant opposition to laboratory and medical testing, is relatively new. Although the movement could be traced back to "anti-vivisectionist" protests of the 19th century, it has only been recently that animal activists have received widespread publicity for protests, litigation, and illegal break-ins to "liberate" test animals. The movement has even invaded the schools where some students have protested against being required to perform the traditional dissection of laboratory specimens in high school biology classes. The animal rights movement has been a cause of alarm to the scientific and medical communities which contend that animal testing is unavoidable when developing new drugs and testing substances for carcinogenic and other adverse effects. In particular, scientists have been upset by militant actions that have ranged from frivolous law suits under the guise of environmental concerns to the wanton destruction of laboratory equipment and scientific records that have negated years of research.

Two teens in three say they support the animal rights movement. A plurality of 41 percent support the movement very much, and are joined by 26 percent who say they are somewhat in favor of it.

17.14 Animal Rights Support

Please tell me how much you support or oppose each of these issues and causes—support very much, support somewhat, oppose somewhat, or oppose very much—Protecting endangered species even if it will cost a lot of money? Animal rights, including bans on all laboratory and medical tests that use animals?

June – July 1991

Support Protecting Endangered Species

Support very much	53%
Support somewhat	34
Oppose somewhat	9
Oppose very much	2
No opinion	2

Support Bans on all Laboratory and Medical Tests Using Animals

Support very much	41%
Support somewhat	26
Oppose somewhat	17
Oppose very much	14
No opinion	2

17.15 Teen Attitudes Towards Animal Programs

Please tell me how much you support or oppose each of these issues and causes—support very much, support somewhat, oppose somewhat, or oppose very much—Protecting endangered species even if it will cost a lot of money? Animal rights, including bans on all laboratory and medical tests that use animals?

	June – July 1991 Support "very much" . . .	
	Support protecting endangered species	Support animal rights
National	53%	41%
Male	51	35
Female	55	46
Ages 13 – 15	56	43
Ages 16 – 17	48	38
White	56	42
Non-white	43	39
White-collar family background	57	42
Blue-collar family background	49	41
Above-average students	54	39
Average and below	49	43
East	55	41
Midwest	48	36
South	54	42
West	56	45
Large city	45	33
Suburb	42	43
Small town, rural area	55	42
Protestant	49	39
Catholic	54	44
Church attender	54	39
Non-attender	43	52

GO 224007; Q. 11

Citizenship

Freedoms and Rights

Respect for minorities

Women's progress and rights

Equal opportunity

Gay rights

CITIZENSHIP AND RIGHTS

Citizenship

Most teens are proud to be Americans, but many have a hazy knowledge of how they and others gained citizenship in this country. Not all teens, for example, realize that they became citizens automatically by being born in this country. Even fewer know that the inhabitants of Puerto Rico also are citizens of the United States. Many others mistakenly believe that getting permission to work in this country or joining the armed services are automatic tickets to U.S. citizenship.

Whether or not people's parents are U.S. citizens, if they are born in this country, they are eligible to be U.S. citizens. This basic right by birth is recognized by nearly nine teens in 10.

The citizens of Puerto Rico have long debated the issue of U.S. statehood vs. independence, but only three mainland teens in 10 appear to understand that Puerto Ricans now are U.S. citizens.

"Green cards" are much coveted by alien residents of the U.S. because the cards allow them to work legally in this country. Many in the past have used the green card as a first step on the path to citizenship. The cards also were used as evidence of U.S. residency by many aliens during the recent immigration amnesty program. Green cards, however, in and by themselves do not automatically confer the right to become a citizen, but only allow people to work as temporary residents in the U.S. Nearly half of the teens mistakenly believe that green cards are an automatic ticket to citizenship.

During the period of Operations Desert Shield and Desert Storm there were reports that many Mexican men were thronging the U.S. consulate offices in that country in hopes of enlisting in the U.S. armed forces. They were disappointed to learn that they were the victims of false rumors that the U.S. was recruiting Mexican mercenaries who, in addition to high pay, could also receive U.S. citizenship in return for their service. Resident aliens have been subject to the military draft in the past, but in recent years the U.S. armed services have relied exclusively upon all-volunteer men and women drawn from the ranks of U.S. citizens, and have not been seeking foreign recruits.

About four teens in 10 hold the erroneous belief that a person can become a U.S. citizen by joining the armed services.

18.1 Knowledge of Citizenship Procedures

	October 1990			
	By being born in the U.S.	By getting 'green card'	By joining armed services	By being born in Puerto Rico
National	**88%**	**46%**	**43%**	**30%**
Male	87	43	43	32
Female	88	47	43	29
Ages 13–15	86	48	48	29
Ages 16–17	86	42	37	32
White	87	44	44	29
Non-white	88	50	41	35
Above-average students	87	43	41	31
Average or below-average	88	49	46	29
White-collar background	87	44	41	34
Blue-collar background	84	45	40	22

Freedoms and Rights

American teens are confident about freedom of the press and freedom of speech in their country, but some are skeptical about minority rights and the separation of church and state.

Teens are most confident about freedom of the press, with 21 percent saying it is excellent and 47 percent that it is good. Freedom of speech receives similar votes of confidence from teens, with 19 percent saying it is excellent and 47 percent that it is good.

In 1985, however, more teens were confident about these basic rights, with 78 percent rating both as excellent or good; in 1988, only 68 percent gave positive marks to freedom of the press and 66 percent to freedom of speech.

In 1988, women's rights in the nation were rated excellent by 13 percent of teens and good by 47 percent. Dissenting were 32 percent, who believed women's rights are only fair, and 7 percent who maintained they are poor. Among young women, 61 percent hold a favorable view of women's rights, compared with 59 percent of the young men who share this opinion. In 1985, 64 percent of the teens viewed women's rights favorably, compared with 60 percent in 1988.

A majority of teens believe the rights of minorities such as blacks and Hispanics are just fair (37 percent) or poor (22 percent). Only 6 percent of teens rate minority rights as excellent, and an additional 34 percent say they are good. Overall, the proportion of teens holding favorable views of minority rights declined between 1985 and 1988, from 47 percent to 40 percent.

Older teens (16 and older) are more likely than those 13 to 15 to rate minority rights as just fair or poor, by a margin of 65 percent to 54 percent. Of non-white teens, seven in 10 say minority rights are only fair (40 percent) or poor (31 percent). Only 4 percent rate their own rights as excellent and 30 percent as good.

Teens are divided on whether the proper separation of church and state is being maintained in the United States. It is rated excellent by 11 percent of teens and good by 38 percent. Disagreeing are 32 percent who say it is fair and 12 percent who believe it is poor. Opinion on the issue has changed little since 1985.

A majority of teens who attend church regularly (51 percent) hold a positive view of the separation of church and state. Agreeing are 45 percent of those who do not go to church regularly. Protestant teens are slightly more likely than Catholics to have a positive opinion of church-state relations, by a margin of 51 percent to 48 percent.

18.2 Opinion of U.S. Freedoms and Rights

For each of the following causes and issues [shown below], do you think we are now doing an excellent, good, fair or poor job in the United States?

Rate 'excellent' or 'good'	1988	1985
Freedom of the Press	68%	78%
Freedom of Speech	66	78
Women's right	60	64
Separation of Church and State	49	51
Rights of minorities such as blacks and Hispanics	40	47

Respect for Minorities

The melting pot of America increasingly is becoming a blend of more colors and alternative lifestyles. As young Americans look around the classroom they are seeing fewer white faces and more people of color who are their own age. The majority of teen-agers believe that America should give more respect to recent immigrants and to members of minority groups.

The 500th anniversary of the "discovery" of America by Christopher Columbus has met with protest from native Americans who feel it unjustly honors an event that launched massive destruction of the original inhabitants of the western world and their cultures. Today, three teens in four still feel that native Americans such as Indians do not receive enough respect from their fellow citizens.

Many Hispanic Americans also are descended at least in part from the original peoples of America, but six teens in 10 say they are not receiving sufficient respect from their fellow citizens.

The proportion of Asian Americans in this country has increased only in recent years because of previously restrictive immigration laws. Although about half the teens say Asian Americans receive too little respect, many others say they are receiving about the right amount. This attitude may stem from the publicity surrounding the academic and economic success achieved by many Asian Americans.

Not all recent immigrants to this country have come legally, and teens show sympathy with the plight of illegal aliens.

Despite the gains that blacks have made in recent years, half of the teens interviewed believe they still do not receive enough respect in this country. Very few teens are worrying that white Americans are not receiving enough respect.

The gay community has made its presence known only in recent years when people of alternative sexual orientation asserted their right to co-exist in the heterosexual world. Over half of the teens say gays still are not receiving enough respect.

18.3 Respect People Receive in the U.S.

	December 1991		
	Too little	About right	Too much
Native Americans such as Indians	73%	22%	5%
Hispanic-Americans	60	36	4
Gays	57	18	24
Illegal aliens	56	20	20
Asian-Americans	53	40	7
Blacks	52	37	11
Whites	5	47	47

Note: "No opinion" (1 – 4 percent) is not shown.

GO 21504500; Q. 28

Women's Progress

More women are now pursuing full-time careers, with results that can range from battles for equal pay and legal rights to demands at home that men now take on a greater share of the household work and do more to help raise their children.

How are women doing? The majority of teens believe that America's women have made many gains over the past 10 years, often achieving greater earnings parity with men and enjoying more equal legal rights. Teens are somewhat less certain, however, that women are receiving greater respect from men or are receiving more help with domestic chores and child raising.

18.4 Progress by Women in Past Ten Years

	December 1991		
	Better off	**About the same**	**Not better off**
Earnings	82%	10%	8%
Legal rights	79	13	8
Respect from men	62	14	24
Help from men in raising children	57	16	27
Housework help from men	53	16	31

Note: "No opinion" (1 – 4 percent) is not shown.

GO 21504500; Q. 32

Opinion of the Women's Movement

"They just don't get it" is a phrase that has been used frequently to describe the insensitivity of some men to women's rights and concerns. A majority of both young men and women agree that American males do not always understand the issues that concern women the most. Despite this insensitivity, however, many teens feel the women's movement has helped women. Comparatively few young women now regard themselves as "feminists."

18.5 Opinion of the Women's Movement

	December 1991		
	Total teens	Young men	Young women
Women's movement has:			
Done a good job	51%	44%	58%
Not gone far enough	33	30	37
Gone too far	15	24	5
Do men understand the issues that concern women the most?			
Yes	40	43	37
No	59	56	62
Have women made gains unfairly at the expense of men?			
Yes	29	30	27
No	67	67	67

GO 21504500; Q. 31, 33–34

Equal Opportunity

Amidst the often heart-rending testimony and acrimonious debates that swirled around the conflicting testimony of Judge Clarence Thomas and of Professor Anita Hill, the American public also witnessed a major event in the progress of civil rights as a parade of bright, well-educated, articulate, powerful, persuasive non-white men and women gave compelling testimony before the U.S. Senate Judiciary Committee.

Some were the proud products of equal opportunity programs that gave them the entry to top schools and their initial jobs that enabled them later to gain high positions; others boasted of having achieved their enviable stations in life "on their own," without the benefit of government programs. Indeed, one of the major underlying conflicts brought to the nation's attention during the hearings was the clash of political and social ideologies between those favoring government intervention to assist the cause of minorities and redress past and present inequalities, vs. those believing this is a matter of individual initiative, pride, and responsibility.

America's teen-agers, in a Gallup Youth Survey conducted just a few months before the Senate hearings, reflect the often ambivalent attitudes of adults towards equal opportunity programs. The great majority of teens believe such programs should be supported, but it would also appear that many probably would prefer to see them replaced by the individual merit approach.

18.6 Support for Equal Opportunity Programs

Support very much	67%
Support somewhat	25
Oppose somewhat	5
Oppose very much	2
No opinion	1

When presented with the opposing view that equal opportunity programs should be dismantled so that people would get ahead in life solely on merit, teen support for the programs wavers somewhat. Preferring the merit approach rather than equal opportunity programs were half of the teens, with 20 percent saying they very much support the elimination of equal opportunity programs.

18.7 Support Elimination of Equal Opportunity Programs

Support very much	20%
Support somewhat	36
Oppose somewhat	20
Oppose very much	18
No opinion	6

18.8 Opinion of Equal Opportunity Programs

Please tell me how much you support or oppose each of these issues and causes — support very much, support somewhat, or oppose very much — Equal opportunity programs for blacks and other minorities to help them get good jobs and into better colleges? Elimination of equal opportunity programs so that people will ahead in life solely on merit?

	June – July 1991	
	Support "very much" . . .	
	Support equal opportunity programs	Should eliminate these programs
National	**67%**	**20%**
Male	61%	20%
Female	72	21
Ages 13 – 15	71	22
Ages 16 – 17	61	18
White	62	18
Non-white	86	29
White-collar background	68	20
Blue-collar background	65	19
Above-average students	64	20
Average and below	70	20
East	71	13
Midwest	71	22
South	63	24
West	63	20
Large city	77	34
Suburb	76	16
Small town, rural area	64	18
Protestant	69	20
Catholic	64	20
Church attender	67	24
Non-attender	67	17

GO 224007; Q. 11

Gay Rights

A majority of teen-agers say they favor greater legal protection and constitutional rights for gays, with 36 percent supporting the guarantees very much, and 18 percent saying they are somewhat in favor of them. Somewhat opposed to gay rights are 18 percent, while an additional 23 percent say they are very opposed. One teen in 20 (5 percent) is undecided.

When asked about support for such actions as prohibiting gay marriages, not allowing gays to teach young children, or banning gays from the U.S. armed services, 15 percent are much in favor and 22 percent somewhat favor such actions. Opposed to these restrictions are a majority of teens, with 28 percent somewhat opposed, and 29 percent very opposed. Six percent are undecided.

Among young women, nearly two in three (63 percent) say they favor rights for gays. The gay rights movement fails to gain majority support from young men, with just 45 percent saying they support gay rights, while a plurality of 49 percent opposes granting them greater rights. Although many young men may oppose giving gays more rights, only 36 percent go to the opposite extreme and argue in favor of greater legal restrictions on gays. They are joined by 38 percent of the young women who support greater restrictions.

Non-whites, who through their own experiences probably can be expected to be more sensitive than whites to matters of minority rights, show greater tolerance for extending rights to gays. Six non-white teens in 10 (61 percent) say they support greater gay rights compared to 53 percent of white teen-agers.

Teens in the East (57 percent) and Midwest (58 percent) are more likely than those from the South (50 percent) or West (42 percent) to support increased rights for gays. Southern and Western teens (42 percent each) also number among those most likely to seek greater legal restrictions against gays.

Churches recently have been the center of controversies concerning gay rights issues, as various denominations have wrestled with issues ranging from gay membership and ordination to the role of the church in the AIDS epidemic. Although gays often are in the news for their protests and disruptions at Catholic church services, Catholic teens appear to be somewhat more liberal than Protestant youth in their attitudes towards gay rights. Six Catholic teens in 10 (61 percent) say they support greater rights for gays, while only 34 percent would like to see more legal restrictions maintained or placed upon them. By comparison, 55 percent of Protestant teens favor greater rights, while 41 percent say they support greater restrictions on the activities of the gay community.

In general, teens who may not be regular church attenders (58 percent) are slightly more likely than those who go more regularly (51 percent) to support the gay rights movement.

18.9 Attitudes towards Gay Rights

Please tell me how much you support or oppose each of these issues and causes—support very much, support somewhat, oppose somewhat, or oppose very much—Greater legal protections and constitutional rights for gays? Laws that would prohibit such things as gay marriages, gays teaching young children, or gays in the armed forces?

	June – July 1991	
	Support gay rights	Support gay restrictions
National	54%	37%
Male	45	36
Female	63	38
Ages 13 – 15	55	37
Ages 16 – 17	53	38
White	43	37
Non-white	61	38
White-collar background	59	41
Blue-collar background	53	29
Above-average students	56	39
Average and below	51	36
East	57	30
Midwest	58	33
South	50	42
West	42	42
Large city	67	34
Suburb	55	31
Small town, rural area	52	38
Protestant	55	41
Catholic	61	34
Attended church last week	51	39
Did not attend	58	39

GO 224007; Q. 11

APPENDIX

Methodology

The Gallup Youth Survey is based upon the sample designs that The Gallup Organization, Inc. employs for its continuing national probability surveys.

The national Gallup telephone samples prior to October 1988 were based upon the area probability sample the organization used for personal surveys. Since that time, they have been based upon an independent random-digit stratified design. In each of the sampling locations selected, a set of telephone exchanges that falls within the geographic boundaries of the sampling location is first identified. Listed telephone numbers in these exchanges are selected randomly and used as "seed numbers" for randomly generating telephone numbers. This procedure results in a sample of listed and unlisted telephone numbers assigned to households within telephone exchanges serving the sampling locations. The final sample of numbers thus reflects the stratification and selection of sampling locations to provide confidence in the representativeness of the area sample.

After the survey data have been collected and processed, each respondent is assigned a weight so that the demographic characteristics of the total weighted sample of respondents matches the latest estimates of the demographic characteristics of the appropriate population available from the U.S. Census Bureau. Telephone surveys are weighted to match the characteristics of the population living in households with access to a telephone. A weighting of personal interview data includes a factor to compensate for the representation of the kinds of people who are less likely to be found at home.

The procedures described above are designed to produce samples approximating the total civilian population living in private households; i.e., excluding those in prisons, hospitals, hotels, religious and educational institutions, and those living on reservations or military bases. Survey percentages may be applied to census estimates of the size of these populations to project percentages into numbers of people. The manner in which the sample is drawn also produces a sample which approximates the distribution of private households in the U.S.; therefore, the survey results also can be projected to numbers of households.

Within the household, an interview is sought with the oldest teen-age male, 13 to 17 years of age. If no young man is present, an interview is sought with the oldest teen-age female in the household. this method of selection within the household has been developed empirically to produce an age distribution by male and female teen-agers separately which compares closely with the age distribution of the population.

Sampling Tolerances

In interpreting survey results it should be borne in mind that all sample surveys are subject to sampling error; i.e., the extent to which the results theoretically may differ from what would be obtained if the entire population surveyed had been interviewed. The size of such sample errors depends largely upon the number of interviews.

The following tables may be used in estimating the sampling error of any percentage in this book. The computed allowances include allowances for the sample design effect upon sampling error. They may be interpreted as showing the range in percentage points (plus or minus the figure shown) within which repeated sampling in the same time period could be expected to vary, 95 percent of the time, if the same sampling procedure, interviewers, and questionnaire were used.

Table A shows how much allowance should be made for the sampling error of a percentage. In comparing survey results in two samples; e.g., young men and young women, the question also arises as to how large must a difference between them be before one can be reasonably certain that it may reflect a real difference.

Table B shows recommended allowance for percentages near 20 or 80.

Table C is for percentages near 50. For percentages in between, the estimated error is between those shown on the two tables.

Sampling Tolerances

TABLE A — Recommended Allowance for Sampling Error of a Percentage
In percentage points (at 95 in 100 confidence level)

Sample Size

	1000	750	600	400	200	100
Percentages near 10	2	3	3	4	5	7
Percentages near 20	3	4	4	5	7	9
Percentages near 30	4	4	4	6	8	10
Percentages near 40	4	4	5	6	8	11
Percentages near 50	4	4	4	6	8	11
Percentages near 60	4	4	5	6	8	11
Percentages near 70	4	4	4	6	8	10
Percentages near 80	3	4	4	5	7	9
Percentages near 90	2	3	3	4	5	7

TABLE B — Recommended Allowance for Sampling Error of the Difference
In percentage points (at 95 in 100 confidence level)

Percentages near 20 or near 80

Size of sample	750	600	400	200
750	5			
600	5	6		
400	6	6	7	
200	8	8	8	10

TABLE C — Recommended Allowance for Sampling Error of the Difference
In percentage points (at 95 in 100 confidence level)

Percentages near 50

Size of sample	750	600	400	200
750	6			
600	7	7		
400	7	8	8	
200	10	10	10	12

Sample Composition

The following table provides the appropriate number of persons interviewed in each group for any single survey. These sample sizes apply to all surveys unless otherwise noted. Gallup Youth Surveys generally have consisted of 500 or 1,000 interviews, and the composition is shown for each.

National	1,000	500
Male	500	250
Female	500	250
Ages 13 – 15	590	295
Ages 16 – 17	410	205
White	760	380
Non-white	240	120
White-collar background	480	240
Blue-collar background	440	220
Above-average students	565	280
Average or below	435	220
Both parents attended college	220	110
One attended college	440	220
Neither attended college	340	170
East	240	120
Midwest	260	130
South	300	150
West	200	100
Large cities	190	95
Suburbs	210	105
Small town	380	190
Rural	220	110
Protestant	520	260
Catholic	300	150
Church attender	480	240
Non-attender	520	260

Index